The Illustrated Directory of

MODERN
COMMERCIAL
AIRCRAFT

The Illustrated Directory of

MODERN
COMMERCIAL
AIRCRAFT

Günter Endres

SALAMANDER

A Salamander Book

Published by Salamander Books Ltd.
8 Blenheim Court
Brewery Road
London N7 9NT
United Kingdom

© Salamander Books Ltd., 2001, 2002

A member of **Chrysalis** Books plc

ISBN 1-84065-287-X

Credits

Project Manager: Ray Bonds
Designers: Interprep Ltd
Reproduction: Studio Tec
Printed and bound in Slovenia

The Author

Günter Endres has been writing for 30 years, on both historic airline subjects and commercial aviation as a whole. He has been Business Reporter and Air Transport Editor of the monthly trade journal *Interavia,* and is currently Yearbook Editor of *Jane's Helicopter Markets and* *Systems,* News Editor of *Jane's Airport Review,* Senior Correspondent for *Airline Business,* and Airline Correspondent for Euromoney's *Airfinance Annual.* He has written a number of books, and some 200 of his articles articles have appeared in most aviation journals.

Contents

Introduction

The number of passengers travelling by air is increasing every year. From time to time, the rate of growth is arrested, as happened in 1986 because of tension and terrorism in the Middle East, in 1991 as a result of the Gulf War, and in 1997, when the financial crisis in Asia threatened the world's biggest growth market. Nevertheless, the overall trend is determinedly upwards, and air freight is increasing even more dramatically than passenger traffic. According to the International Civil Aviation Organisation (ICAO), some 1.6 billion passengers travelled on scheduled services in 2000. At the same time, the world's airlines carried 3.7 million tonnes of cargo. With average annual growth rates of around 5-6%, these figures will spiral to around 5 billion passengers and 12 million tonnes respectively by 2020.

Based on these expectations, aircraft manufacturers predict that over the next 20 years the world's airlines, according to Airbus, will need some 15,400 new aircraft. Boeing pitches its forecast even higher. The vast majority will be required to meet new demand, with a large number also required to replace older types nearing the end of their design lives.

Gathered together in this book are brief development histories, descriptions of variants, technical specifications and illustrations of more than 150 aircraft, in a consistent format to make possible direct comparisons. These range from the most important airliners in mainline service, to older types now only operated in small numbers, as well as business jets and noteworthy utility aircraft with a capacity of at least

nine passengers and used on commuter and air taxi services. Aircraft under development and due to enter service within the next few years are also covered, and include the new giant double-deck Airbus A380, set to become the largest passenger aircraft when it goes into service in 2006, with a potential capacity for up to 1,000 people. In short, aircraft in this book range from the largest wide-body jets to small piston-engined twins, from the slow to the supersonic, from designs that trace their origins to before World War Two, to those advanced new-technology types that entered commercial service in the last decade of the 20th Century.

Many of the manufacturers whose aircraft appear in this book are little more than a distant memory. Following the take-over by Boeing of McDonnell Douglas in 1997, the large aircraft market is now being fought over only by the European Airbus and Boeing. Both now have a half-share of the world market. The 30- to 100-seat regional aircraft market has been notable for the appearance of the small regional jet, now covering the whole range. As a result, turboprop manufacturers are feeling the pinch, and Saab has already stopped its production line, with others sure to follow. Fokker, building both jets and turboprops, slipped quietly into bankruptcy in 1996. The main players are now Bombardier, Embraer and Fairchild Dornier. In Russia, shortage of funding has produced few new aircraft, and rather more paper designs, some more fanciful than others. Tupolev remains the most prolific manufacturer, but Sukhoi, better known for its stunning military aircraft, is quietly moving into the commercial market.

Aerospatiale/BAC Concorde

SPECIFICATION

(Aerospatiale/BAC Concorde)

Dimensions: Wingspan 25.56m (83ft 10¼in); length overall 62.10m (203ft 9in); height overall 11.4m (37ft 5in), wing area 358.25m^2 (3,856ft^2).

Power Plant: Four Rolls-Royce Snecma Olympus 593 Mk610 turbojets, each rated at 169.3kN (38,05lb) static thrust.

Weights: Operating weight empty 78,700kg (173,500lb); max take-off 185,065kg (408,000lb); max landing 111,130kg (245,000lb); max payload 11,340kg (25,000lb).

Performance: Max cruising speed 1,176kt (2,179km/h); service ceiling 18,290m (60,000ft); take-off field length 3,415m (11,200ft); landing field length 2,225m (7,300ft); range with typical payload 3,360nm (6,225km).

Accommodation: Flight crew of two. Single-aisle cabin layout, seating typically 100 passengers, although a maximum of 144 is possible. Baggage/cargo compartments under the floor and in rear fuselage have a total volume of 19.74m^3 (607ft^3).

Having celebrated 20 years of successful revenue service in the hands of British Airways and Air France in January 1996, Concorde has a history that goes back to 1955. In that year, member companies of the British aerospace industry and government agencies undertook preliminary design work that led

Below: The British-assembled prototype made its first flight from Filton on 9 April 1969.

Above: British Airways planned to provide Concorde services to Australia, but never got beyond Singapore.

to the establishment in 1956 of a Supersonic Transport Aircraft Committee (STAC) to study the feasibility of an SST. Among the project studies looked at by STAC was the Bristol Type 198 – a design number covering several different aircraft configurations, of which the most favoured came to be a slender delta-winged layout with eight engines and able to operate across the North Atlantic at Mach 2.0. Through a process of continuous refinement, this evolved into the smaller Type 223, with four engines and 110 seats for a London to New York operation. While this work went on in the UK, a similar process was under way in France, leading by 1961 to evolution of a project called the Super Caravelle that was strikingly similar to the Bristol 223. At government behest, the British and French designers were merged into a single project, and a protocol of agreement was signed between the two governments on 29 November 1962. Principal airframe companies were BAC (which had absorbed Bristol) and Aérospatiale (incorporating Sud), and the engine companies were Rolls-Royce (which had meanwhile acquired the Bristol Siddeley engine company in which Concorde's Olympus engines originated) and SNECMA. The Concorde programme was handled in a number of stages, embracing the construction and testing of two prototypes, known as Concordes 001 and 002; two pre-production aircraft, originally known as Concordes 01 and 02 and subsequently as Concordes 101 and 102; and a production sequence commencing with Concorde 201. Production of an initial batch of 16 aircraft was authorised by the

two governments and production of major airframe and engine components was divided between companies in the UK and France without duplication. Separate final assembly lines were set up at Toulouse and Filton, alternate aircraft being assembled in the UK and France. Concorde 001 made its first flight Toulouse on 2 March 1969, its first supersonic flight on 1 October 1969, and its first excursion to Mach 2 on 4 November 1970 (on its 102nd flight). Concorde 002 was the first to fly in the UK (at Filton) on 9 April 1969.

VARIANTS

Concordes 001 and 002 were slightly smaller than the production standard, which introduced lengthened front and rear fuselages, revised nose visors, changes to the wing geometry and uprated engines. These new features were progressively introduced on Concorde 101, first flown from Toulouse on 17 December 1971, and Concorde 102, flown at Filton on 10 January 1973. The more definitive production standard was represented by Concorde 201, flown ▶

Below: British Airways, through innovative charter programmes including regular flights to Barbados and specialist round-the-world charters, has made a success of operating the small number of Concordes. The record for the flight from London to New York is under three hours.

at Toulouse on 6 December 1973, and Concorde 202 flown at Filton on 13 February 1974. Production aircraft 203 to 216 flew alternately from the two assembly lines, the last two on 26 December 1978 and 20 April 1979 respectively.

SERVICE USE

Certification of the Concorde for full passenger carrying operations was obtained on 13 October 1975 in France and on 5 December 1975 in the UK, leading to introduction into service by British Airways and Air France simultaneously on 21 January 1976. The routes, respectively, were London to Bahrain and Paris to Rio de Janeiro (via Dakar). Services to Washington began on 24 May 1976 (extended in 1985 to Miami and New York in December 1977). BA flew a service from London to Singapore (via Bahrain) jointly with Singapore Airlines in 1979/80, and in the same period Braniff leased aircraft time from Air France and BA to extend the Washington services to Dallas/Fort Worth. For a time Air France flew scheduled services to Caracas and to Mexico via

Washington; many other destinations around the world have been served under an extensive programme of charters. Thirteen aircraft were flown by British Airways (7) and Air France (6) on the London-New York and Paris-New York schedules until a tragic accident of an Air France aircraft on 25 July 2000, the aircraft's first, led to the withdrawal of Concorde's certificate of airworthiness (CofA) on 16 August 2000. Modifications to the fuel tanks and hydraulic and electrical lines are being tested, which was expected to enable Concorde to regain its CofA and resume service by June 2001. A British-Airways-led life extension programme, designed to increase airframe life from 6,700 to 8,500 reference flights – a reference flight is defined as one flight on a long-haul sector at a take-off weight in excess of 170,000kg (375,000lb) – should keep the youngest aircraft in service until 2017.

Below: Air France was the only other operator of the Concorde, serving only the Paris-New York route on a scheduled basis. One of its aircraft is pictured landing on a charter flight in New Zealand.

Aerospatiale (Nord) 262

SPECIFICATION

(Nord 262C)

Dimensions: Wingspan 22.60m (74ft 2in); length overall 19.28m (63ft 3in); height overall 6.21m (20ft 4in), wing area 55.0m² (592.0ft²).

Power Plant: Two 843kW (1,130shp) Turboméca Bastan VIIA turboprops, with Ratier Forest four-blade propellers.

Weights: Operating weight empty 7,225kg (15,929lb); max take-off 10,800kg (23,810lb); max landing 10,450kg (23,040lb); max payload 3,075kg (6,781lb).

Performance: Max cruising speed 224kts (415km/h); initial rate of climb 6.1m/s (1,200ft/min; service ceiling 7,160m (23,500ft); take-off field length 820m (2,690ft); landing field length 630m (2,060ft); range with max payload 550nm (1,020km).

Accommodation: Flight crew of two. Seating for up to 29 passengers, three-abreast with single aisle. Total baggage volume 4.50m³ (159.0ft³).

This small regional airliner evolved from a design by Max Holste, whose company flew on 20 May 1959 the prototype of a utility transport powered by Pratt & Whitney Wasp radial piston engines and based on a square-section fuselage. Known as the MH-250, this was followed by the MH-260 with Bastan turboprops, flown on 29 July 1960. State-owned Nord (now merged into Aérospatiale) undertook further development of the basic design and produced as a result the Nord 262, which differed from the MH-260 primarily in having a pressurized circular-section cabin large enough for 24-26 passengers. A prototype flew on 24 December 1962. This and three pre-production aircraft were known as the 262B, with the definitive production being the Nord 262A. After the Nord 262A and 262B with Bastan IVC engines, the models 262C and 262D were evolved with higher-powered Bastan VIIC, which flew in July 1968, although most sales were in military guise as the 262D Frégate to the Armée de l'Air. The designation Mohawk 298 was adopted for a variant developed in the USA and flown on 7 January 1975 with Pratt & Whitney Canada PT6A-45 turboprops, to meet FAR 298 regulations. The modification programmed was

Above: British scheduled and charter airline Dan-Air was the only UK airline to operate the high-wing Nord 262. It was in service from July 1970 to February 1972.

managed by Mohawk Air Services and undertaken by Frakes Aviation in Texas, at the instigation of Allegheny Airlines whose associate Ransome Airlines was the initial operator. Apart from the engines and new wingtips, the Mohawk 298 incorporated many new systems. The Nord 262 was certificated on 16 July 1964 and entered service with Air Inter. Total production amounted to 110 aircraft, but only 10 remained in service at 1 January 2001.

Left: Air Ceylon bought a single aircraft new from the manufacturer for local services. It was later bought by Dan-Air.

Aerospatiale (Sud-Est) Caravelle

SPECIFICATION
(Caravelle 10B3)
Dimensions: Wingspan 34.30m (112ft 6in); length overall 33.01m (108ft 3½in); height overall 8.72m (28ft 7in), wing area 146.7m² (1,579ft²).
Power Plant: Two 63.2kN (14,000lb) Pratt & Whitney JT8D-1 or -7 or 64.5kN (14,500lb) JT8D-9 turbofans.
Weights: Operating weight empty 30,055kg (66,259lb); max take-off 56,000kg (123,457lb); max landing 49,500kg (109,127lb); max payload 9,100kg (20,062lb).
Performance: Max cruising speed 445kts 825(km/h); take-off field length 2,090m (6,850ft); landing field length 1,580m (5,180ft); range with max payload 1,450nm (2,685km).
Accommodation: Flight crew of three. Seating for up to 100 passengers, five-abreast with single aisle. Aft baggage volume 4.2m³ (148ft³).

At the end of 1952, SNCA Sud-Est (one of the state-owned companies later merged to form Aérospatiale) was selected by the French air ministry to develop a twin-jet civil transport for short/medium-range operations. Designs had been submitted to meet the official specification drawn up in 1951; that by Sud-Est selected for further development featured engines mounted on the rear fuselage – an innovative idea at that time, and one which had a number of attractions. Two prototypes were funded by the French government and made their first flight on 27 May 1955 and 6 May 1956, powered by Rolls-Royce Avon RA.26 Mk 521.

French certification was achieved on 2 April 1959, with US FAA endorsement following on 8 April. The first service was flown by Air France on 6 May that same year. The initial production versions were the Caravelle I and

Below: The Caravelle was operated by many leading European airlines, including France's Air Inter.

Above: Denmark's biggest charter airline was one of the most prolific users of the Caravelle, operating a number of different models including the VI-R, 10B3 and 12.

IA with Avon RA.29 Mk 522 and Mk 526 turbojets respectively, later converted to Series III standard, which had Avon Mk 527s and increased weights. A further change of engine to the Mk 531 produced the Srs VI-N, first flown on 10 September 1960 and then, with thrust reversers on Mk 532R or 533R engines, the Srs VI-R. The Caravelle 10B1R, flown on 18 January 1965, was similar, but had Pratt & Whitney JT8D-1 or -7 turbofan engines. The General Electric-powered Srs VII led to the Caravelle 10A, with a 1.0m (3ft 4in) longer fuselage, while the Srs 10B3 (Super B) was identical except for having JT8D-1, -7 or -9 engines. The Caravelle 11R was the 10BR with a forward side cargo door for mixed passenger/cargo operations. The final variant was the still longer Caravelle 12, which first flew on 29 October 1970. Production ended in March 1973 after 282 had been built, but only 10 remained in service at 1 January 2001.

Airbus A300

SPECIFICATION

(Airbus A300-600R)

Dimensions: Wingspan 44.84m (147ft 1in); length overall 54.08m (177ft 5in); height overall 16.53m (54ft 3in), wing area 260.0m^2 (2,798.6ft^2).

Power Plant: Two General Electric CF6-80C2A5 rated at 273kN (61,500lb) each, or 262kN (59,000lb) Pratt & Whitney PW4158 turbofans. Other options available.

Weights: Operating weight empty 90,339kg (199,165lb); max take-off 171,700kg (378,535lb); max landing 140,000kg (308,645lb); max payload 39,735kg (87,600lb).

Performance: Max cruising speed 484kts (897km/h); service ceiling 12,200m (40,000ft) take-off field length 2,240m (7,350ft);landing field length 1,555m (5,100ft); range with typical payload 4,050nm (7,500km).

Accommodation: Flight crew of two. Twin-aisle cabin layout, seating typically 266 passengers in two classes, or up to 361 in 9-abreast high-density tourist configuration. Total baggage volume 24.98m^3 (882ft^3).

Product of a truly international programme of development and manufacture, the A300 was the first of the Airbus family of wide-body jetliners that challenged long-held US primacy in the production of transport aircraft. Design activity began in 1965 as an Anglo-French initiative to develop a large-capacity transport for BEA and Air France; West German participation dates from 1967, with signature of a memorandum of understanding by the three governments on 26 September 1967. The initial tri-nation project was for 149,700kg (330,000lb) aircraft with two Rolls-Royce RB.207 engines, but this was scaled down after the British government withdrew on the grounds that a market could not be guaranteed, leaving Hawker Siddeley to maintain a British share on a privately-financed basis. The smaller A300B emerged in December 1968 with a 125,000kg (275,575lb) gross

Above: The A300 found a ready market in the Far East, including with China Airlines in Taiwan.

Below: UK charter airline Monarch operates the A300-600R in a high-density layout for 361 passengers.

weight, two British or American engines each of about 200kN (45,000lb) thrust and accommodation for 252 passengers. Two prototypes were built in this configuration: under the designation A300B1, these two aircraft first flew on 28 October 1972 and 5 February 1973 at Toulouse with General Electric CF6-50A turbofans. These had a fuselage length 2.65m (8ft 8in) less than that of the production models, as described under the Variants heading below. Production of the A300 family is shared between the Airbus partners, comprising Aérospatiale in France, Daimler-Benz Aerospace (Dasa) in West Germany, British Aerospace in the UK and CASA in Spain, with Fokker in the Netherlands as an associate in the programme. All final assembly takes place in Toulouse, with major components ferried in from the other national production centres.

VARIANTS

Production began with the A300B2, later known as A300B2-100, with CF6-50C or C2 engines and first flown on 28 June 1983. The A300B2K (later A300B2-200) introduced wing-root leading-edge Krueger flaps for better field performance, and first flew 30 July 1976. Pratt & Whitney JT9D-59A engines were introduced on the A300B2-220 (and A300B2-320 with higher zero-fuel and landing weights), first flown 28 April 1979. The A300B4 (later A300B4-100 with CF6 engines, and A300B4-120 with JT9D engines) was

introduced as a long-range version, with more fuel capacity and higher weights; the first flight of this variant was made on 26 December 1974. A higher-weight option, with structural strengthening, is the A300B4-200, which could also have more fuel in the rear cargo hold. A two-man forward-facing cockpit distinguishes the A300F4-200, first flown on 6 October 1981. A convertible freighter version is designated A300C4, based on the B4 with a forward side-loading door and reinforced floor, the first example flew in mid-1979. The A300-600 was launched in 1980 as an advanced version of the B-4, with a number of significant improvements including a rear fuselage of A310 profile, allowing two more seat rows in the cabin; a two-crew EFIS cockpit; use of composites and simplified systems for reduced structure weight; and advanced engines as quoted above, or the 249kN (56,000lb) thrust PW4156, 258kN (58,000lb) PW4158 or 236kN (53,000lb) RB.211-524D4A. The first A300-600 flew on 8 July 1983 with JT9D-7R4HI engines, and an A300-600 with CF6-80C2 engines flew on 20 March 1985. The A300-600R, first flown on 9 December 1987, differed in having small wingtip fences, a tailplane fuel tank with a computerised fuel trimming system, increased take-off weight and extended range capability. A small number of A300- ▶

Below: Short-lived Mexican charter airline Latur used an A300-600 to fly U.S. holidaymakers to Mexican resorts.

600 Convertibles were also produced, whose main differences are a large forward upper deck cargo door, reinforced floor and a smoke detection system in the main cabin. Interest from Federal Express (FedEx) in a freighter version launched the A300-600F which first flew in December 1993. Many older models are also being converted for cargo use.

SERVICE USE

French and West German certification of the Airbus A300B2 was obtained on 15 March 1974, and service use began on 30 May 1974 with Air France. The first A300B2K was delivered to South African Airways on 23 November 1976. The Airbus A300B4 was certificated in France and West Germany on 26 March 1975, gained approval in the UYnited States on 30 June 1976, and entered service with Germanair on 1 June 1975. The A300B4-200FF was certificated on 8 January 1982 and entered service with Garuda. The

convertible Airbus A300C4 entered service with Hapag-Lloyd at the end of 1979. The first Airbus A300-600 was delivered to Saudi Arabian Airlines on 26 March 1984, and the first improved Airbus A300-600 to Thai Airways International in October 1985. Deliveries of the A300-600R to launch customer American Airlines began on 21 April 1988 and the first A300-600F freighter was delivered to FedEx on 27 April 1994. A large number of Airbus A300 B4s are now being converted for freight use with the installation of a forward freight door and strengthened floor. The first conversion (for HeavyLift Cargo) was introduced at the 1997 Paris air show. At 1 January 2001, Airbus had orders for 522 A300s of all versions, of which 496 had been delivered and 427 remained in operation.

Below: Start-up Compass Airlines used the A300-600R to break the two-airline stranglehold in Australia, but failed.

Airbus A310

SPECIFICATION
(Airbus A310-300)
Dimensions: Wingspan 43.89m (144ft 0in); length overall 46.66m (153ft 1in); height overall 15.80m (51ft 10in), wing area 219.0m^2 (2,357.3ft^2).
Power Plant: Two 262kN (59,000lb) General Electric CF6-80C2A8, or Pratt & Whitney PW4156A turbofans, rated at 249kN (56,000lb). Other options available.
Weights: Operating weight empty 72,000kg (158,840lb); max take-off 164,000kg (361,550lb); max landing 124,000kg (273,375lb); max payload 32,117kg (70,805lb).
Performance: Max cruising speed 484kts (895km/h); service ceiling 12,200m (40,000ft); take-off field length 2,560m (8,400ft); landing field length 1,555m (5,100ft); range with typical payload 5,150nm (19,537km).
Accommodation: Flight crew of two. Twin-aisle cabin layout, seating typically 210-250 passengers in two class layout. Certificated for maximum of 280 passengers. Total cargo/baggage volume 102.1m^3 (3,605ft^3).

Shortly after the A300 had been launched, Airbus Industrie began to investigate a number of possible future derivatives of the basic aircraft. These acquired designations from A300B5 onwards, and by 1974 interest was centred upon the B9, a fuselage-stretched variant; the B10, a fuselage shortened version; and the B11, with an enlarged wing and four engines. Of this trio, the B9 and B11 became the subject of further evolution under the TA9 and TA11 designations (now the A330 and A340), while the B10 was launched as the A310. Interest in a short/medium-range, medium-capacity transport crystallised in the mid-1970s as several European airlines indicated a need for such an aircraft for service from 1983 onwards. To achieve this timescale, Airbus made a marketing launch decision in July 1978, at which time 'pre-contracts' were obtained from Swissair, Lufthansa and Air

Above: The Royal Thai Air Force uses a single A310 as a VIP transport.

Below: Mexican holiday charter airline Aerocancun used its A310-300 on flights to the United States and Latin America.

France. The A310, as the A300B10 now became known, was not finally defined until the end of 1978, when the fuselage length was set at 13 frames less than the basic A300, but with some reprofiling of the rear fuselage to allow seating to extend farther aft. The wing was to remain structurally similar to that of the A300, but aerodynamically was completely new, taking advantage of extensive development work by British Aerospace at Hatfield. With government approval, British Aerospace (which had meanwhile absorbed the original Hawker Siddeley share in the A300) became a full partner in Airbus Industrie on 1 January 1979, with a 20 per cent share, and this is reflected in the work-sharing on the A310, with participation of Aérospatiale, Dasa, CASA and Fokker on a basis similar to that of the A300. The first A310 flew at Toulouse on 3 April and the second on 3 May 1983, both powered by JT9D-7R4 engines; the third aircraft, flown on 5 August 1982, had CF6-80A3 engines.

VARIANTS
Short and medium-range versions of the A310 were at first designated A310-100 and A310-200, at maximum take-off weights of 121,000kg (266,755lb) and 132,000kg

(291,010lb) respectively. The former version was dropped, however, and the A310-200 was developed to have optional higher weights of 138,600kg (305,560lb) and 142,000kg (313,055lb) with a fuel capacity of 54,900l (12,077Imp.gal) in all versions. To extend the range of the basic aircraft, the A310-300 was developed with the tailplane trim tank to increase fuel capacity, and optional under floor tanks. The A310-300 is available at two weights as listed above, and has small wing tip fences, which also were retrospectively adopted for the A310-200. The first extended range A310-300, with JT9D-7R4E engines, flew on 8 July 1985 and the second, with CF6-80C2 engines, on 6 September 1985. Wingtip fences introduced as standard on A310-200 from Spring 1986. Airline preferences for the longer-range model soon indicated that the A310-200 had run its course, and from 1988, only the A310-300 was built. With the advances in power plants, a number of engines have been used, with current options for the A310-200 ▶

Below: CSA Czech Airlines began its transition from a Soviet fleet to modern Western aircraft with the acquisition of the A310-300.

and -300 models being the 237kN (53,250lb) General Electric CF6-80C2A2 and the 231kN (52,000lb) Pratt & Whitney PW4152. A higher-gross weight version of the A310-300 has more powerful 262kN (59,000lb) CF6-80C2A8 and 249kN (56,000lb) PW4156A turbofans. Martinair Holland took delivery of the only example to date of a cargo-convertible A310-200C on 29 November 1984. Many used aircraft are now being converted to full freighter configuration under the designation A310-200/300F, through the addition of a large 3.58 x 2.57m (141 x 101in) main deck cargo door on the left hand side, replacement of the passenger window panes with fire resistant metal plates and reinforced floor. A multi-role tanker transport (MRTT) version is being offered to military customers.

SERVICE USE
The A310-200 was certificated in France and West Germany on 11 March 1983, in the UK

in January 1984 and in the USA early in 1985. First deliveries to Lufthansa and Swissair were made on 29 March 1983, and the first revenue services were flown on 12 and 21 April 1983 respectively. The A310-300 with JT9D engines gained French and West German certification on 5 December 1985, and service use by Swissair began on 16 December 1985 on routes linking Geneva and Zürich with points in Africa. Certification with alternative CF6-50C2 and PW4152 engines was granted in April 1986 and June 1987 respectively, and Wardair (Canada) received the first aircraft with additional centre tanks soon after certification in November 1987. At 1 January 2001, Airbus had received orders for 260 A310s, of which 255 had been delivered. All but eight of these remain in service.

Below: Trans-European Airways used two A310-300s on world-wide charters but went bankrupt a few months later.

Airbus A318

SPECIFICATION
(Airbus A318-100)
Dimensions: Wingspan 34.09m (111ft 10¼in); length 31.45m (103ft 2⁰in); height overall 12.56m (41ft 2½in); wing area 122.60m² (1,319.7ft²).
Power Plant: Two 97.9kN (22,000lb) thrust Pratt & Whitney PW6122, or two 106.8kN (24,000lb) PW6124, or two 97.9kN (22,000lb) CFM International CFM56-5B turbofans.
Weights: Operating weight empty 38,950kg (85,870lb); max take-off 59,000kg (130,075lb); max landing 56,000kg (123,460lb); max payload 14,050kg (30,975lb).
Performance: Max cruising Mach 0.82; service ceiling 11,890m (39,000ft); take-off field length 1,430m (4,695ft); range with typical payload 1,500nm (2,780km).
Accommodation: Flight crew of two. Twin-aisle cabin layout, seating typically 107 passengers in a two-class configuration. Max high-density seating for 129 passengers. Cargo/baggage volume 21.90m³ (773ft³).

The A318 is a derivative of the A320 and the smallest aircraft in the Airbus family. Essentially a truncated version of the A320, it was announced at the Farnborough Air Show in September 1998, and formally launched on 26 April 1999 with orders, commitments and options for 109 aircraft, replacing the cancelled AVIC/AIA/STPL AE316/317 venture. The first customer was the International Lease Finance Corporation (ILFC), which had signed a memorandum of Understanding (MoU) on 17 November 1998 for up to 30 aircraft, followed by a firm order on 30 April 1999. These will be leased to Air France. The prototype is scheduled to fly in the first quarter of 2001, with airline services to begin in the last quarter of 2002. Production will be at the EADS (formerly DaimlerChrysler Aerospace Airbus) plant at Hamburg in Germany, with AVIC of China sharing some of the production to compensate

Below: British Airways will use the A318 on regional services as part of a move towards and Airbus regional fleet.

Above: The A-318, the smallest member of the family, is essentially a truncated version of the A320.

it for the loss of the projected A316/317 work.

High commonality (about 95%) with other A320 family members is achieved in the A318, largely through the adoption of the A319 wing, engine pylon and interface. For the first time in any airliner, laser welding, rather than riveting, will be used to reduce costs and weight. The fuselage of the A318 is 2.39m (7ft 10in) shorter than the A319, with 1¹/₂ frames removed forward of the wing and three frames aft, providing accommodation for in a two-class layout for 107 passengers, or up to 129 in single-class high-density configuration. No containerised freight will be carried, because baggage doors had to be reduced to maintain the same engine nacelle clearance for loading vehicles as the A319. Other external changes include a dorsal fillet on the fin, and a slight modification to the wing camber. Launch engines are the 97.9kN (22,000lb) thrust Pratt & Whitney PW6122 or 106.8kN (24,000lb) thrust PW6124 turbofans. The 97.9kN (22,000lb) CFM International CFM56-5B was announced on 4 August 1999 as an alternative engine, and will enter service in mid-2003.

VARIANTS
The only version announced by January 2001 is the A318-100 baseline aircraft.

SERVICE USE
At 1 January 2001, Airbus had firm orders for 161 aircraft.

Airbus A319

SPECIFICATION
(Airbus A319-100)

Dimensions: Wingspan 34.09m (111ft 10¼in); length 33.84m (111ft 0¼in); height overall 11.76m (38ft 7in); wing area 122.60m² (1,319.7ft²).

Power Plant: Two CFMI International CFM56-5A4 or IAE V2522-A5 turbofans, each rated at 97.9kN (22,000lb) thrust. Higher-powered available options include the CFM56-5A5, CFM56-5B/P and V2524-A5, each giving 104.5kN (23,500lb) static thrust.

Weights: Operating weight empty 40,160kg (88,537lb); max take-off 64,000kg (141,095lb); max landing 61,000kg (134,480lb); max payload 16,840kg (37,125lb).

Performance: Max cruising speed Mach 0.82; service ceiling 11,890m (39,000ft); take-off field length 1,820m (5,975ft); landing field length 1,470m (4,825ft); range with typical payload 1,830nm (3,385km).

Accommodation: Flight crew of two. Twin-aisle cabin layout, seating typically 124 passengers in a two-class configuration. Max high-density seating for 145 passengers.

This short-fuselage version of the A320 was launched in June 1993 and made its first flight at Hamburg on 29 August 1995. Two aircraft (the second flew on 31 October 1995) were used in a 650-hour flight test programme leading to certification with the CFM56-5A engine on 10 April 1996. JAA 120-minute ETOPS approval was granted on 14 February 1997. The A319 is seven fuselage frames shorter than the A320, reducing its overall length by 3.73m (12ft 3in) to 33.84m (111ft 0¼in), but is otherwise little changed. It seats typically 124

Above: Airbus is also offering the A319 as a corporate Jetliner which can be customised to suit individual requirements.

Below: German regional airline Eurowings put the A319 into service in Spring 1997. It has a total of six aircraft on order.

passengers in a two-class layout, or up to 145 passengers in an all-economy arrangement. Assembled in Germany alongside the stretched A321 by EADS (formerly DaimlerChrysler Aerospace Airbus).

VARIANTS

The basic production version is the A319-100, which is available with a choice of two standard engines, the 97.9kN (22,000lb) CFMI International CFM56-5A4 turbofan or the IAE V2522-A5 with the same thrust rating. Three, more powerful options include the CFM56-5A5, CFM56-5B/P or IAE V2524-A5, each rated at 104.5kN (23,500lb) static thrust. A corporate Jetliner, the ACJ, was announced at the Paris Air Show in June 1997 and first flew on 12 November 1998. It can be customised to suit individual requirements, but standard aircraft carries 40 passengers over a distance of 4,200 nautical miles (7,770km). With just 12 executives, the range increases to more than 6,000nm (11,100km). On 16 June 1999, the ACJ set a world non-stop record, flying the 6,918nm

(12,812km) distance from Santiago de Chile to Le Bourget in 15 hours 13 minutes. The ACJ can easily be converted back to airline configuration.

SERVICE USE
The first CFM56-powered A319-100 was delivered to ILFC on 25 April 1996 and leased five days later to Swissair, which put the type into service on the Zurich-Rome route on 8 May. The first V2500-powered aircraft made its maiden flight on 22 May 1996 and received certification on 18 December that year. Delivery of the first ACJ was made on 8 November 1999 to UK-based Twinjet Aircraft, which operates the aircraft for the first customer Mohamed Abdulmohsin Al Kharafi of Kuwait. At 1 January 2001, the A319 had logged a total of 694 orders, including 26 for the ACJ, with deliveries totalling 305 aircraft.

Below: Air Canada is one of several North American carriers to operate the successful A319.

Airbus A320

SPECIFICATION
(Airbus A320-200)
Dimensions: Wingspan 33.91m (111ft 3in); length overall 37.57m (123ft 3in); height overall 11.80m (38ft 8½in), wing area 122.4m² 1.317.5ft²).
Power Plant: Two 117.9kN (26,500lb) CFM International CFM56-5B4, or 111.2kN (25,500lb) IAE V2525-A5 turbofans. Other options available.
Weights: Operating weight empty 42,059kg (92,746lb); max take-off 77,000kg (Úị169,755lb); max landing 64,500kg (142,195lb); max payload 18,931kg (41,735lb)
Performance: Max cruising speed 487kts (900km/h); service ceiling 12,200m (40,000ft); take-off field length 2,286m (7,500ft); landing field length 1,442m (4,730ft); range with typical payload 2,900nm (5,370km).
Accommodation: Flight crew of two. Single-aisle cabin layout, seating typically 150 passengers in two class layout. Certificated for maximum of 179 passengers. Total cargo/baggage volume 38.76m³ (1,368.8ft³).

The 'decision in principle' to launch a short/medium-range jetliner in the 150-seat category was taken by Airbus Industrie in June 1981, and followed some 10 years of design activity in which all major European aircraft manufacturers had been either directly or indirectly involved, individually or in various collaborative groupings. Most directly a forerunner of the aircraft that became the A320 was the Aérospatiale AS200- actually a

family of project designs that the French company studied in the mid-1970s. In 1977 Aérospatiale joined with British Aerospace, MBB and VFW-Fokker in the Joint European Transport (JET) study group, the objective of which was to provide a short/medium-range transport with 'a new order to quietness, fuel efficiency and operating economy'. The JET work was brought under Airbus Industrie direction when British Aerospace formally became an Airbus partner on 1 January 1979, and the studies continued under the SA (single-aisle) designation. The resulting SA-1, SA-2 and SA-3 had different fuselage lengths. The designation A320 was adopted early in 1981 as refinement of the design continued, while the optimum size remained under study. The aircraft was widely described as a '150-seater'. This being the typical, mixed-class capacity that was thought likely to be required by the airlines in the last decade of the present century. At the time of the marketing launch, however, there was still some interest in a somewhat larger capacity, so A320-100 and A320-200 projects were on offer with one-class accommodation at 32in (81cm) pitch, 154- and 172-seat capacities being provided by different fuselage lengths. Air France was the first to announce an intention to purchase the A320, in both these versions, but before Airbus was able to announce a full launch ▶

Below: Hong Kong-based Dragonair took delivery of its first A320 in February 1993. Its aircraft are fitted out either in a two-class layout with 12 Club and 144 economy seats, or in a 168-seat single-class configuration.

with the necessary financial backing on 2 March 1984, the decision had been made to concentrate on a single body size to accommodate 162 passengers, but still at two different weights, with different fuel capacities. The A320 made its maiden flight at Toulouse on 22 February 1987. Four aircraft were used in the development and certification programme culminating in JAA certification on 26 February 1988. The A320 was a wholly new design, the structure of which is based on well-proven principles used in the A300 and A310. Much use is made of the latest materials (including composites) and of advanced technology features in systems and equipment, with a quadruplex fly-by-wire control system, sidestick controllers for the two pilots, computerised control functions, an electronic flight instrument systems (EFIS) and electronic centralised aircraft monitor. Construction of the A320 is shared between the Airbus Industrie partners in the same way as those of the A300 and A310, with with BAE Systems Airbus (20%) of

the workshare responsible for the wing; EADS Airbus (formerly Aerospatiale Matra) (37.5%) for the forward fuselage and nose; EADS Germany (frrormerly DaimlerChrysler Aerospace Airbus) (37.5%) for the centre and rear fuselage; CASA (4.2%) for the rear fuselage panels and tailplane; and Belairbus for the wing leading edge.

VARIANTS
The two variants of the A320 are the A320-100 and A320-200, which have the same overall dimensions but different fuel capacities and operating weights. The A320-100, ▶

Below: Air Jamaica has re-equipped with an all-Airbus fleet, including this A320-200, typically seating 150 passengers.

however, gave way to the A320-200 after the 20th aircraft, which is now the only production model, simply referred to as the A320. The A320-100 was powered by the 104.5kN (23,500lb) thrust CFM International CFM56-5A1, but a choice between the CFM56 and International Aero Engines (IAE) V2500 turbofans is available in the A320-200. Aircraft are now being delivered with either the 120.1kN (27,000lb) thrust CFM56-5B4/P, or 117.9kn (26,500lb) thrust V2527E-A5 turbofan.

SERVICE USE

First deliveries of the A320-100 were made to Air France and British Caledonian (B.Cal) or

Above: Air Malta is one of many European flag-carriers operating the A320 on both scheduled and charter services.

28 and 31 March 1988 respectively, although the B.Cal aircraft entered service with British Airways, following its take-over with effect from the next day. JAA certification for the CFM56-powered A320-200 was granted on 8 November 1988, and the first delivery was made to Ansett Australia 10 days later. Adria Airways took delivery of the first A320-200 with IAE V2500 engines on 18 May 1989. At 1 January 2001, the A320 order book stood at 1,423 aircraft, with 880 delivered.

Airbus A321

SPECIFICATION
(Airbus A321-100)
Dimensions: Wingspan 34.09m (111ft 10in); length overall 44.51m (146ft 0in); height overall 11.81m (38ft 9in), wing area 122.4m² (1.317.5ft²).
Power Plant: Two 133.4kN (30,000lb) CFM International CFM56-5B1 or IAE V2530-A5 turbofans. Two 137.6kN (31,000lb) CFM56-5B2 engines optional.
Weights: Operating weight empty 47,776kg (105,330lb); max take-off 85,000kg (187,390lb); max landing 75,000kg (166,350lb); max payload 21,725kg (47,895lb).
Performance: Max cruising speed 487kts (900km/h); service ceiling 11,890m (39,000ft); take-off field length 2,345m (7,695ft); landing field length 1,587m

(5,208ft); range with typical payload 2,300nm (4,260km).
Accommodation: Flight crew of two. Single-aisle cabin layout, seating typically 185 passengers in two class layout, or 220 in an all-economy arrangement. Total cargo/baggage volume 52.04m³ (1,838ft³).

The A321 stretched version of the single-aisle A320 was announced on 22 May 1989 and officially launched on 24 November. The A321 incorporates several airframe changes, the most noticeable being the insertion of a 4.27m ▶

Below: All Nippon Airways of Japan operates this A321 in a special 'film roll' colour scheme.

(14ft 0in) fuselage plug forward of the wing and a 2.67m (8ft 9in) plug immediately aft, to provide 24 per cent more seating. Other changes include modified wing trailing-edges with double-slotted flaps, local structural reinforcement, uprated landing gear, repositioned and larger emergency exits, higher take-off weights, and more powerful CFMI or IAE engines. First Airbus aircraft assembled in Germany by Daimler-Benz Aerospace Airbus' plant at Hamburg. Front fuselage plug is produced by Alenia, rear fuselage by British Aerospace. First flight with V2500 lead engine took place on 11 March 1993 at Hamburg, followed by a CFM56-5B-powered model in May. Four aircraft were used in the certification programme, completed with JAA approval for the V2530-powered aircraft on 17 December 1993. Cross-crew qualification of all models in the A319/A320/A321 family is a significant advantage.

VARIANTS

The initial version produced was the A321-100, offering a choice of two standard engines, including the CFM International CFM56-5B1 and IAE V2530-A5 turbofans, both rated at 133.4kN (30,000lb) thrust, plus a more powerful option. An extended-range version, the A321-200, was launched in April 1995 and made its first flight on 12 December 1996. It features further structural

Above: Spanish flag-carrier Iberia took delivery of its first two A321-200s in summer of 1999.

einforcement, higher thrust versions of existing engines and additional centre uel tank, and longer range. A higher MTOW version was launched in January 999. Airbus was reported to be considering to offer a corporate jet variant, the A321ACJ, with additional fuel tanks, but no formal launch had been announced by the beginning of 2001.

SERVICE USE

German flag-carrier Lufthansa accepted the first A321-100 with V2530 engines on 27 January 1994, and put the type into service on 18 March 1994 JAA certification with the A321-100 powered by the CFM56-5B2 was achieved on 15 February 1994 and the first of this model went into service with Alitalia at the end of March. Launch customer Aero Lloyd, a German holiday airline, put the A321-200 into service in February 1998 on its Mediterranean charters. The first higher-gross weight version went into service with Spanair in September 2000. At 1 January 2001, Airbus had obtained firm orders for 377 A321s of both versions, of which 172 had been delivered.

Airbus A330

SPECIFICATION

(Airbus A330-300)

Dimensions: Wingspan 60.30m (197ft 10in); length overall 63.68m (208ft 11in); height overall 16.84m (55ft 3in), wing area 363.1m² (3,908.4ft²).

Power Plant: Two 300kN (67,500lb) st General Electric CF6-80E1A2 or 285kN (64,000lb) Pratt & Whitney PW4164 or 300kN (67,500lb) Rolls-Royce Trent 768 turbofans. Higher thrust versions are also available.

Weights: Operating weight empty 122,200kg (269,400lb); max take-off 230,000kg (507,000lb); max landing 179,000kg (394,625lb); max payload 46,800kg (103,175lb).

Performance: Max cruising speed 500kts (925km/h); service ceiling 12,500m (41,000ft); take-off field length 2,255m (7,400ft); landing field length 1,815m (5,955ft); range with typical payload 4,850nm (8,982km).

Accommodation: Flight crew of two. Twin-aisle cabin layout, seating typically 335 passengers in two class layout with six-abreast in economy, or 440 maximum high density.

After studying a number of possible stretched versions and other derivatives of the basic A300 widebody twin-jet in the late 1970s to maintain its competitive position vis-a-vis the major US manufacturers, Airbus had narrowed

own the choice to two designs. At the initial project stage, these were eferred to as the A300B9 and A300B11. The latter grew into a four-engined ong-range design and led to the TA11, later re-designated A340, which flew efore the twin-engined model. Further into the study process, the medium-ange large-capacity twin-engined A300B9 was renamed the TA9. As the 'TA' esignation indicated, it was a twin-aisle design, based on the use of the basic A300 fuselage cross-section. As the project definition was firmed up and reliminary marketing efforts were initiated, the TA9 officially became the A330 n January 1986. Airbus offered a choice of General Electric CF6-80C2 and Pratt ˣ Whitney PW4000-series turbofans and in 1987, Rolls-Royce engines became n option for the first time on an Airbus aircraft. Official launch, together with he A340, took place on 5 June 1987. Design features include an all-new wing vith high-lift devices from root-to-tip on both leading and trailing edges to nsure optimum low-speed efficiency, A320-derived fly-by-wire control system, omputer-managed fuel transfer system to control centre-of-gravity position nd reduce drag, centralised maintenance system (CMS), and increased thrust ersions of proven engines. Maximum use is made of advanced materials and ▶

Below: Belgian flag-carrier Sabena operates the shorter, but longer-range A330-200.

processes, including composites, superplastic forming and diffusion bonding and robotic assembly. The A330, together with the A340, is part of a uniqu manufacturing and operating concept, whereby two different bu complementary types benefit from substantially common structures, system and assembly line, but serving different market sectors. The A330 has bee optimised for high-density regional and extended-range international routes an can typically carry 335 passengers a distance of 4,500 nautical miles. First fligh of the A330, powered by General Electric CF6 engines, was made from Toulouse on 2 November 1992, followed by a PW4168-engined aircraft on 1 October 1993. A 1,100-hour flight test programme with GE engines led to the first ever simultaneous European and US certification of an airliner on 2 October. The first Rolls-Royce Trent-powered aircraft flew on 31 January 199 Certification with Pratt & Whitney engines was obtained on 2 June 1994 an with the Rolls-Royce Trent on 22 December 1994.

VARIANTS
The basic production version is the A330-300, which was certificated with

Above: Airbus put the A330-300 through its paces at the high-altitude and hot environment of Lhasa Airport in Tibet.

maximum take-off weight of 212,000kg (467,375lb). A longer-range, higher 18,000kg (480,603lb) weight model, previously designated A330-300X, is now available, as is a still higher gross weight version with strengthened wing and a take-off weight of 230,000kg (507,060lb). Range is increased by 00nm (1,300km) to 10,200km. On 24 November 1995, Airbus launched he short-fuselage, extended-range A330-200, formerly referred to as the 330M10, as a direct competitor to the Boeing 767-300ER. This differs in aving a 10-frame reduction in fuselage length to 59.00m (193ft 6³/4in) and maximum take-off weight of 230,000kg (507,060lb). It can carry 256 assengers in three classes a distance of 6,400nm (11,850km). First flight ook place on 13 August 1997. At the Farnborough Air Show in July 2000, irbus promoted the A330-500 (formerly the A330-100), a short-fuselage ariant of the A330-200. Reducing the length from 59.00m to 54.60m (179ft ³/4in) through removing for frames forward of the wing and four frames aft, ▶

the A330-500 will also feature new cockpit systems developed for the A340-500/600 models. Airbus is promoting two gross weight options of 228,000kg (502,650lb) and a lighter 195,000kg (429,900lb), providing respective ranges with 222 passengers of 7,000nm (12,950km) and 4,350nm (8,050km). Design definition is expected to be frozen by the third quarter of 2001, with planned first flight in third quarter 2003 and service entry at the beginning of 2004.

SERVICE USE

First deliveries of the A330-300 were made to launch customer Air Inter (now Air France Europe) on 30 December 1993 and the type entered service on 17 January 1994 with a flight from Paris Orly to Marseille. Aer Lingus flew the first

service across the Atlantic in May 1994, after the GE-powered version was granted 120-minute ETOPS approval, since extended to A330s powered by Pratt & Whitney and Rolls-Royce. First orders for the new A330-200 came from ILFC and Korean Air in March and May 1996. First delivery of the CF6-80E1-engined A330-200, to ILFC for lease to Canada 3000, was made on 29 May 1998. Korean Air received the first PW4000-powered model in June that same year. The first Rolls-Royce Trent-powered version first flew on 24 June 1998 and was delivered to Air Transat following JAR and Transport Canada certification in January 1999. At 1 January 2001, the A330 had won 342 firm orders, of which 171 had been delivered.

Below: US Airways is taking delivery of 10 A330-300s.

Airbus A340

SPECIFICATION
(Airbus A340-300)

Dimensions: Wingspan 60.30m (197ft 10in); length overall 63.65m (208ft 10in); height overall 16.74m (54ft 11in), wing area 363.1m² (3,908.4ft²).

Power Plant: Four CFM International CFM56-5C engines at various thrust levels, including 138.8kN (31,200lb) each in -5C2, 114.6kN (32,500lb) in -5C3 and 151.2kN (34,000lb) in -5C4.

Weights: Operating weight empty 129,806kg (286,175lb); max take-off 275,000kg (606,275lb); max landing 190,000kg (418,875lb); max payload 48,194kg (106,250lb).

Performance: Max cruising speed 494kts (914km/h); service ceiling 12,500m (41,000ft); take-off field length 2,790m (9,150ft); landing field length 1,855m (6,090ft); range with typical payload 7,300nm (13,520km).

Accommodation: Flight crew of two. Twin-aisle cabin layout, seating typically 335 passengers in two class layout with eight-abreast in economy, or 440 maximum high density.

In the 1970s, Airbus began studying a number of possible stretched version and other derivatives of the A300 twin-jet to build on its success in havin broken the US manufacturers' monopoly of widebody aircraft. These studie eventually crystallised into two distinct, but parallel designs, initially referred t as the A300B9 and A300B11. The A300B9 grew into a twin-engined medium range aircraft and led to the TA9, later re-designated A330, but it was the fou

Below: Virgin Atlantic flies the A340-300, but also has the longer A340-500 on order.

Above: Air Tahiti Nui's sole A340-200 links Tahiti with the US West Coast.

engined A300B11 which took priority in the development of the new widebody family. After first being redesignated TA11, TA standing for twin-aisle, the aircraft was given the next number in the Airbus sequence, namely A340, in January 1986. The A340 was jointly launched with the A330 on 5 June 1986. Using the same all-new wing, A320-derived fly-by-wire system, centre-of-gravity management system and advanced materials and manufacturing processes of the A330, the A340 diverged in the choice of power plant and engine-related systems. With four engines, a smaller turbofan was required and Airbus decided on using a higher thrust version of the CFM International CFM56 turbofan used in the A320/A321, with FADEC (Full Authority Digital Engine Control) as standard. No other suitable engine was available. Airbus had planned to power the A340 with the SuperFan, a ultra-high bypass development of the CFM56 or V2500 engines, but this came to nothing. Nevertheless, the choice of engine provides important commonality benefits with the single-aisle family. The A340, together with the A330, is also part of a unique concept, whereby two different but complementary types benefit from substantially common structures and systems, but serving different market sectors. The A340 has been optimised for medium-density long-range routes and typically carries 295 passengers a distance of over 7,000nm (13,000km). The A340-300 took

off from Toulouse on its maiden flight on 25 October 1991, followed on 1 April 1992 by the shorter A340-200. Six aircraft (four A340-300 and two A340-200) were used in the flight test programme, which was concluded with the simultaneous certification of both versions by the European joint airworthiness authorities (JAA) on 22 December 1992. FAA certification was granted in May 1993.

VARIANTS

The first two versions to enter service were the A340-300 high-capacity model, intially powered by four 138.8kN (31,200lb) CFM56-5C2 engines and capable of transporting 295 three-class passengers, and the shorter-fuselage, but longer-range A340-200, with reduced three-class capacity of 263 passengers. The extended-range A340-300E and first flown on 25 August 1995, can carry a typical 295-passenger load over a distance of 7,150nm (13,242km) and is powered by higher 151.2kN (34,000lb) thrust CFM56-5C4 engines. Three additional fuel tanks in the rear cargo hold, ▶

Below: Turkish Airlines now operates five A340-300s, having taken delivery of its first aircraft in July 1993. They are used on long-haul services, fitted out in three-classes.

strengthened fuselage and wings of the A340-200 produced the A340-8000 growth version, first announced in November 1995, offering a range of over 8,000nm (15,000km) in a 253-seat three-class configuration. Announced at the 1997 Paris Air Show and formally launched in December that year, the A340-600 is a stretched derivative of the A340-300, with 249kN (56,000lb) Rolls-Royce Trent 556 turbofans, improved aerodynamics, additional fuel capacity, strengthened and modified four-wheel central landing gear, and a maximum take-off weight of 365,000kg (804,675lb). Compared to the A340-300, it is 11.70m (38ft 4½in) longer and capable of carrying 380 passengers in a three-class layout over a distance of 7,515nm (13,900km). It was due to make its first flight in January 2001. The A340-500, an ultra long-range version of the A340-600, was also launched in December 1997. It is six frames longer than the A340-300, adding up to 4.20m for a total length of 67.80m (222ft 5¼in), and also features an increased span of 63.60m (208ft 8ni0, taller vertical stabiliser, new horizontal stabiliser, and strengthened and modified landing gear. Maximum take-off weight is 365,000kg (804,675lb).

but a higher weight of 372,000kg (820,125lb) is under consideration. With a typical three-class compliment of 313 passengers, the aircraft will have a range of 8,415 nm (15,570km). It will be powered by the 236kN (53,000lb) Rolls-Royce Trent 553. First flight is scheduled for mid-2001.

SERVICE USE
The A340-300 and A340-200 entered service in March 1993 with Air France and Lufthansa respectively. Singapore Airlines took delivery of the first high gross weight A340-300E on 17 April 1996 and the Sultan of Brunei received the first A340-8000, configured in a VVIP arrangement, in 1997. The A340-500 will enter service with Air France in Mid-2002, with launch customer Virgin Atlantic Airways, which placed the first firm order for eight on 15 December 1997, expected to put the A340-600 into service in early 2002. By 1 January 2001, Airbus had orders for 307 A340s, with 186 delivered.

Below: The new A340-600 during rollout in September 2000.

Airbus A380

SPECIFICATION (provisional)
(Airbus A380-100)
Dimensions: Wingspan 79.80m (261ft 9³/₄in); length 73.00m (239ft 6in); height overall 24.10m (79ft 0³/₄in).
Power Plant: Four 298kN (67,000lb) thrust Rolls-Royce Trent 900 or Engine Alliance GP7200.
Weights: Operating weight empty 267,000kg (588,625lb); max take-off 540,000kg (1,190,500lb); max landing 381,000kg (839,950lb); max payload 85,000kg (187,395lb).
Performance: Max cruising speed Mach 0.85+; take-off field length 3,350m (11,000ft); range with typical payload 7,650nm (14,165km).
Accommodation: Flight crew of two. Four-aisle cabin layout on two decks, seating typically 555 passengers in a two-class configuration.

In parallel with the eventually inconclusive joint studies between Airbus members and Boeing, the European consortium decided in May 1994 to continue feasibility studies into its own A3XX high-capacity aircraft. In March 1996, Airbus set up a Large Aircraft Division tasked with preparing the launch and to enter into discussions with key airlines to establish a design definition. Following commitments for 50 aircraft from six customers (Air France, Emirates, ILFC, Qantas, Singapore Airlines and Virgin Atlantic), Airbus formally launched the A3XX as the A380 on 19 December 2000. Airbus is currently offering the double-deck A380 in three basic versions, with several specific models projected within these three. The baseline version is the 550-seat A380-100, which will also be made available in -100C Combi variants with

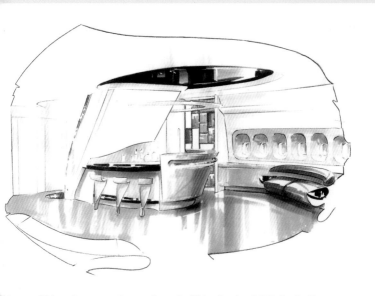

Above: Airbus is promoting various facilities in the A380, including a lower deck bar area.

Below: Emirates was the first airline to commit to Airbus' new double-deck 'super jumbo'.

typically 421 passengers and 11 freight pallets, the increased range -100R, and the -100F freighter with a capacity for 57 pallets and the same main deck rear cargo door as the Combi version. The A380-200 is 6.40m (21ft 0in) longer and will seat 656 passengers in a three-class layout, or up to 1,000 in high-density configuration. A reduction of 5.10m (16ft 8³⁄₄in) in fuselage length compared to the -100 baseline aircraft, produces the A380-50R 481-passenger version. All models have the same wingspan of 79.80m (261ft 9³⁄₄in), keeping all models within the 80 x 80m 'box', which requires minimum adaptation of existing airports. Maximum design take-off weight is 590,000kg (1,300,725lb). Dual-lane stairs will permit four-aisle boarding, with typically 10-abreast layouts on the main deck and 8-abreast on the upper deck. Shops, bars, restaurants, fitness centres and many other passenger facilities on the lower deck are being offered to customer airlines. Two power plants are offered, the Rolls-Royce Trent 900 or Engine Alliance (General Electric and Pratt & Whitney) GP7200. Manufacture of the A380 will be undertaken by the Airbus members in France, Germany, Spain and the United Kingdom. First flight is due in mid-2004, with customer deliveries early in 2006.

Airbus (SATIC)
A300-600ST Beluga

SPECIFICATION
(A300-600ST)

Dimensions: Wingspan 44.84m (147ft 1in); length overall 56.16m (184ft 3in); height overall 17.25m (56ft 7¼in).

Power Plant: Two 262.45kN (59,000lb) General Electric CF6-80C2A8 turbofans.

Weights: Operating weight empty 86,500kg (190,700lb); max take-off 155,000kg (341,700lb); max landing 140,000kg (308,645lb); max payload 47,300kg (104,280lb).

Performance: Max cruising speed 420kts (778km/h); range with max payload 900nm (1,667km).

Accommodation: Flight crew of two. Main-deck cargo volume 1,400 m³ (49,440ft³).

On 20 October 1991, Aerospatiale and Deutsche Aérospace Airbus (now EADS Germany), two of the partners in Airbus Industrie, set up the Special Air Transport International Company (SATIC), to undertake engineering production and certification work for a new specialist freighter to replace the four Super Guppys, which have transported Airbus parts between the various manufacturing locations since 1971. Dubbed the A300-600ST Beluga Super Transporter, the aircraft is based on the A300-600R, but almost equals the construction of a new aircraft, since little similarity is retained. The main

Below: The Beluga Super Transporter bears little resemblance to the Airbus A300-600R from which it is derived. The giant 'whale-like' aircraft has now taken over from the Super Guppy in carrying Airbus assemblies across Europe. Five are in service. Airbus is also examining similar outsize freighter concepts based on its larger A330/A340 models.

Above: The Beluga transports whole assemblies of Airbus aircraft between the various manufacturing locations.

elements of the work involve the relocation of the cockpit 1.5m (4ft 11in) forward of the main cargo deck and to a lower level, allowing the cargo door - the largest ever - to be positioned in the nose above. A new upper fuselage, which enlarges the diameter to 7.40m (24ft 3¼in), permits a greatly increased cargo volume. The tailplane has been strengthened, and to maintain longitudinal stability during the flight, horizontal stabilisers have been modified and equipped with auxiliary fins. New components for the Beluga are being produced by 12 main sub-contractors in five European countries. Final assembly is at Toulouse. The first aircraft made its maiden flight on 13 September 1994 and was delivered to Airbus in September 1995, immediately following certification. Airbus has placed orders for five aircraft, the last of which was due for delivery on 31 December 2000. The new freighter will also be targeted at the general commercial and military market.

Airtech (CASA/IPTN) CN-235

SPECIFICATION
(CN-235-100)
Dimensions: Wingspan 25.81m (84ft 8in); length overall 21.40m (70ft 2½in); height overall 8.18m (26ft 10in), wing area 59.10m² (636ft²).
Power Plant: Two General Electric CT9-7C turboprops each flat rate at 1,305kW (1,750shp). Four-blade Hamilton Standard 14RF-21 propellers.
Weights: Operating weight empty 9,800kg (21,605lb); max take-off 15,100kg (33,289lb); max landing 14,900kg (32,849lb); max payload 4,000kg (8,818lb).
Performance: Max cruising speed 228kts (422km/h); rate of climb 9.65m/s (1,900ft/min); service ceiling 6,860m (22,500ft); take-off field length 1,290m (4,235ft); landing field length 772m (2,530ft); range with max fuel 810nm (1,501km); range with typical payload 2,350nm (4,352km).
Accommodation: Crew of two on flight deck plus one cabin attendant. Commuter configuration for 44 passengers in four-abreast seating with central aisle. Baggage compartment volume 7.0m³ (247.2ft³).

Details of the CN-235 were made public in June 1981, when Construcciones Aeronauticas SA (CASA) in Spain and P T Nurtanio in Indonesia (now IPTN

announced their intention to develop and produce the aircraft on an equally-shared basis for both commercial and military applications. Subsequently, a company known as Aircraft Technology Industries (Airtech) was set up in Madrid to handle the programme. With accommodation for up to 44 passengers or 48 troops, the short-range CN-235 entered what appeared to be an overcrowded marketplace for aircraft of approximately the same capacity, but it differed noticeable from its several competitors in being designed as much for military use as commercial application, as indicated in particular by the provision of a large rear ventral loading and supply dropping ramp/door, and the retractable tandem wheel main landing gear units suitable for rough field operations. The size of the cabin in the circular cross-section fuselage was such as to offer a high degree of comfort in commuter airline layouts; at the same time, the military aspects of the design made the aircraft potentially useful also ▶

Below: Binter Mediterraneo and Binter Canarias, both part of Spanish flag-carrier Iberia, are two of only four airlines using the high-wing turboprop transport. Binter Canarias serves the Canary Islands, while Binter Mediterraneo links southern Spain with the Balearics.

for mixed traffic and quick-change operations or as a pure commercial freighter able to carry, for example, 18 passengers and two LD3 containers, or four standard LD3s or five LD2s. The agreement between CASA and Nurtanio provided for each company to be responsible for 50 per cent of the development and production of the CN-235, without duplication of manufacturing effort but with final assembly lines at the CASA works in Madrid and those of IPTN (previously Nurtanio) at the Husein Sastranegara Air Force Base at Bandung in Indonesia. So far as manufacture is concerned, CASA is responsible for the forward and centre portions of the fuselage, the wing centre section and inboard flaps. IPTN produces the rear fuselage section, outer wings complete with flaps and ailerons, and the entire tail unit. Preliminary design activities concerned with the CN-235 began in January 1980, with manufacture of two prototypes commencing in May 1981 and final assembly starting in 1983. Simultaneously, the two prototypes were rolled out on 10 September 1983, one in Madrid and the other at Bandung. First to fly was the CASA-assembled aircraft on 11 November 1983, the Indonesian following on 30 December of the same year. Spain and Indonesian certification was obtained 20 June 1986 and deliveries began on 15 December from Indonesian production and on 4 February 1987 from CASA. A total of 50 aircraft are being assembled under licence by Tusaş Aerospace Industries (TAI) to fulfil a Turkish order. The first Turkish-assembled aircraft flew on 24 September 1992, with deliveries starting on 13 November that same year. The CN-235 is certificated to FAR Parts 25 and 36 and to the European JAR 25. FAA certification was grated on 3 December 1986.

VARIANTS
Initial production version, of which 15 were built in each location, was the CN

235-10 with General Electric CT7-7A engines. This was replaced in 1988 by the CN-235-100/110, incorporating 1,305kW (1,750shp) CT7-9C engines in composite nacelles and a number of systems improvements. The designation –100 distinguishes Spanish-built models from the Indonesian –110 production. Structural reinforcements, higher operating weights and increased range produced the CN-235-200/220. Civil versions are available in passenger, cargo or quick-change (QC) passenger/cargo configurations. Military aircraft are the CN-235M transport, CN-235-330 Phoenix, and the CN-235 MP Persuader and CN-235 MPA for maritime patrol missions. A CN-235 AEW airborne early warning aircraft is proposed. Civil and military versions have the same overall dimensions. A stretched development of the CN-235M, the C-295M is being built in Spain. It made its first flight on 28 November 1997.

SERVICE USE

Of the many CN-235 originally entered into the order book, only 26 are in airline service today. Many of the initial options taken out by Spanish and Indonesian operators, including Aviaco, Bouraq, Deraya, Dirgantara and Mandala, never materialised and the main commercial operators are Merpati Nusantara, which put the type into service on 1 March 1988 and has 14 Series 10 in service and another 16 Series 210 on order; and Spanish regional airlines Binter Canarias and Binter Mediterraneo with seven. The aircraft has achieved greater success in the military market.

Below: CASA announced the stretched C-295 at the 1997 Paris air show. Although targeted at the military market, it may find applications as a commercial transport.

Alliance Starliner

SPECIFICATION (provisional)
(Alliance Starliner SL-200)
Dimensions: Wingspan 28.00m (91ft 101/4in); length 27.81m (91ft 3in); height overall 10.03m (32ft 11in).
Power Plant: Two 60kN (13,500lb) thrust BR700.
Weights: Operating weight empty 20,275kg (44,700lb); max take-off 35,600kg (78,500lb); max landing 34,020kg (75,000lb); max payload 8,165kg (18,000lb).
Performance: Max cruising speed 350kts (648km/h); take-off field length 1,370m (4,500ft); landing field length 1,070m (3,500ft); range with typical payload 2,400nm (4,440km).
Accommodation: Flight crew of two. Single offset aisle cabin layout, seating typically 70 passengers.

New US company Alliance Aircraft Corporation announced the fast track development of a new family of regional jets on 20 January 2000, with letters of intent from 30 unnamed customers. During the Farnborough Air Show in July 2000, Alliance revealed firm orders for another 250 aircraft plus a further 200 options, from New York-based Global Airlines. The Starliner family is of conventional construction with twin wing-mounted turbofan engines, and a circular fuselage with off-set aisle to permit five abreast seating. Baseline engine is the Rolls-Royce Deutschland BR700. The company is proposing to build three models with different seating capacities. The first two to be delivered in 2003 are the 70-seat SL-200 and 90-seat SL-300 variants, powered by two turbofans in the 60kN (13,500lb

Antonov An-12

SPECIFICATION
(Antonov An-12)
Dimensions: Wingspan 38.00m (124ft 8in); length overall 33.10m (108ft 7¼in); height overall 10.53m (34ft 6½in), wing area 121.7m² (1,310ft²).
Power Plant: Four 2,983kW (4,000shp) Ivchenko AI-20K turboprops with four-blade constant-speed feathering and reversing AV-68 propellers.
Weights: Operating weight empty 28,000kg (61,730lb); max take-off 61,000kg (134,480lb); max payload 20,000kg (44,090lb).

Performance: Max cruising speed 361kts (670km/h); initial rate of climb 10.0m/s (1,970ft/min; service ceiling 10,200m (33,500ft); take-off field length 700m (2,300ft); landing field length 500m (1,640ft); range with max payload 1,940nm (3,600km).
Accommodation: Flight crew of five. Seating for up to 100 in troop-carrying version. Total usable cabin volume for freight 97.2m³ (3,433ft³). Rear ramp/door for direct loading.

The An-12 freighter had its origins in the An-10, which appeared in 1957 as one of the first of Aeroflot's turboprop transports, entering service in 84-seat form and being developed into the 100-seat An-10A. The An-12 appeared in 1959 as a dedicated freighter and became numerically more important than the An-10, entering service both with Aeroflot and with the Soviet military forces

Below: The Starliner is a proposed new regional aircraft family.

and 71.2kN (16,000lb) thrust class respectively. The third version, to be delivered from 2004, is the smaller SL-100, which will typically carry 35-50 passengers.

Above: An-12 freighters are often seen in the West, including this version operated by Bulgarian carrier Inter Trans Air, photographed at Manston, UK.

Its military significance was shown by the provision of a twin-gun tail turret, and this feature (less the guns) was usually retained in aircraft operated by Aeroflot on freight services and supply missions outside the Soviet Union, for which the An-12 continues to be widely used. The type was also exported to several Soviet bloc air forces and to the airlines of some countries in the Soviet sphere of influence, including Bulgaria, China, Cuba, Iraq, Poland and Guinea. A version similar to the Soviet An-12BP production model has been manufactured in China as the Hanzhong Y-8, with Chinese-built Wojiang WJ-6 turboprops. The NATO reporting name for the An-12 variant is 'Cub'.

Antonov An-24/26/30/32

SPECIFICATION

(Antonov An-24V)

Dimensions: Wingspan 29.20m (95ft 9½in); length overall 23.53m (77ft 2½in); height overall 8.32m (27ft 3½in), wing area 74.98m² (807ft²).

Power Plant: Two Ivchenko AI-24A turboprops, each rated at 1,902kW(2,550shp). An-24RV has auxiliary turbojet in starboard nacelle, rated at 8.82kN (1,984lb) thrust.

Weights: Operating weight empty 13,300kg (29,321lb); max take off 21,000kg (46,296lb); max landing 21,000kg (46,296lb); max payload 5,500kg (122,125lb).

Performance: Max cruising speed 243kts (450km/h); rate of climb 8.0m/s (1,575ft/min); service ceiling 8,400m (27,560ft); take-off field length 1,720m (5,645ft); landing field length 1,590m (5,215ft); range with max fuel 2,293nm (2,400mn); range with typical payload 296nm (550mn).

Accommodation: Flight crew of two plus one cabin attendant. Standard layout for 52 passengers in paired seats four-abreast with central aisle. Rear baggage hold 2.8m³ (99ft³).

The design bureau headed by the late Oleg K. Antonov began the development in 1958 of a twin-turboprop transport intended to replace the large numbers of piston-engined twins (such as the Lisunov Li-2 and the Ilyushin Il-12 and Il-14) used on internal routes in the Soviet Union. First flown in April 1960, the An-24 (NATO reporting name 'Coke') is a conventional high

ving monoplane seating 44/52 passengers and one of the most widely
xported of Soviet post-war transports.

VARIANTS

he standard 50-seat production version of the Antonov transport was
designated An-24V and was powered by (1,902kW) 2,550shp AI-24 engines. It
vas followed in production by the An-24V (Series 2 which had improved AI-24A
ngines (with water injection), increased chord on the wing centre section, and
arger flaps . For aircraft operating in 'hot and high' conditions, 2,103kW
2,820shp) AI-24T engines could be fitted. The designation An-24T referred to a
pecialised all-freight variant which incorporated a loading door in the rear of the
abin floor, hinged to open upwards into the rear fuselage. To allow both the
N-24V and An-24T to carry bigger payloads out of 'difficult' airfields, an
ptional installation was an RU19-300 auxiliary turbojet in the starboard engine
acelle in the An-24RV and An-24RT versions. Developed in 1971 the An-24P
vas a special fire fighting version, with provision to drop firefighters and ▶

*Below: The high-wing An-24 and its derivatives were delivered to all
Soviet Republics and to friendly nations around the world. The line-up of
An-24RVs at Riga in Latvia shows the remnants of the large fleet of
atavio, once the flag-carrier of this small, now independent, Baltic
epublic.*

equipment by parachute. Primarily intended for military duties, the An-26 wa
based on the An-24RT and, first seen in public in 1969, incorporated
completely new rear fuselage with a 'beaver tail' and a unique rear door whic
could either hinge down conventionally as a loading ramp or slide forward unde
the fuselage to provide a clear exit for parachuting. Many variants wer
produced. A specialised version of the An-24 for aerial survey duties i
designated An-30, and appeared in 1973. A hot-and-high version of the An-2€
the An-32, intended primarily for military use, first became known in May 1977
Licence-production of the An-24 family is continuing in China as the Xian Y7
powered by Chinese-built WJ5A-1 turboprops based on the AI-24A. The Y7-10
has Western avionics and winglets, while further improvements, including Prat
& Whitney engines were incorporated in the Y7-200A Combi and the stretche
Y7-200B. A civil derivative of the An-26 is the Y7-500, certificated on 15 Jun
1994. An improved Y7-200A was first shown in model form at Asian Aerospace

Antonov An-38

SPECIFICATION
(Antonov An-38-100)
Dimensions: Wingspan 22.06m (72ft 4½in); overall length 15.54m (51ft 0in);
overall height 4.30m (14ft 1¼in); wing area
Power Plant: Two AlliedSignal TPE331-14GR-801E turboprops each rated at
1,227kW (1,645shp) for take-off, with Hartzell HC-B5MA five-bladed propellers.
Weights: Operating weight empty 5,087kg (11,215lb); Max take-off weight
8,800kg (19,400lb); max payload 2,500kg (5,510lb).
Performance: Normal cruising speed around 200kts (370km/h); take-off field
length 790m (2,590ft); range with max payload 324nm (600km).
Accommodation: Flight crew of two. Seating for up to 27 passengers, two-
abreast with central aisle.

Developed from the Polish-built Antonov An-28, primarily to replace large numbers o
Let L-410 Turbolets and to a lesser extent the Antonov An-24 and the small Yakovle
Yak-40 trijet, the high-wing An-38 is distinguished by a lengthened passenger cabin

ingapore, in February 2000, designated MA-60, which will also be built in a maritime patrol version as the MA-MPA.

SERVICE USE

The An-24 entered service with Aeroflot in September 1963 on the routes between Moscow, Voronezh and Saratov. It became widely used in the Soviet Union, and was also exported (for airline use) to some 14 other airlines, including most of those of the Soviet bloc nations. Production ended in the Soviet Union in 1978, with about 1,360 An-24s reported to have been built. Close on 100 have been produced in China to date, with orders for the MA-60 exceeding 60 aircraft. Approximately 1,400 An-26s were built between 1968 and 1985, before being superseded by the An-32, which remains in production, being built in several specialised versions. Although the An-24 family of aircraft is no longer in frontline airline use, some 825 remain in service across the world.

provide accommodation for typically 26 passengers seated three-abreast and a high content of western equipment, to make it more attractive on the world market. As its predecessor, it has a high degree of self-sufficiency for operation in outlying areas, in all conditions and from unpaved runways. An initial batch of six aircraft was produced, with the prototype making its first flight at Novosibirsk on 23 June 1994. Production started by Novosibirsk Aircraft Production Association in 1995. Initial variants include the An-38-100, powered by two 1,227 kW (1,645 shp) Honeywell TPE331-14GR-801E turboprops; An-38-200 with alternative 1,029 kW (1,380 shp) Omsk MKB 'Mars' TVD-20 turboprops; and the An-38K, a convertible version of the -100 with a large upward-opening side door at the rear to permit loading of LD-3 cargo containers, and a built-in cargo handling system. Specialised versions are available for a number of different utility and specialist applications. First delivered to Vostok Airlines in 1998, but less than 10 built by 1 January 2001.

Below: The 26-passenger An-38 was developed mainly to replace large numbers of the smaller Let L-410 Turbojet.

Antonov An-72/An-74

SPECIFICATION
(Antonov An-72)
Dimensions: Wingspan 31.89m (104ft 7½in); length overall 28.07m (92ft 1in); height overall 8.75m (28ft 8½in), wing area 98.53m² (1,060.6ft²).
Power Plant: Two 63.75kN (14,330lb) ZMKB Progress/Lotarev D-36 Series 1A turbofans.
Weights: Operating weight empty 19,500kg (42,990lb); max take-off 34,500kg (76,059lb); max payload 10,000kg (22,046lb).
Performance: Max cruising speed 374kts (692km/h); service ceiling 11,800m (38,715ft); take-off field length 930m (3,050ft); landing field length 465m (1,525ft); range with max payload 540nm (1,000km).
Accommodation: Flight crew of three. Seating for up to 38 passengers.

The An-72 was developed as much for military duties as for commercial use. It is unique as a production aircraft for its use of upper surface blowing (USB) as a means of increasing lift and thus providing STOL performance. The two high-bypass turbofans are mounted well ahead of the high-positioned wing which causes the airflow to attach itself to the wing upper surface with the result of enhanced lift and good low-speed performance. Other notable features are the multi-leg main landing gear contained in fuselage side blisters and its rear-loading provisions, indicative of its military applications and the requirement to operate from unprepared airstrips. The first of two prototypes, built at Kiev, flew on 22 December 1977, but after eight pre-series aircraft production was transferred to Kharkov. The first Kharkov-built production aircraft made its maiden flight in 1985. The An-74 Polar version was announced in February 1984.

VARIANTS
The An-72 (NATO reporting name 'Coaler C') is the standard transport version with ZMKB Progress D-36 Series 2A engines each rated at 63.74kN (14,330lb) thrust, but many specialised mission aircraft are available including the An-72 for maritime patrol, An-72S military VIP transport, two-crew export An-72V, and the dedicated civilianised An-72-100. Variants of the An-74 'Coaler B'

bove: The giant Soviet airline Aeroflot used the An-72 to service utlying areas with unprepared airstrips.

clude the basic Arctic model; An-74-200 freighter with increased payload; n-74T-200A with longer hold, loading winch and roller conveyors, and the milar An-74T-100 with navigator station; An-74TK-200 convertible with twin lding seats for 52 passengers and the similar An-74TK-100, but with avigator and flight engineer stations. A stretched version, the An-74-400 is to e offered in both passenger and freight versions. The An-74T-300 and An-4TK-300 are proposed derivative versions announced with the overwing ngine arrangement changed to the more normal podded, underslung engine nfiguration. Studies have also begun into the An-174, a stretched version ith 74.3kN (16,700lb) ZMBK Progress D-436T1 turbofans.

ERVICE USE

lore than 160 An-72/74s believed built to date, with 50 in non-military ervice.

Left: The convertible passenger/cargo Antonov An-74TK was demonstrated at the 1997 Paris Air Show. Like many Antonov designs, it has the capability to operate from unprepared airstrips.

Antonov An-124

SPECIFICATION

(Antonov An-124-100)

Dimensions: Wingspan 73.30m (240ft 5¾in); length overall 69.10m (226ft 8 ½in); height overall 21.08m (69ft 2in), wing area 628.0m² (6,760ft²)

Power Plant: Four ZMKB Progress (Lotarev)D-18T turbofans, each rated at 229kN (15,590lb).

Weights: Operating weight empty 175,000kg (385,800lb); max take-off 392,000kg (864,200lb); max landing 330,000kg (727,513lb); max payload 120,000kg (264,550lb).

Performance: Max cruising speed 467kts (865km/h); service ceiling 12,200m (40,000ft); take-off field length 3,000m (9,840ft); landing field length 900m (2,955ft); range with max fuel 8,900nm (16,500km); range with max payload 2,430nm (4,500km).

Accommodation: Six or seven flight crew plus 10-12 technician and load masters. Cabin for up to 88 passengers, Cargo volume 1,000m³ (35,315ft³).

The An-124 was first reported to be under development in the late 1970s when the designation was thought to be an An-40, later changed to An-400. The definitive designation of An-124 emerged on May 1985 when an example of this very large transport made an appearance at the Paris air show. The first flight of the prototype had been made on 26 December 1982, and production examples were reported to be in service by January 1986. Loads carried by the An-124 range from the largest tanks to complete SS-20 nuclear missile systems, and from earth movers to oil well equipment; it is therefore of value in major civil engineering schemes and is now used to transport heavy and outsize equipment across the world. The An-124 is of conventional aerodynamic design but makes extensive use of composite materials in it

Below: Antonov's giant An-124 Ruslan is the largest commercial freighter in service. Its ability to operate from an unprepared airfield in remote locations, makes it sought-after for the carriage of large and heavy pieces of equipment and machinery.

bove: The Antonov Design Bureau operates the An-124 on commercial argo flights.

:ructure, representing some 1,500m² (16,150sq ft) of surface area and saving 800kg (3,970lb) of weight. The floor of the main hold is fabricated from :anium, and the flight control system is completely fly-by-wire. A 24 wheel nding gear (10 main wheels on each side of the fuselage and four nose heels) helps to spread the weight of the An-124, which is the largest ʳoduction aircraft in the world, and allow it to operate from unprepared fields, ʳard-packed snow and ice-covered swampland, although not necessarily at its aximum weights. The An-124 has large front and rear loading access quipped with fold-down hydraulic ramps for roll-roll-on/roll-off capability. Its avernous cargo hold is fitted with two overhead cranes, each with a 10-tonne ting capacity. Two further optional cranes can increase lifting capacity to 37 ʳnnes. NATO reporting name is 'Condor'.

ARIANTS
asic model is the An-124, used largely by Aeroflot and the military. On 20 ecember 1992, the aircraft was certificated by AviaRegistr of Interstate viation Committee of CIS for commercial operations as the An-124-100, with stricted take-off weight and payload. A prototype An-124-100M was ɔmpleted in late 1995, equipped with Western avionics, reducing crew to four. ʳew is further reduced to three in EFIS-equipped An-124-102. A firefighting ater-bomber, capable of dropping 200 tonnes of retardant, is under ɔnsideration as the An-124FFR, as is the An-124-200 with 263kN (59,100lb) rust General Electric CF6-80C2 turbofan engines.

SERVICE
ʳe An-124 entered service in January 1986 in Aeroflot markings. First foreign ɔerator was UK airline Air Foyle, which began operations in September 1989 a joint venture with the Antonov Design Bureau, followed by another joint ɛnture between HeavyLift Cargo Airlines (UK) and Volga-Dnepr of Russia. ʳound 85 aircraft are believed to have been built.

Antonov An-140

SPECIFICATION
(Antonov An-140)
Dimensions: Wingspan 24.50m (80ft 43/4in); length 22.60m (74ft 2in); height overall 8.23m (26ft 113/4in).
Power Plant: Two 1,839kW (2,466shp) Motor-Sich AI-30 Series I turboprops.
Weights: Max take-off 19,150kg (42,218lb); max landing 19,100kg (42,108lb); max payload 6,000kg (13,227lb).
Performance: Max cruising speed 310kts (575km/h); cruising altitude 7,500m (24,600ft); take-off field length 1,350m (4,430ft); range with typical payload 486nm (900km).
Accommodation: Flight crew of two. Single-aisle cabin layout, seating typically 52 passengers four-abreast. Cargo/baggage volume 9.0m³ (318ft³).

The twin-turboprop Antonov An-140 is of traditional high-wing design and closely resembles the An-24 which it is intended to replace, offering twice the fuel efficiency and range, as well as a high cruise speed of 310kt (575km/h). Production of this new aircraft was committed in 1994, following receipt of orders from unnamed Ukrainian and Russian airline companies, and the first prototype was rolled out at the Ukrainian design bureau's Kiev base on 6 June 1997 and made its maiden flight. on 17 September that year. On that same day, Air Ukraine signed Letter of Intent for up to 40 aircraft for delivery between 2000 and 2010, followed later by orders from Samara Airlines and another LoI from Aeroflot. In series production since 1999. at the Kharkov State Aircraft Manufacturing Company and Kiev State Aviation Plant, Ukraine and by Aviacor in Samara, Russia, the An-140 is

rue joint venture programme, with aerodynamic research by TsAGI, the 2,500shp turboprop engines designed by Klimov but assembled by Motor-Sich, wings by KhGAPP, the AB-140 propellers by Aerosila, landing gear by Aviagregat and the AI-9-3B auxiliary power unit by Motor-Sich. Western input is provided by French companies Auxilec and Eros, providing power supply and oxygen systems respectively, while MAN of Germany supplies the toilet system. It is also being assembled by HESA in Iran for the local market.

VARIANTS

The baseline aircraft is the An-140 with two 1,839kW (2,466shp) AI-30 Series I turboprops (Klimov TV3-117VMA-SBM1 built under licence by Motor-Sich), which was certificated in May 2000. Aircraft ordered by Aeroflot will have 1,864kW (2,500shp) Pratt & Whitney PW127A and Hamilton Sundstrand propellers, and be designated An-140A. The An-140T is a proposed freighter with a large cargo door at the rear, while the An-140TK convertible model will carry 3,650kg (8,050lb) of cargo in the forward cabin and 20 passengers at the rear. Another proposal, under development since 1997, is a 68-seat version with a 3.80m (12ft 5½in) longer fuselage, given the designation An-140-100. Also under development is the An-142 with a forward-retracting rear loading ramp. The An-140M is being offered to the military for patrol, surveillance, photographic and other missions.

SERVICE USE

Air Ukraine took delivery of the first An-140 in 2000.

Left: The An-140 is intended to replace the large numbers of An-24s that remain in service.

Antonov An-225 Mriya

SPECIFICATION
(Antonov An-225)
Dimensions: Wingspan 88.40m (290ft 0in); length overall 84.00m (275ft 7in); height overall 18.20m (59ft 8in), wing area 905m² (9,742ft²).
Power Plant: Six 229.8kN (51,640lb) ZMKB Progress/Lotarev D-18T turbofans
Weights: Max take-off 600,000kg 1,322,770(lb); max payload 250,000kg (551,000lb).
Performance: Max cruising speed 459kts (850km/h); take-off field length 3,500m (11,485ft); range with max payload 1,350nm (2,500km).
Accommodation: Flight crew of six. Seating for up to 70 passengers in passenger cabin, in addition to the carriage of 250 tonnes of freight.

The An-225 Mriya (Dream) was the first aircraft to fly at a gross weight exceeding one million pounds and remains the world's largest aircraft by some distance. It was developed principally to carry on its back the Soviet space shuttle orbiter *Buran*, together with Energyia rocket elements, between the Moscow production plant and the Baikanour Cosmodrome. Based on the An-124 heavy freighter, Antonov stretched the wings by adding a new centre section which increased the overall wingspan by 15.10m (49ft 6 1/2in), and lengthened the fuselage to enlarge the aircraft by about 50% compared to the An-124. The basic fuselage cross-section was unchanged, as were the turbofan engines, although the heavier weight required six Progress/Lotarev D-18T turbofans, each generating 230kN (51,650lb) thrust, instead of four engines. It has an upward-hinged visor-type nose door, identical to the An-124, but no rear ramp/door. The prototype was rolled out at Kiev on 30 November 1988 and first flew on 21 December. It made its first flight with the *Buran* space shuttle on its back on 13 May 1989 and has since also been used on a number of commercial tasks to support the energy sector in Russia, the Ukraine and other CIS countries, ferrying equipment and personnel into remote and inhospitable regions. It has a freight-carrying capacity of 250 tonnes, as well as an upper passenger cabin for 60-70 people. One aircraft has been built, but a second is planned to be completed in 2001 to be put into commercial service with Antonov Airlines, carrying outsize cargo. NATO reporting name is Cossack.

Above: The 250-tonne payload An-225 Mriya was built to support the Soviet space programme carrying the Buran space shuttle, but is undergoing modifications to obtain its civil certification.

Left: The giant An-225 is the largest aircraft in the world. On 22 March 1989, flown by Alexander V Galunenko, it set a total of 106 world and class records during a 3-hour flight from Kiev, taking off at a weight of 508,200kg (1,120,370lb), with a payload of 156,300kg (344,576lb).

Avions de Transport Régional ATR 42

SPECIFICATION

(ATR 42-500)

Dimensions: Wingspan 24.57m (80ft 7½in); length overall 22.67m (74ft 4½in); height overall 7.59m (24ft 10¾in), wing area 54.50m^2 (586.6ft2).

Power Plant: Two Pratt & Whitney Canada PW127E turboprops, derated from 2,051kW (2,750shp) to 1.610kW (2,160shp) for normal operation and max take-off power of 1,788kW (2,400shp). Six-blade Hamilton Standard/Ratier-Figeac 568F propellers with electronic control.

Weights: Operating weight empty 11,250kg (24,802lb); max take-off 18,600kg (41,005lb); max landing 18,300kg (40,345lb); max payload 5,450kg (12,015lb).

Performance: Max cruising speed 305kts (565km/h); service ceiling 5,485m (18,000ft); take-off field length 1,475m (4,840ft); landing field length 1,095m (3,595ft); max range 1,000nm (1,850km).

Accommodation: Flight crew of two. Two-abreast seating each side of the central aisle for 46 to 50 passengers. Baggage volume, including overhead bins 9.9m^3(350ft^3).

The Avions de Transport Regional (ATR) organisation, now a partnership between EADS (50%) and Alenia Aerospazio (50%), was set up on February1982 under French law as a Groupement d'Intérêt Economique (GIE to manage the programme of development, production and management of a regional airliner known as the ATR 42. The aircraft in question had been launched some three months earlier, on 29 October 1981, as a joint product o Aérospatiale in France and Aeritalia (now Alenia) in Italy, in continuation of a preliminary accord reached by the two companies in July 1980. Before that time, both companies had been studying the market for a regional airliner with 30-40 seats and had produced project designs under the designation Aérospatiale AS-35 and Aeritalia AIT 320. These projects were of generally similar configuration, and the ATR 42 was a continuation of the same theme, with a high wing, two turboprop engines, fuselage-side blisters fo the main landing gear units, and a T-tail. Sizing of the aircraft was a matter for careful study, with 42 seats eventually adopted as the norm, a few more than in the earlier independent project designs (as their designation indicated). The division of labour between the two companies provides fo Aérospatiale to manufacture the wing while Alenia produces the fuselage

Below: French regional Air Littoral operates the ATR 42-500 in a colourfu 'Mediterranean' scheme.

ATR 42-320

Above: The ATR 42 has been a popular regional aircraft out in the Far East. Lao Aviation acquired this model-320, which features PW121 turboprop engines for increased 'hot-and-high' performance.

nd tail unit. The Italian company is also responsible for the hydraulic, air-conditioning and pressurisation systems, while the French partner looks fter the flight deck and cabin, the power plant, and the electrical and flight-ontrol systems. Civil passenger versions of the ATR 42 are assembled and est flown at Toulouse; the ATM 42-F military cargo version and any civil reighters with rear loading ramp are assembled at Naples. Flight testing of ne ATR 42 began on 16 August 1984, the second development aircraft eing flown on 31 October of that year and the first production ATR 42 on 0 April 1985.

▶

VARIANTS

The designations ATR 42-100 and ATR 42-200 were at first applied to versions with gross weight of 14,900kg (32,848lb) and 15,750kg (34,722lb) respectively, the latter having a redesigned interior that allowed accommodation to be increased from 42 to 50 without any change in external dimensions. By the time production deliveries began, the ATR 42-200 had become the standard aircraft, with the ATR-42-300 available as a high gross weight option at 16,150kg (35,604lb), with a range of 890nm (1,650km) carrying the full passenger payload. Other designated variants of the basic aircraft include the ATR 42-F commercial freighter and the ATM 42 military freighter, the latter with a rear-loading ramp. The ATR 42-320 is identical except for optional PW 121 engines for improved hot-and-high performance. Further performance enhancements were incorporated in the ATR 42-400, which features PW121A engines with six-blade Hamilton Standard/Ratier-Figeac propellers. This version made its first flight on 12 July 1995. An uprated ATR 42-500 with more powerful PW127E engines derated from 2,051kW (2,750shp) to 1.610kW (2,160shp) for normal operation and max take-off power of 1,788kW (2,400shp), and a 'new look' interior flew before the -400, on 16 September 1994. Also available are the ATR 42 Cargo with a quick-change interior, the ATR 42F military/paramilitary freighter, the ATR 42 L with a lateral cargo door, and the SAR 42, a surveillance and rescue version based on the ART 42-400 and fitted with a chin-mounted FLIR/TV camera, ventral radome and ESM antennae. In December 2000, Farnai

Europe launched the cargo conversion programme with an order for one ATR 42-320. The conversion, which will feature a large 116 x 71 inch cargo door and provide accommodation for LD3 containers and 88 x 108 inch pallets, will be undertaken by Aeronavali.

SERVICE USE

Simultaneous certification to JAR 25 by DGAC of France and Italy's RAI was granted for the ATR 42-200 and ATR 42-300 on 24 September 1985, followed by US FAR Part 25 on 25 October 1985. Deliveries began on 3 December 1985 to French regional Air Littoral, which began revenue service with the type on 9 December. Command Airways became the first US operator in March 1986. DGAC certification for the ATR 42-400 was received on 27 February 1996 and two were delivered to CSA Czech Airlines on 14 March 1996. The ATR 42-500 was certificated in July 1995 and first delivered to Air Dolomiti in October 1995. In November 1996, the ATR 42-500 received certification for 120 minutes ETOPS (Extended-range twin-engine Operations). The Italian customs service ordered two SAR 42 in mid-1996 and took delivery in early 1997. At 1 January 2001, a total of 259 aircraft of all versions had been delivered.

Below: The ATR 42-500 is the latest and most powerful of the family, providing much enhanced performance.

Avions de Transport Régional ATR 72

SPECIFICATION
ATR 72-200)

Dimensions: Wingspan 27.05m (88ft 9in); length overall 27.17m (89ft 1¾in
height overall 7.65m (25ft 1¼in), wing area 61.0m² (656.6ft²).

Power Plant: Two Pratt & Whitney Canada PW124B turboprops, rated a
1,611kW 2,160shp). Four-blade Hamilton Standard 14SF-11 propellers.

Weights: Operating weight empty 12,500kg (27,558lb); max take-off 21,500k
(47,400lb); max landing 21,350kg (47,068lb); max payload 7,200kg (15,873lb).

Performance: Max cruising speed 285kts (527km/h); service ceiling 2,680r
(8,800ft); take-off field length 1,408m (4,620ft); landing field length 1,210r
(3,970ft); max payload range 645nm (1,195km).

Accommodation: Flight crew of two. Two-abreast seating each side of the centra
aisle for 64 to 74 passengers. Typical baggage/cargo volume 10.6m³ (375ft³).

The family concept of the ATR regional aircraft design was put int
development soon after the ATR 42 entered flight testing. First announce
at the 1985 Paris Air Show and officially launched on 15 January 1986, the ATI
72 was a stretched derivative with more power, greater wingspan and a longe
fuselage for up to 74 passengers. Structurally similar to the ATR 42, the ATR 7
is distinguished by a fuselage stretched by 4.50m (14ft 9¼in) to 27.17m (89¹
13⁄4in) and a 2.48m (8ft 2¾in) greater wingspan of 27.05m (88ft 9in). Accom
modation for up to 74 passengers in a high-density configuration is possible

Above: The ATR 72 was used by KLM uk on its Channel Islands routes.

Below: Charter carrier British World Airlines upgraded to the ATR 72 from the Viscount, to service its Shell contract in support of the North Sea oil business.

and a second cabin attendant's seat is also provided. Three developmen
aircraft were built and these made their first flights on 27 October 1988, 2
December 1988 and April 1989.

VARIANTS
The first version, still in production, is designated ATR 72-200. Powered by tw
PW124B turboprops, each rated at 1,611kW (2,160shp), it is available in bot
passenger configuration with 74 seats in a high-density layout, and for cargc
capable of carrying 13 small containers. More powerful 1,849kW (2,480shp
PW127 engines for better hot-and-high performance produced the ATR 72-21C
which first flew in 1992. To keep ahead of requirements, AI(R) introduced th
ATR 72-210A (later referred to as the ATR 72-500) to the family portfolio in earl
1997. This model features higher operating weights to accommodate new
passenger regulations, increased range and improved airfield performance, an
has the same powerful 2,052kW (2,750shp) PW127E engines and Hamilto
Standard/Ratier-Figeac propellers fitted to the ATR 42-500. Cabin comfort als
matches the ATR 42-500 in terms of appearance, comfort, low noise an
vibration levels and overhead locker volume. Announced as long ago as Apr
1992 but yet to be put into production is the ATR 52C, a rear-loading civil/militar
cargo version of the ATR 72-210. The main difference, apart from the rear ram

ype door, is a 3.18m (10ft 5¼in) shorter fuselage. A proposed stretch, designated ATR 82, was shelved in favour of a jet development, now also cancelled. A cargo conversion programme was announced for the ATR 72 at the Farnborough Air Show in July 2000. Like the ATR 42, it features a large cargo door, with all passenger amenities stripped.

SERVICE USE

French DGAC and US FAA certification was obtained on 25 September and 15 November 1989 respectively, with deliveries to Finnish airline Karair from 27 October 1989. The ATR 72-210 received French and US certification on 15 and 8 December 1992 respectively, and this improved type went into service that same month with American Eagle carrier Simmons Airlines. The ATR 72-500 made its first flight on 19 January 1996 and received its certification on 14 January 1997. The first delivery to American Eagle was made on 31 July 1997. At 1 January 2001, a total of 254 of all versions had been delivered.

Below: **The recent development of regional air services in the Asia/Pacific area has created a good market for the larger-capacity ATR 72, seen here in the earlier markings of Vietnam Airlines, which operates a fleet of six, carrying up to 74 passengers.**

Ayres Loadmaster

SPECIFICATION
(Ayres LM200)
Dimensions: Wingspan 19.51m (64ft 0in); length 19.61m (64ft 4in); height overall 7.00m (22ft 111/2in); wing area 42.55m² (458ft²).
Power Plant: One 2,013kW (2,700shp) LHTEC CTP800-4T.
Weights: Operating weight empty 4,082kg (9,000lb); max take-off and landing 8,618kg (19,000lb); max payload 3,946kg (8,700lb).
Performance: Max cruising speed 200kts (370km/h); service ceiling 7,620m (25,000ft); take-off field length 465m (1,525ft); landing field length 532m (1,745ft); range with typical payload 1,590nm (2,944km).
Accommodation: Flight crew of one or two. Single-aisle cabin layout, seating typically 19 passengers plus freight. Max high-density seating for 34 passengers. Four LD3 containers in all-cargo layout. Total cargo volume 54.5m³ (1,925ft³).

The high-wing Ayres LM200 Loadmaster was officially launched November 1996, following receipt of an order for 50 cargo versions from Federal Express. Production was assigned to Dothan, Alabama, with subsidiary Le

Right: The FedEx order is vital to the success of the Loadmaster.

unovice in the Czech Republic building the wing and tail unit assemblies. It is also intended that a second production line will be set up by Let. Three protoypes re under construction, but the programme is running three years late, with the first ight now scheduled for mid-2001. Further uncertainty has been created with a ankruptcy petition filed against Let. The Loadmaster is powered by a single ,013kW (2,700shp) LHTEC CTP800-4T 'twin barrel' propulsion system of two oupled engines, driving a single six-bladed Hamilton Sundstrand propeller through GKN Westland combining gearbox. This arrangement of linked turboshafts ircumvents the prohibition of single-engine commercial night flights that exists in nany countries. A shoulder-wing design, the Loadmaster can accommodate a pilot nd optional co-pilot/observer, as well as four LD3 or Demi freight containers and eneral cargo. It is being offered in cargo, combi, 19-passenger versions under the M200 designation, and as a military freighter as the LM250. Firefighting, econnaissance, and long-range patrol variants are also under development, as is ne Searchmaster, a remote earth sensing aircraft with two operators' consoles in ne cargo hold. Other options are a rear loading ramp and amphibious operations. t 1 January 2001, firm orders exceeded 100 aircraft but the company envisages narket for up to 600 aircraft by 2010.

Beech 99 Airliner

SPECIFICATION
Beech C99 Airliner)
Dimensions: Wingspan 13.98m (45ft 10½in); length overall 13.58m (44ft 6¾in); height overall 4.37m (14ft4¼ in), wing area 25.98m² (279.7ft²).
Power Plant: Two 533kW (715shp) Pratt & Whitney Canada PT6A-36 turboprops, Hartzell three-blade constant-speed fully-feathering reversible-pitch propellers.
Weights: Operating weight empty 2,946kg (6,494lb); max take-off 5,125kg (11,300lb); max landing 5,125kg (11,300lb); max payload 1,474kg (3,250lb).
Performance: Max cruising speed 268kts (497km/h); initial rate of climb 11.1m/s (2,220ft/min); service ceiling 8,560m (28,080ft); range with max payload 578nm (1,072km).
Accommodation: Flight crew of two. Seating for up to 15 passengers, two-abreast with central aisle. Total baggage volume front and rear 1.72m³ (60.9ft³).

Beech entered the commuter airliner market in 1965 using the twin piston Queen Air as a base for development. Using a wing similar to the Queen Air and a lengthened fuselage to accommodate 15 passengers, the new model was identified as the Beech 99. A standard feature of the design was an airstair incorporated in the main cabin door, but a wide cargo-loading door was offered to facilitate use of the aircraft in a mixed passenger/cargo configuration. Beech flew a development airframe in the shape of a long fuselage piston-powered Queen Air in December 1965, but in July 1966 this prototype began a new series of trials with Pratt & Whitney Canada PT6A-20 turboprops. It represented the Model 99 in all respects and formed the basis for FAA certification on 2 May 1968. Deliveries began the same month, the first entering service with Chicago-based Commuter Airlines. The first production aircraft were powered by 410kW (550shp) PT6A-20 engines. When 507kW (680shp) PT6A-27 turboprops were introduced, the designation became A99, although these engines were flat-rated to the

Below: GP Express Airlines was one of many US commuters using the 15-seat Beech C99.

Above: Air Vegas uses the Beech C99 Airliner between Las Vegas and the Grand Canyon.

ame power as the orginal PT6A-20s. The B99 had a higher gross weight, vas otherwise identical. Production ended in 1974 after 164 had been built, ut a new version, announced as the Commuter C99, was included in eechcraft's plans to re-enter the commuter airliner market in May 1979. he improved C99 Airliner, as it became officially known, first flew on 20 une 1980 and entered service with Christman Air System on 30 July 1981. total of 75 were sold, with production ending in 1986. Most aircraft were elivered for airline use, though an executive version was also produced. Of he 239 aircraft of all models built, some 170 remained in passenger and argo service at 1 January 2001.

Beech 1900

SPECIFICATION
(Beech 1900D)

Dimensions: Wingspan 17.67m (57ft 11¾in); length overall 17.63m (57ft 10in); height overall 4.72m (15ft 6in), wing area 28.80m² (310ft²).

Power Plant: Two Pratt & Whitney Canada PT6A-67D turboprops, each flat rated at 954kW (1,279shp). Four-blade Hartzell composite propellers.

Weights: Operating weight empty 4,815kg (10,615lb); max take-off 7,688kg (16,950lb); max landing 7,530kg (16,600lb).

Performance: Max cruising speed 276kts (511km/h); rate of climb 13.3m/s (2,625ft/min); service ceiling 10,058m (33,000ft); take-off field length 1,140m (3,740ft); landing field length 844m (2,770ft); typical range with reserves 1,500nm (2,778km).

Accommodation: Crew of one or two on flight deck. Commuter seating for 19 passengers in single seat rows each side of a central aisle. Baggage volume 6.34m³ (223.9ft³).

Having stopped production of the Beechcraft 99 in 1975, and thus separate itself from the developing market for small commuterliners and regiona airliners, Beech Aircraft announced in 1979 its intention to develop one or mor new types of aircraft suitable for this portion of the market. Design studie were already in hand for a pressurised aircraft in the 30/40-seat category but t provide a more immediate entry into the regional airliner market place, variant of the Super King Air 200 were projected. One such, known as the Model 130 used the same airframe as its progenitor with a cabin arranged to seat 1 passengers (hence the designation), whilst the Model 1900 was to have lengthened fuselage (for 19 passengers) and uprated engines, With indicatio of airline interest, development of the Model 1900 was continued and in 198

Below: Canadian airline Central Mountain Air, based at Smithers, British Columbia, has operated Beechcraft since its foundation in 1987. It has now upgraded to the 1900D, providing regional business-class service.

bove: Morocco's first regional carrier, Regional Air Lines, took delivery
f four Beech 1900Ds in Spring 1997. The airline links its base at
asablanca with the cities of Agadir, Fes, Marrakech, Rabat and Tangier.

ork began on three flying prototypes, a static test airframe and a fuselage for
ressure-cycle testing. The first two flying prototypes made their maiden flights
n 3 September and 30 November 1982. The third, after being used for function
nd reliability testing, equipment certification and demonstration, was
•furbished for customer delivery. Before the first flight of the prototype,
•sting of the PT6A-65 engine began in a Super King Air flying test bed on 30
•pril 1981. Based as it is on the Super King Air 200, the Model 1900 had the
•ame fuselage cross section, the parallel section of the fuselage being
•ngthened by some 14ft (4.27m). Most other major components, including the
•ing centre section and the tail unit, are dimensionally similar to those of the
•uper King Air, but strengthened structurally where necessary to permit ▶

operations at higher weights. The PT6A-65B engines are flat-rated in order to provide constant power in elevated ambient temperatures. An unusual feature of the Beechcraft 1900 is its use of auxiliary horizontal fixed tail surfaces, known to Beech as stabilons, on each side of the rear fuselage just forward of the tailplane which is mounted atop the fin. Small 'tail-let' vertical fins are also mounted beneath each tailplane half, near the tips. A 'wet' wing was also developed for the Model 1900, with integral tankage replacing the five bladder tanks in the original design increasing fuel capacity by some 60 per cent and maximum range by an impressive 85 per cent. Beech revisited the 13-seat development of the Super King Air and in January 1988 announced the go-ahead for the Model 1300 for long thin routes Deliveries began on 30 September that same year. A new development of the Model 1900 with stand-up headroom and a 28.5 per cent increase in cabin volume was announced at the US Regional Airlines Association (RAA) meeting in 1989 Known as the Model 1900D, it first flew on 1 March 1990 and received its FAA certification to FAR Pt 23 Amendment 34 in March 1991.

VARIANTS
The basic 19-seat commuterliner was given the designation 1900C. It is powered by two Pratt & Whitney PT6A-65B turboprops each rated at 820kW (1,100shp) and incorporates a passenger door forward and upward hinged cargo-loading door in the port side of the rear fuselage. Accommodation is provided in two single seat rows each side of a central aisle. The Model 1900C Exec-Liner has a standard passenger door in this position and seats from 12-16 passengers. All doors are fitted with integral airstairs. From September 1987

ıe USAF took delivery of six 1900C aircraft, designated C-12J, for Air National uard mission support. The Model 1900D replaced the 1900 Series on the roduction line from November 1991. Main differences are more powerful T6A-67D turboprops each flat rated at 954kW (1,279shp), a flat floor with tand-up headroom, winglets for better hot-and-high performance, and twin antral strakes for improved directional stability.

₄ SERVICE

ıe Model 1900 was certificated under FAR Part 41C regulations on 22 ovember 1983, which included single-pilot approval under FAR 135 Appendix . The first Model 1900C entered service with Bar Harbor Airlines in February 984, and the first 1900 Exec-Liner was delivered to the General Telephone ompany of Illinois in July 1985. A total of 248 1900C, mostly to US ommuter/regional airlines, were sold before being replaced by the Model 900D. Following the initial delivery to Mesa Airlines, which ordered a large umber of the stand-up 1900D, this latest model is steadily making inroads in ıe export market and a total of more than 400 1900DS had been delivered by January 2001. It is also available in executive configuration, the first of which as delivered in April 1995.

elow: Holiday Airlines was one of several US commuter airlines perating the 1900C from the beginning in February 1983. This model ad the normal cabin height which, at 1.45m (4ft 9in) was not a stand-up ıbin and gave rise to the 1900D's development.

Beech Beechjet 400

SPECIFICATION
(Beechjet 400A)

Dimensions: Wingspan 13.25m (43ft 6in); length 14.75m (48ft 5in); heigh overall 4.24m (13ft 11in); wing area 22.43m² (241.4ft²).

Power Plant: Two 13.2kN (2,965lb) Pratt & Whitney JT15D-5 turbofans.

Weights: Operating weight empty 4,919kg (10,850lb); max take-off 7,303k (16,100lb); max landing 7,121kg (15,700lb).

Performance: Max cruising speed 468kts (867km/h); service ceiling 13,240 (43,450ft); take-off field length 1,270m (4,170ft); landing field length 900 (2,950ft); range with typical payload 1,575nm (2,915km).

Accommodation: Flight crew of two. Standard club layout seats eigh passengers. Cargo/baggage volume 1.09m³ (38.4ft³).

This twin-engined, short- to medium-range business jet started life in Japa where it was designed by Mitsubishi as the MU-300 Diamond I, which firs flew on 29 August 1978 and received its FAA certification on 6 November 198 A total of 65 Diamond Is were produced before it was replaced by the Diamon IA from January 1984. This featured uprated Pratt & Whitney JT15D-4 engines, higher gross weight and improved avionics. Only 27 were built befor it too was replaced by the Diamond II, with a new interior and JT15D-5 engine of which only one was built, making its first flight in June 1984. Beechcra acquired the rights to the Diamond II in December 1985, and, after makin some improvements including adding a tailcone baggage compartment an extended-range tanks, renamed the aircraft Beechjet 400. The first Beec assembled Beechjet 400 rolled out at Wichita on 19 May 1986 and a total of 6 were built. At the 1989 NBAA show, Beech announced the Beechjet 400 which featured a more spacious cabin (within the same overall dimensions), modern 'glass' cockpit with Collins Pro Line 4 EFIS, and a higher certificate operating altitude. The 400A first flew on 22 September 1989 and received i

bove: Beechjet 400A in service with Hainan Airlines in China.

AA certification on 20 June 1990, leading to first deliveries that November. The
S Air force acquired 180 Beechjet T-1A Jayhawks between July 1991 and July
997 to meet its Tanker Transport training System (TTTS) requirement, and nine
milar aircraft have been sold to the Japan Air Self Defense Force (JASDF) as
e T-400. Total deliveries of all models, including the early Diamond series
xceeded 600 at 1 January 2001.

elow: Beechjet T-1A Jayhawk used by USAF.

Beech King Air/Super King Air

SPECIFICATION
(Beech Super King Air B200)
Dimensions: Wingspan 16.61m (54ft 6in); length overall 13.34m (43ft 9in); height overall 4.57m (15ft 0in); wing area 28.15m² (303ft²).
Power Plant: Two Pratt & Whitney Canada PT6A-42 turboprops, each flat rated at 634kW (850shp). Four-blade Hartzell propellers.
Weights: Operating weight empty 3,675kg (8,102lb); max take-off 5,670kg (12,500lb); max landing 5,670kg (12,500lb).
Performance: Max cruising speed 289kts (536km/h); rate of climb 12.45m/s (2,450ft/min); service ceiling 10,670m (35,000ft); take-off field length 786m (2,580ft); landing field length 632m (2,075ft); typical range with reserves 1,190nm (2,204km).
Accommodation: Crew of one or two on flight deck. Typical seating 7-9 passengers. Baggage volume at rear of cabin 1.51m³ (53.5ft³).

The King Air family was derived from the Queen Air, which itself entered production in 1958 as the largest of the Beechcraft twins. The King Air provided the basis for development of the Beechcraft 1900 Airliner, but variants of the smaller King Air are also used as third-level airliners and as air taxis by number of operators in various parts of the world. Development of the King Air began with a installation of PT6A turboprops in a Queen Air airframe, leading to construction of a true King Air prototype which first flew on 20 January 2964. Initial deliveries of the Model 90, with PT6A-6 engines began later in 1964, the model being superseded by the A90 and B90 with slightly more powerful PT6A-20s and the C90 and C90-1 with PT6A-21s and cabin improvements. The C90 introduced 'pitot' cowlings with reduced-area intakes to increase ram-air flow to the engines. The improved C90B became the standard production model from 1991. A C90SE (Special Edition) was first delivered in October 1994. The King Air 100, introduced in 1969, featured more powerful PT6A-28 engines,

Below: Norwegian commuter and business airline Air Stord operated a fleet of King Air 100s and Super King Air 200s on scheduled and charter services from its island base at Stord.

above: The versatile Beech B200 Super King Air is being used as a corporate transport and as a commuter airliner.

ngthened cabin to provide up to 13 seats in airline commuter configuration, and duced wing span. The A100 had a series of refinements and the B100 switched 536kW (715shp) Garrett TPE331-6-252B engines. The E90 combined the frame of the C90 with PT6A-28 engines of the A100 and the F90, which appeared 1979, combined the basic Model 90 fuselage with the short span wings of the del 100 and the T-tail of the Super King Air 200. The F90-1 features PT6A-135 gines and 'pitot' intake as on the C90A-1. The larger Super King Air family has a stinctive T-tail configuration. The Super King Air 200, powered by twin Pratt & itney PT6A-41 turboprops, received certification to FAR Part 25 on 14 December 73. It was replaced by the B200 in March 1981, which was generally similar cept for the installation of higher performance PT6A-42 turboprops. The B200C fered in having a 1.32m x 1.32m (4ft 4in x 4ft 4in) cargo door. Wingtip tanks of e maritime patrol B200T and the cargo door are combined in the B200CT. A ecial edition B200SE, certificated in October 1995, has improved avionics and ▶

three-blade propellers. Further improvements led to the Super King Air 300 wi
783kW (1,050shp) PT6A-60A engines, introduced in January 1984, and th
300LW (Light Weight) development for the European market in 1988. Th
'stretched' Model 350 replaced the 300 in Spring 1990. It has a fuselag
lengthened by 0.86m (2ft 10in) to provide accommodation for up to 1
passengers, but retains the power plant of the Model 300. The 350C has

above: The 'stretched' Beech King Air 350.

argo door and built-in airstairs passenger access, and 350 Special Missions
nd RC-350 Guardian ELINT versions are also available. The B200 Super King
ir has been popular with commuter airlines. More than 5,000, including both
vil and military versions, had been delivered by 1 January 2001.

Bell Boeing 609

PRELIMINARY SPECIFICATION
Dimensions: Proprotor diameter 7.92m (26ft 0m); length overall 13.41m (44ft 0m); width overall 18.29m (60ft 0m).
Power Plant: Two 1,447kW (1,940shp) Pratt & Whitney PT6A-67A turboshafts with three-bladed propellers.
Weights: Operating weight empty 4,763kg (10,500lb). Max take-off weight 7,258kg (16,000lb); Useful payload 2,495kg (5,5001b).
Performance: Max cruising speed 275kt (509km/h); service ceiling 7,620m (25,000ft), max range 750nm (1,388km).
Accommodation: Flight crew of one or two, and 6-9 passengers in single seats each side of a central aisle.

In early 1996, Bell and Boeing announced a design study into a nine-seat, twin engined civil tilt-rotor, based on the military V-22 Osprey. Originally designated D-600, the innovative aircraft, which combines the speed of a turboprop aircraft with the speed of a turboprop aircraft with the vertical take-off and landing capability of a helicopter, is targeted primarily at inter-city transport, offshore support, emergency medical service and search and rescue. Decision to move into design made in November 1996 with design configuration frozen in May 1997. Manufacturing started in August and the first of four prototypes is scheduled to fly in early 2001, with first deliveries following in 2002. By the end of 1997, the manufacturers claimed commitments for 50 aircraft, including one from Petroleum Tiltrotor international (PTI) in the Middle East, the world's first company specifically founded to operate tiltrotor aircraft. The 609 is a high-wing aircraft with a T-tail empennage and forward swept wings. It will use the same hybrid, composite skin/aluminium frame construction and three-blade composite rotor blades used on the V-22. The 609 features fly-by-wire flight control and is equipped with three-across colour LCD displays in the cockpit and an engine indication and crew alerting system (EICAS). Power is provided by two Pratt & Whitney PT6C-67A turboshaft engines, each rated at 1,447kW (1,940shp). Accommodation is one or two crew and seating for 6-9 passengers. Bell assumed Boeing's 49% stake in the programme in February 1998, and risk sharing partnership with Agusta announced during the Farnborough Air Show the following September. Agusta will assemble the aircraft in Italy for the European market. The BA 609 will be the initial baseline version, but the HV-609 multi-mission variant has been proposed for the US Coast Guard, and a UV-609 utility variant for the US Army. A larger 20-seat version is under consideration. At 1 January 2001, orders and commitments had been received for 80 aircraft.

Above: The new BA 609 version of the V-22 Osprey tiltrotor is targeted at finding applications for business transport.

Left: The Bell/Agusta BA 609 will become the world's first commercial tiltrotor aircraft when it enters service in 2001.

Boeing 707/720

SPECIFICATION
(Boeing 707-320C)

Dimensions: Wingspan 44.42m (145ft 9in); length overall 46.61m (151ft 11in) height overall 12.93m (42ft 5in), wing area 283.4m² (3,050ft²).

Power Plant: Four Pratt & Whitney JT3D-7 turbofans, each rated at 84.55kN (19,000lb) st.

Weights: Operating weight empty 66,406kg (146,400lb); max take-off 151,315kg (333,600lb); max landing 112,037kg (247,000lb); max payload 23,856kg (52,593lb).

Performance: Max cruising speed 525kts (973km/h); rate of climb 20.3m/s (4,000ft/min); service ceiling 11,885m (39,000ft); take-off field length 3,055m (10,020ft); landing field length 1,950m (6,400ft); range with max fuel 5,000nm (9,270km); range with typical payload 3,150nm (5,840km).

Accommodation: Flight crew of three. Maximum one-class layout for 189 passengers six-abreast. Underfloor baggage/cargo volume 48.15m3 (1,700ft³). Upper deck cargo volume 161.2m³ (5,693ft³).

The first of the company's jetliners and first US jet transport to enter service, the Boeing 707 had its origins in the design studies conducted by the company in the late 1940s and early 1950s for a new tanker for the USAF as a successor to the C-97/KC-97 family. From a number of turboprop and turbojet designs studied, Boeing selected its Model 367-80 for prototype construction and this aircraft, which later became best known simply as the 'Dash 80', made its first flight on 15 July 1954 at Renton, powered by four Pratt & Whitney JT3C turbojets. The Model 367-80 successfully demonstrated its potential to the USAF, which subsequently purchased many hundred KC-135A tankers and related reconnaisance and special-purpose variants, similar in size and configuration to the prototype. For airline use, however, Boeing decided that the cross-section of the fuselage should be increased so that more comfortable ▶

Below: The Boeing 707 was once found in all the major airlines' fleets. It opened up long-distance jet travel in the 1960s, but has now been relegated to the carriage of cargo.

107

six-abreast seating could be provided and the new commercial project becam
identified as the Model 707. With 57.85kN (13,000lb) JT3C-6 engines, th
Model 707 was offered in 'short-body' and 'long-body' versions, and the latte
was chosen by Pan American when it placed a launch order on 13 October 195
(more than three years after the de Havilland Comet had become the world
first jet airliner in service). The first two Boeing 707s, used for certificatior
were flown on 20 December 1957 and 3 February 1958, and Boeing adopted
series of designation suffixes by which the first number of a three-numerica
group indicated the model variant and the second and third numbers served a
a means of identifying the particular customer.

VARIANTS

Most early orders were for the so-called 'long-body' variant of the Boeing 70⁷

*bove: Delivery of the Boeing 720B in mid-1961 enabled Northwest to
reatly expand its jet service.

20; only Qantas ordered the 'short-body' version of the -120 (this being the
`odel 707-138, with 38 referring to the customer, Qantas). With the same
`selage length as the 'long-body -120, the Model 707-220 introduced 70.30kN
`5,800lb) JT4A-3 or 5 engines for hot-and-high performance but was specified
`ly by Braniff, the first flight being made on 11 June 1959. These same
`gines – or the 74.76kN (16,800lb) JT4A-9 or 77.88kN (17,500lb) JT4A-11 –
`ere then adopted for the third model, the Model 707-320. This was the
`tercontinental versions of the aircraft, whereas the -120 was the
`anscontinental model, and it has the fuselage lengthened enough to
`commodate up top 189 passengers, and a larger wing to cope with the higher ▶

weights. The first Model 707-320 flew on 11 January 1959, and was followed on 20 May 1959 by the first Model 707-420, which featured 73.4kN (16,500lb) Rolls-Royce Conway 505 engines. In 1957 Boeing offered a short/medium range version of the basic aircraft as the Model 720, featuring a fuselage 0.51m (1ft 8in) longer than that of the short-body Model 707-120 used by Qantas, a lightened structure, lower fuel capacity 53.40kN (12,000lb) JT3C-7 engines and extended chord on the inboard wing leading edges. The Model 720 first flew on 23 November 1959. In 1960 Boeing introduced versions of the Models 707 and 720 with the newly-developed JT3D turbofan engines, identified by 'B' designation suffix. The Model 707-120B, with the aerodynamic refinements of the Model 720, first flew on 22 June 1960, and the first Model 720B flew on the 6 October 1960. The turbofan-engined Model 707-320B, which first flew on 31 January 1962, also had new low-drag wing tips with a span increase of 1.0m (3ft 3½in), slotted leading-edge flaps and improved trailing-edge flaps. The passenger/cargo convertible version, with side-loading cargo door, was designated Model 707-320C and flew on 19 February 1963. One Model 707 was flown (starting on 27 November 1979) with CFM56 turbofans, but proposed retrofit programme for these engines did not proceed, and variants some with lengthened fuselages, designated up to Model 707-820, also

emained in the project stage.

SERVICE USE

The first model of the Boeing 707 was certificated on 23 September 1958 and revenue service was inaugurated by Pan American on 26 October across the North Atlantic. Key dates for other variants were: Model 707-220 certificated on November 1958 and first service by Braniff on 20 December 1959; Model 07-320 certificated on 15 July 1959 and first service by Pan American on 10 October 1959; Model 707-420 certificated on 12 February 1960 and first service y BOAC in May 1960; Model 720 certificated on 30 June 1960 and first service y United on 5 July 1960; Model 707-120B certificated on 1 March 1961 and Model 720B on 3 March 1961, first service by American Airlines on 12 March 961; and Model 707-320B certificated on 31 May 1961 and first service by Pan American in June 1963. Boeing built a total of 917 Model 707s (excluding irframes for the E-3 and E-6 military programmes), made up of 63 -120, 78-20B, five -220, 60 -320, 174 -320B, 337 -320C, 37 -420, 65 -720 and 89 -720B ariants. Some 100 remain in service, most converted for cargo use.

Below: Ecuatoriana's 720B was used to link Ecuador with the USA.

Boeing 717

SPECIFICATION
(Boeing 717-200)
Dimensions: Wingspan 28.45m (93ft 4in); length 37.80m (124ft 0in); height overall 8.86m (29ft 1in); wing area 92.97m² (1,000.7ft²).
Power Plant: Two Rolls-Royce Deutschland BR 715 A1-30, rated at 82.3kN (18,500lb) thrust, or the 93.4kN (21,000lb) BR 715 C1-30.
Weights: Operating weight empty 31,674kg (69,830lb); max take-off 51,710kg (114,000lb); max landing 46,265kg (102,000lb); max payload 12,220kg (26,940lb).
Performance: Max cruising speed 438kts (811km/h); service ceiling 11,280m (37,000ft); take-off field length 1,905m (6,250ft); landing field length 1,400m (4,600ft); range with typical payload 1,460nm (2,700km).
Accommodation: Flight crew of two. Single-aisle cabin layout, seating typically 106 passengers in a two-class configuration. Max high-density seating for 117 passengers. Cargo/baggage volume 26.5m³ (936ft³).

Known as the McDonnell Douglas MD-95 prior to the take-over of the company by Boeing in August 1997, this smallest version of Douglas' twin engined series of jet aircraft was first revealed at the Paris air show in June 1991. Approximating in size to the earlier DC-9-30, the 717 features a mixture of low cost systems and advanced technology avionics, based on the flight deck of the, now discontinued, MD-90. It includes a Honeywell flight management system (FMS), inertial reference system (IRS), digital flight guidance system (DFGS), digital air data computer and windshear detection system, six-across electronic flight instrumentation system (EFIS), and the MD-11 advanced flight control system (AFCS). Lightweight structure is similar to the MD-80/MD-90. The aircraft has typical seating for 106 passengers in a five

breast arrangement in a new modern cabin. The 82.3kN (18,500lb) thrust BMW Rolls-Royce BR 715 was selected to power the aircraft in March 1994. Construction of a development prototype was began in late 1994, using a modified DC-9-30 airframe, and the first prototype made its maiden flight on 2 September 1998. The aircraft had been formally launched on 19 October 1995, with an order for 50, plus 50 options, from US low-cost carrier ValuJet, now AirTran Airways. Many partners contribute to the 717 production, among them Alenia (fuselage), Korean Air (nose and forward door areas) and Halla Engineering (wing sets), with final assembly at the former Douglas Long Beach plant.

VARIANTS

Basic production version is the 717-200, available in basic and high gross weight versions, and is the only model built to date. It received its FAA/JAA certification on 1 September 1999. A flight computer upgrade was certificated in December 2000. Several models are being studied, although no launch decision had been made by the end of 2000. These include the 80-seat 717-100X (formerly the MD-95-20) which would be 1.90m (6ft 3in) shorter; the 717-100X Lite, a proposed 75-seat model; and the 717-300, a 130-seat design based on the MD-95-50, which would be 2.38m (7ft 10in) longer than the -200.

SERVICE USE

Launch customer AirTran Airways put the first 717-200 into service in October 1999. At 1 January 2001, Boeing had received orders for 151 aircraft, of which 44 had been delivered.

Below: The Boeing 717 started life as the McDonnell Douglas MD-95, designed to replace the DC-9 series of trijets.

Boeing 727

SPECIFICATION
(Boeing 727-200)
Dimensions: Wingspan 32.93m (108ft 0in); length overall 46.69m (103ft 2in); height overall 10.36m (34ft 0in), wing area 157.9m² (1,700ft²).
Power Plant: Three Pratt & Whitney JT8D turbofans, each rated at 64.52kN (14,500lb) (JT8D-9A) or 66.75kN (15,000lb) (-11) or 68.98kN (15,500lb) (-15) or 71.2kN (16,000lb) (-17) or 73.0kN (16,400lb) (-17R).
Weights: Operating weight empty 46,164kg (101,773lb); max take-off basic 83,820kg (184,800lb); max landing 70,081kg (154,500lb); max payload 18,598kg (41,000lb).
Performance: Max cruising speed 530kts (983km/h); initial cruise altitude 10,060m (33,000ft); take-off field length 3,035m (9,950ft) landing field length 1,495m (4,900ft); range with max fuel 2,400nm (4,449km); range with max payload 2,140nm (3,967km).
Accommodation: Flight crew of three. Basic two-class layout for 135 passengers, with maximum six-abreast tourist configuration for 189 passengers.

The Model 727 was the second member of the Boeing jet family to appear design work on a 'junior partner' for the Boeing 707/720 series having begun a full two years before the first Model 707 entered service. Many possible configurations were studied before Boeing decided to adopt the tri-jet arrangement with one engine in the rear fuselage and the other two on the sides of the rear fuselage in pods. By the autumn of 1959 the design had been frozen, based on three Allison-built Rolls-Royce Speys (which had also been specified for the Hawker Siddeley Trident, launched in 1958 with a nearly identical layout). By the time a launch decision was made on 5 December 1960, however, with orders for 40 aircraft each placed by Eastern and United A

ines, Pratt & Whitney JT8D engines had been chosen, and these were
estined to be used, in progressively more powerful versions, in every Model
27 built. The new airliner was designed to have as much commonality as
ossible with the Model 707, and this applied in particular to the entire upper
obe of the fuselage (from the cabin floor up), thus permitting closely-similar
abin layouts and fitments to be used. At the time of its launch, the Model 727
ad the most advanced aerodynamics of any commercial aircraft, with greater
ving sweep back than was then and is now common, and a combination of
igh-lift devices on the leading and trailing edges to ensure reasonable field
erformance. The first flight of the Model 727 was made on 9 February 1963,
he second aircraft following on 12 March 1963.

VARIANTS
he original Model 727 production aircraft had an overall length of 40.59m
(33ft 2in) and were later designated Model 727-100; engine options were
he 62.3kN (14,000lb) JT8D-1 or 7, and the 64.6kN (14,500lb) JT8D-9, and
naximum take-off weight went from 68,965kg (152,000lb) to 72,595kg
(160,000lb). A convertible passenger/cargo version with side-loading freight
oor flew as the Model 727C (later Model 727-100C) on 30 December
965. The 'stretched' Model 727-220 flew on 27 July 1967 and became the
tandard aircraft, initially with JT8D-7 engines and 76,680kg (169,000lb)
naximum take-off weight but later with engine and weight options as listed
bove. Introducing a number of refinements, improved cabin and greater
uel capacity, the Advanced 727 first flew on 3 March 1972, with JT8D-15 ▶

*Below: Although the use of the Boeing 727 tri-jet is being limited by
oughening noise regulations, some airlines, like UK charter operator
Sabre Airways' 727-200, have fitted hush-kits.*

engines and a 83,660kg (191,000lb) gross weight. A pure freighter, wit
cabin windows blanked off, was the final Model 727 variant to appear , i
1983, and was known as the Model 727-200F, with a maximum payload (fc
the Federal Express 'small package' operation) of 26,650kg (58,750lb
Many have now been fitted with hush-kits in order to comply with stricte
noise regulations.

SERVICE USE

FAA Type Approval of the Model 727-100 was obtained on 24 December 196.
and the first revenue services were flown by Eastern on 1 February and t
United Airlines on 6 February 1964. The first operator outside the USA wa
Lufthansa which introduced the type into service on 16 April 1964. Lufthans
later also acquired the quick-change (QC) version and large numbers of th
bigger 727-200. The Model 727C was certificated on 13 January 1966 an
entered service with Northwest on 23 April 1966. Boeing obtained certificatio

*bove: Many Boeing 727s have found their way to corporate owners,
quipped with high-quality furnishings and equipment. This 727-100 was
hotographed at London's Stansted Airport.*

the Model 727-200 on 29 November 1967, and Northwest flew the first
ervice on 14 December, while All Nippon Airways was the first to fly the
dvanced 727 in July 1972 following certification on 14 June. The first Model
27 with automatic thrust reverse on its Pratt & Whitney JT8D-17R engines
ew with Hughes Airwest on 27 May 1976, and Federal Express took delivery
the last Model 727 built, on 18 September 1984, bringing total production to
832 of all variants. These consisted of 408 Srs 100 (including one test aircraft
t delivered to customer), 164 Srs 100C and QC (Quick Change), 1, 245 Srs
00 and 15 Srs 200F. Some 1,175 Boeing 727s remain in service, including 275
odel 100s and 900 Model 200s, more than half of these are serving with
lines in the Americas.

Above: Saudi-registered Boeing 727-200 photographed at Basel.

Boeing 737-100/200

SPECIFICATION
(Boeing 737-200)

Dimensions: Wingspan 28.35m (93ft0in); length overall 30.53m (100ft 2in); height overall 11.28m (37ft 0in), wing area 102.0m² (1,098ft²).

Power Plant: Two Pratt & Whitney JT8D turbofans, each rated at 62.2kN(14,000lb) JT8D-7 or 64.52kN (14,500lb) (-9) or 68.98kN (15,500lb) (-15/15A) or 71.2kN (16,000lb) (-17/17A) or 73.0kN (16,400lb) (-17R).

Weights: Operating weight empty 27,310kg (60,201lb); max take-off standard 52,391kg (115,500lb); max landing 46,720kg (103,000lb; max payload 15,781kg (34,790lb).

Performance: Max cruising speed 488kts (905km/h); take-off field length 1,830m (6,000ft); landing field length 1,350m (4,430ft); range with standard fuel and 115 passengers 1,855nm (3,439km).

Accommodation: Flight crew of two. Basic arrangements for 115 passenger six-abreast, or 130 in high-density configuration. Underfloor cargo/baggage hold volume 24.78m³ (875ft³).

The model 737 is the 'baby' of the Boeing jetliner family and the third of th series of commercial jet transports to appear from the Seattle compan

Below: The 737-200, which has largely been replaced in first line service with major airlines by later models, has found a niche with low-fare operators across the United States. This -200 belonging to New Jersey-based Eastwind was photographed at Baltimore Washington International Airport.

*bove: TAP Air Portugal was one of many European airlines to
se the 737-200 on its short-haul scheduled services. These are
ow gradually being replaced by single-aisle Airbus types.*

ven though it started late, the family became Boeing's most successful
rcraft. Boeing announced its intention to develop a twin jet with 80-100 seats
November 1964, by which time two other new types in a similar category, ▶

the BAC One-Eleven and the Douglas DC-9, were already well advanced. B
contrast with its two rear-engined competitors, however, the Boeing desig
featured a more conventional layout with underwing engines and a low tailplan
position; for commonality with the Models 707 and 727, Boeing also chose t
use the same basic cabin cross-section (from the floor up), allowin
comfortable six-abreast seating and interchangeability for passenger facilitie
galley equipment, etc, for airlines using more than one of the Boeing jetline
types. Named Model 737 to continue the Boeing family of designations tha
had begun with the Model 707, the new type won a launch order fror
Lufthansa on 19 February 1965 – the first time that a non-US airline had bee
in the position of ordering a new American airliner that was not already i
production for at least one major US operator. As launched, the Model 737 wa
sized for 100 seats and powered by 62.3kN (14,000lb) Pratt & Whitney JT8D-
engines. Design work on the 737 began on 11 May 1964 and the first flight, b
a company-owned prototype, was made on 9 April 1967.

VARIANTS
Only 30 aircraft were built in the original Model 737-100 configuration, th

ersion quickly being superseded by the Model 737-200, with a fuselage 'stretch' of 1.82m (6ft) to allow basic accommodation for 119 and, eventually, a maximum of 130. United Airlines was the first to order this variant, and the fifth example of the Model 737 to fly, on 8 August 1967, was the first stretched Model 737-200. A passenger/cargo convertible version, with a forward side door similar to that of the Model 727-200C, was flown in August 1968 and designated Model 737-200C. Aircraft from no.135 onwards introduced a series of modifications to the thrust reversers (switching from clamshell to target type) and wing flaps, and another series of changes to the leading edge and trailing-edge devices, nacelle mountings and other items led to the introduction of the Advanced 737, whose first flight was made on 15 April 1971. The Model 737-200 first appeared at a maximum take-off weight of 43,999kg (97,000lb), but this has been progressively increased. As noise regulations at airports became more stringent, Boeing introduced in 1973 a Quiet Nacelle modification, and an optional gravel runway kit was offered, including deflection ▶

Below: LanChile operates a large fleet of 737-200 Advanced on domestic services.

shields on the main and nosewheel legs, fuselage abrasion protection, flap protection, blow-away jets beneath the engine intakes and other speci features. Several schemes for stretching the Boeing 737 were studie during the late 1970s, eventually leading to the launch of the Model 737-3C as described separately. Several Model 737s have been sold as corpora or executive transports and the designation 77-32 is used for aircraft in th role.

SERVICE USE

The Boeing 737-100 was certificated on 15 December 1967, and this varia entered service with Lufthansa on 10 February 1968. Type Approval for th Model 737-200 followed quickly, on 21 December 1967, and United operate the first services on 28 April 1968. Wien Consolidated was the first operator

*bove: There are few areas of the world where the 737 has not been
en regularly. Egyptair, a prolific Boeing user, had a fleet of 737-200s;
e is seen here at Cairo.*

e Model 737-200C towards the end of 1968, after certification in October. The
dvanced 737-200 gained its Type Approval on 3 May 1971, allowing All Nippon
ways to become the first operator of this model in June 1971; the first
ample with a 'wide look' interior was operated by Air Algerie in January 1972,
d Eastern Provincial Airways was the first to receive the Quiet Nacelle
odification in October 1973. Total production of the Boeing 737 amounted to
Model 100, 219 Model 200 and 865 Model 200 Advanced totalling 1,114
craft. Some 825 remain in service today with a wide spectrum of the world's
lines, some of which have considerable fleets of 737s.

Boeing 737-300/400/500

SPECIFICATION
(Boeing 737-300)

Dimensions: Wingspan 28.88M (94ft 9in); length overall 33.40m (109ft 7in); height overall 11.13m (36ft 6in), wing area 105.4m² (1,135ft²).

Power Plant: Two CFM International CFM56-3C-1 turbofans each rated at either 89.0kN (20,000lb) or 97.9kN (22,000lb).

Weights: Operating weight empty basic 32,704kg (72,100lb); max take-off basic 56,470kg (124,500lb); max landing 51,720kg (114,000lb).

Performance: Max cruising speed 491kts (908km/h); initial cruise altitude 10,195m (33,450ft); take-off field length 2,286m (7,500ft); landing field length 1,433m (4,700ft); range with typical payload 2,270nm (4,204km).

Accommodation: Crew of two. Typical mixed-class layout for 128 passengers with maximum of 149 six-abreast. Underfloor baggage/cargo volume 30.24m³ (1,068ft³).

Development of a stretched version of the Boeing 737 began in 1979, when market studies began to show the need for what Boeing was later describe as 'a longer-bodied version of the popular 737 twinjet, designed burn less fuel per passenger and provide reduced noise levels for the short-ha markets of 1985 and beyond'. As has been the case with many programmes 'stretch' an existing aircraft, the exact degree of lengthening that was desirab remained open to question for some time, as airline reactions were studied ar launch customers sought. By early 1980, the Model 737-300 designation ha been adopted for the proposal and, when details were published by Boeing the course of the Farnborough Air Show later that year, a stretch of 2.13m (84i was indicated, compared with earlier studies that provided for a lengthening only 1.02m (40in). However much the aircraft was lengthened, engines mo

Below: The Boeing 737-300 forms the main fleet of UK low-fare, no-frills airline easyJet. Based at London's Luton Airport, the airline sells tickets direct to the public, hence the huge reservations number on the side of the fuselage.

bove: Seen here in the markings of Luxair, the 737-400 was the largest f the second-generation 737 models.

dvanced and more powerful than the JT8Ds used in the Model 737-200 were eeded, with fuel efficiency and low noise levels the two most important naracteristics. As plans for the Model 737-300 were confirmed it became clear at the CFM56 was the only suitable engine which could be developed with a uitable thrust and in the required time-frame. The latter, based on launch rders announced in March 1981 from USAir and Southwest Airlines, was stablished with an entry into service date of late 1984. By the time of the unch, the fuselage had grown again, by a further 0.51m (20in), with a 1.12m 4in) plug head of the wing and a 1.52m (60in) plug aft of it. This allowed the aximum seating to be increased to 149 and gave the Model 737-300 some 21 ore seats than the Model 737-200 in a comparable all-tourist layout. Apart ▶

from (and to some extent because of) the higher weights at which the Model 737-300 was to operate, some airframe modifications were made, including wing tip extensions that added 230mm (9in) to each tip, some changes to the leading-edge slots, revised trailing-edge 'flipper' flaps and flap track fairings, an addition to the dorsal fin area, and a lengthened nosewheel leg to provide adequate ground clearance for the engines. To fit the larger-diameter CFM56 engines under the wings, their accessory drives were located on the sides of the engines, resulting in a somewhat unusual flat-bottomed nacelle shape. The first Model 737-300, destined for delivery eventually to USAir, flew at Seattle on 24 February 1984.

VARIANTS

The Model 737-300 is available at two maximum weights, the higher weight being required when the optional fuel tanks are carried in the aft cargo bay. Uprated CFM56-3B2 engines are available for operation in hot-and-high conditions. Corporate/executive versions of the stretched aircraft carry the designation 77-33. Soon after launching the Model 300, Boeing was considering both a lengthened and shortened version, initially known as the 737-300L and 737-100L(Lite) respectively, later given the designations 737-400 and 737-500. Details of the 737-400 were announced in June 1986 and the first aircraft made its maiden flight on 19 February 1988, receiving FAA certification on 2 September. The new model was stretched 3.05m (10ft 0in) by means of two 'plugs', forward and aft of the wing, providing up to 170 passengers in an all-tourist layout. Other changes were a tail bumper, strengthened outer wing and landing gear and additional emergency exits. Power plant was either the 97.86kN (22,000lb) thrust CFM56-3B-2 as used on the 737-300, or the 104.5kN (23,500lb) CFM56-3C. A high gross weight version with a ramp weight of

Visit www.Waldenbookstores.com

PV# 002448

CHANGE	-.27
CASH	5.00
GIFT CARD ACCOUNT BALANCE:	0.00
601736587492797·35 G/C RDM	20.00
S/VALUELINK AUTH: 286797	
TOTAL	24.73
7.700% TAX	1.77
SUBTOTAL	22.96
04 068191201·4	6.99
03 068142560·0	5.99
02 068161699·6	2.99
01 068179081·4	6.99

REL 7./6/1.05   44   14:23:45

SALE   0702   102 4448 04-27-04

W A L D E N B O O K S

8,265kg (150,500lb) was rolled out on 23 December 1988. Combining the advanced technology of both the -300 and -400 models, but with a fuselage shortened to 29.95m (101ft 9in), almost the same size as the 737-200, the 737-00 was first announced on 20 May 1987 and made its maiden flight on 30 June 1989. It is powered by CFM56-3C1 turbofan engines of 88.97kN 0,000lb) thrust, or derated to 82.29kN (18,500lb) according to gross weight.

ERVICE USE

AA certification of the Model 737-300 was obtained on 14 November 1984, nd Boeing began delivering the new variant on the 28th day of that month, then USAir accepted its first aircraft, followed two days later by Southwest irlines. The latter operator flew the first revenue service on 7 December 1984, ith USAir following on 18 December. The first delivery to a non-US customer as made to Orion Airways in the UK on 29 January 1985, with service entry n 22 February, and Pakistan International Airlines took delivery of the first lodel 737-300 with the uprated -3B2 engines on 31 May 1985, for first service n 1 July. First delivery of the 737-400 was made to launch customer Piedmont irlines on 15 September 1988 and the higher gross weight version followed n 21 March 1989. Southwest Airlines accepted the first 737-500 on 28 ebruary 1990, 16 days after FAA certification. Launch customer Braathens AFE of Norway received its first aircraft on 7 March 1990. Production of these lodels ceased in 2000, with the last of 1,988 delivered in February. The total cludes 1,113 737-300s, 486 -400s and 389 -500s. Some 1,945 remained in ervice at 1 January 2001.

elow: Braathens SAFE in Norway paints one aircraft each summer in a pecial colour scheme. This is a 737-500.

Above: The 737-500, which first entered service in February 1990, is the 'baby' of the second-generation twin-jet series. It is seen here in British

G-MSKA

...irways markings, but operated by franchisee Maersk Air out of ...irmingham.

Boeing 737-600/700/800/900

SPECIFICATION
(Boeing 737-600)
Dimensions: Wingspan 34.31m (112ft 7in); length 31.24m (102ft 6in); height overall 12.57m (41ft 3in); wing area 125.00m² (1,345.5ft²).
Power Plant: Two CFM International CFM56-7B18, each rated at 86.7kN (19,500lb) thrust, or the 101.0kN (22,700lb) CFM56-7B22.
Weights: Operating weight empty 37,104kg (81,800lb); max take-off 65,090kg (143,500lb); max landing 54,655kg (120,500lb).
Performance: Max cruising speed M0.785; service ceiling 12,5000m (41,000ft); take-off field length 1,796m (5,890ft); landing field length 1,342m (4,400ft); range with typical payload 1,340nm (2,480km).
Accommodation: Flight crew of two. Single-aisle cabin layout, seating typically 108 passengers in a two-class configuration. Max high-density seating for 132 passengers. Cargo/baggage volume 20.4m³ (720ft³).

In 1991 Boeing began working with more than 30 airlines to develop a new generation derivative family of its highly-successful twin-engine 737 airliner. The new 737-X was to be offered in three sizes, approximately matching the 737-300, 400 and -500 models. Boeing stressed that the earlier versions would continue t

e produced alongside the new models, for as long as customers demanded. After
arrowing down design parameters, Boeing's board of directors authorised the
ffering for sale of the 737-X on 29 June 1993, with full launch into production
ollowing an order for 63 Model 737-700 (32 converted from options for the 737-
00), plus 63 new options, from Southwest Airlines on 18 November 1993.
oeing's decision to proceed was also strongly influenced by the inroads made into
ne market by the more advanced Airbus A320, which was itself being expanded
to a three-member family. Key design features of the new 737s are a modified
ring, enlarged in area by 25 per cent through increased chord and a 4.88m (16ft
n) extension of the wingspan, larger tail surfaces, increased tankage to provide US
anscontinental range, and new quieter, cleaner and more fuel-efficient CFM
ternational CFM56-7B (previously CFM56-3XS) turbofans with full authority digital
ngine control (FADEC). The CFM56-7B combines the core of the CFM56-5 with
ne improved low pressure compressor of the CFM56-3. It will have a 10 per cent
gher thrust capability than the -3C which powers the existing 737s. A new
dvanced flight deck, similar in many respects to those of Boeing's other new ▶

*Below: The Boeing Business Jet (BBJ) is a corporate version of the
37-700.*

airliners, will emulate their electronic flight instrumentation system (EFIS) an
primary flight display – navigation display (PFD-ND). These improvements wi
provide greater range (approximately 900nm further), higher speeds and altitude
reduced fuel burn, as well as lower noise signatures and emission levels, while
maintaining commonality with earlier 737s. The first of the three models, the 737
700, was rolled out on 8 December 1996 and took off on its maiden flight from
Seattle on 9 February 1997. The flight-test programme involved aircraft, including
four 737-700, three 737-800 and three 737-600. The 737-800 flew on 31 July 1997
and the smallest member, the 737-600 made its maiden flight on 22 January 1998.
On 10 November, Boeing launched the stretched 737-900 (formerly 737-900X), with
an order for 10, plus 10 options, from Alaska Airlines.

VARIANTS
The first model was the 737-700, which uses the fuselage of the 737-300, but
is 0.23m (9in) longer due to an increased tail span. Wingspan is 5.45m (17ft

0in) greater at 34.31m (112ft 7in). It seats between 126 and 149 passengers nd is powered by two wing-mounted CFM56-7B24 turbofans, each rated at 01N (22,700lb) static thrust. The -700 is also planned to be made available in n extended-range version, presently designated 737-700ERX, and as a 737-'00C Combi model. Roughly equivalent to the 737-400, the new 737-800 is tretched to carry from 162 to 189 passengers and has more powerful 121.4kN 27,300lb) thrust CFM56-7B27 engines to take account of the heavier weight. he 737-600 is the smallest variant, similar in size to the 737-500, providing eating for 108 to 132 passengers. It is powered by the CFM56-7B22 engine, ated at 101kN (22,700lb). Boeing flew the 737-900 on 3 August 2000. The rgest of the next-generation 737s, it has been stretched by a total of 1.64m 5ft 3¹/₂in) to provide seating from 177 to 189 passengers. Boeing has also ▶

Below: UK charter airline Excel Airways, formerly known as Sabre Airways, operates a fleet of 737-800s on charters to the Mediterranean.

developed two corporate versions, first launched on 2 July 1996. The BBJ i
based on the 737-700 and typically carries 8 passengers (max 63) non-stop ove
a range of 6,200nm (11,480km). The larger BBJ 2 has been developed from th
737-800 and was launched on 11 October 1999. The BBJ first flew on
September 1998. Both BBJs are distinguished by new blended winglets, whic
are also an option on the basic passenger models.

IN SERVICE

The Boeing 737-700 was the first to enter service with launch custome
Southwest Airlines in October 1997. The first European delivery was made t
Maersk Air of Denmark. Launch customer Hapag-Lloyd took delivery of the firs

Above: The new-generation 737 family is set to continue the success story of this twin-engined aircraft, with more than 1,700 orders received.

37-800 on 22 April 1998, following JAA certification 13 days earlier. The first 37-600 was certificated on 18 August 1998 and delivered to launch customer AS Scandinavian Airlines on 18 September that year. Delivery of the first 737-00 to Alaska Airlines is scheduled for April 2001. First customer delivery of the BJ took place on 23 November 1998. At 1 January 2001, Boeing had received ders for 1,741 next-generation 737s, including 86 for the -600, 781 for the -0, 56 for the -700BBJ, 772 for the -800, and 46 for the -900 model. A total of 5 of all models had been delivered.

Boeing 747-100/200/SP

SPECIFICATION
(Boeing 747-200B)
Dimensions: Wingspan 59.64m (195ft 8in); length overall 70.66m (231ft 10in);
height overall 19.33m (63ft 5in), wing area 511m² (5,500ft²).
Power Plant: Four General Electric CF6-50E2 turbofans, each rated at
233.5kN (52,500lb) or Pratt & Whitney JT9D-7R4G2 at 243.5kN (54,750lb) or
Rolls-Royce RB211-524D4 at 236.25kN (53,110lb).
Weights: (P&W engines) Operating weight empty 169,961kg (374,400lb); max
take-off 377,840kg (833.000lb); max landing 285,765kg (630,000lb); max
payload 68,855kg (151,800lb).
Performance: Max cruising speed 507kts (940km/h); cruise ceiling 13,715m
(45,000ft); take-off field length 3,170m (10m400ft); landing field length 2,120m
(6,950ft); range with max fuel 7,100nm (13,135km); range with max payload
6,150nm (11,380km).
Accommodation: Flight crew of three. Typical mixed-class layout for 452
passengers, with maximum of 516 ten-abreast, all with twin aisles. Underfloor
baggage/cargo volume 147.0m³ (5,190ft³).

Boeing's development of its fourth individual jetliner design, and the largest
built to date, began in the early 1960s as a by-product, in the first instance
of the work done on a large military logistics transport, the CH-X. When
Lockheed won the military order with the C-5A Galaxy, Boeing studied civil
alternatives of its military project, with 'double-bubble' fuselage arrangement
and a mid-wing layout, but eventually adopted a more orthodox Model 707-type
configuration, though at much larger scale. The design that became the Model
747 then evolved around the concept of a single main deck, wide enough over
most of its length for 10-abreast seating with two aisles, whilst the flight deck
was at a higher level, with a small passenger cabin in the fuselage behind it and
reached by a spiral staircase from the main deck. By 1965, the basic concept of
this very large jetliner, with seating for up to 500 passengers, had been settled
and the all-new Pratt & Whitney JT9D turbofan chosen to power it. The launch
order, from Pan American, came on 14 April 1966, and the production go-ahead
was given in July after orders were placed by Lufthansa and JAL. The first flight
was made on 9 February 1969 at Everett, Washington, where Boeing
established a completely new production facility for the massive new transport
which soon became known as the Jumbo Jet. Subsequently evolution of the
design has produced a number of variants as set out below, most of which have
retained the same external dimensions and shapes of the original. The Model
747-300 with a longer upper deck, the Model 747-400 with the same upper
deck plus an extended wing and winglets, and possible further stretches of the
basic Model 747, are described separately.

VARIANTS
The original Boeing 747 was introduced with JT9D-1 or -3 engines at 193.6kN
(43,500lb) and a certificated gross weight of 322,140kg (710,000lb). Other
engines used were the JT9D-3A, -3W, -7 and -7W, and higher gross weights
were approved in due course. These early variants all became the Model 747-
100 when the designation Model 747-200B was adopted for a version first
flown on 11 October 1970 with the increased weight, more fuel and uprated
engines. A reduced gross weight, shorter-range version introduced in 1973 as
the Model 747SR later became the Model 747-100B and in used primarily in
Japan. Versions of the Model 747-200 were developed as pure freighters
(Model 747F) or convertible passenger/freighter (Model 747C) with upward-
hinged nose for straight-in freight loading; the first Model 747F flew on 3

Above: The early Boeing 747s, now often referred to as the 'Classic', have shown themselves to be particularly suited to the carriage of cargo, and many were produced both as pure freighters and as passenger/cargo combis. Europe's major all-cargo operator Cargolux flies an all 747 fleet including these 747-200Cs.

November 1971, and the first Model 747C on 23 March 1973. A version with a large side-loading freight door aft of the wing appeared in 1974 as the Model 747 Combi, sometimes combined with the nose-loading door. All the foregoing Model 747 variants are dimensionally similar, but the Model 747SP (Special Performance), first flown on 4 July 1975, has a fuselage shortened by 14.6m (48ft) for a typical mixed-class accommodation of 288, and a taller fin and rudder, together with other less obvious changes. Retaining the full tankage of the basic aircraft, the Model 747SP achieves a full payload range of 5,750nm (10,660km). There have been a number of increases in the maximum permitted weights of the basic Model 747-200, hand-in-hand with the introduction of more powerful engines, including the options quoted above. Other engine variants applicable have included the JT9D-7J, -7Q, -7AW and 7O, the CF6-50D, 50E and -45AZ and the RB.211 -524B2 and -524C2.

SERVICE USE

The Model 747 was originally certificated on 30 December 1969, and Pan American put the 'jumbo' into service on the North Atlantic on 21 January 1970. The Model 747-200B was certificated on 23 December 1970 and entered service with KLM early in 1971. Type Approval of the Model 747F was obtained on 7 March 1972 and service use by Lufthansa began on 19 April 1972; and the ▶

Model 747C convertible with nose-loading door entered service with World Airways after certification on 24 April 1973, while Sabena was first to operate the Model 747 Combi in 1974. The 'lightweight' Model 747SR entered service with Japan Air Lines on 9 October 1973, and the short-body Model 747SP with Pan American in May 1976. Boeing built 643 of these 747 models, including 205 -100, 393 -200 and 45 SP. Some 440 remained in active service at 1 January 2001.

*Below: The 'dumpy' 747SP (Special Performance) was built at the behest
of Pan American World Airways to provide non-stop range between New
York and Tokyo. Only 45 were built, as the improvements of the larger
models soon provided similar performance. Syrianair was one of the few
airlines to purchase it. Others still operating the type include Iran Air,
Saudi Arabian Airlines, Corsair and South African Airways.*

Boeing 747-300/400/X

SPECIFICATION
(Boeing 747-400)
Dimensions: Wingspan 66.44m (211ft 5in); length overall 70.66m (231ft 10in); height overall 19.41m (63ft 8in), wing area 524.9m² (5,650ft²).
Power Plant: Four General Electric CF6-80C2B1F, each rated at 252kN (56,750lb) or Pratt & Whitney PW4056 also rated at 252kN (56,750lb) or Rolls Royce RC211-524G/H rated at 258kN (58,000lb).
Weights: (P&W engines) Operating weight empty 180,958kg (399,000lb); max take-off 362,875kg (800,000lb); max landing 260,360kg (574,000lb) max payload 62,690kg (138,206lb).
Performance: Max cruising speed 507kts (938km/h); initial cruise altitude 10,030m (32,900ft); take-off field length 3,322m (10,900ft); landing field length 2,072m (6,800ft); range with max fuel 8,400nm (15,540km); range with max payload 7,125nm (13,180km).
Accommodation: Two flight crew with seats for two observers. Typical three class layout for 421 passengers.

Having launched the Model 747 in 1966, Boeing soon turned its attention to the possibility of 'stretching' the basic aircraft in a number of possible ways. Increasing engine power, fuel capacity and operating weights enhanced the aircraft's economics and broadened its operational spectrum, but plans to increase the passenger-carrying ability matured more slowly. It was not until 1980 that a modest stretch proposal emerged in which the upper passenger deck, behind the flight deck, was extended aft by 7.11m (3ft 4in) effectively doubling the 'upstairs' seating area. This proposed new variant was identified at first as the Model 747SUD (stretched upper deck), later as the Model 747EUD (extended upper deck) and finally as the Model 747-300. The importance of the upper deck seating area as a revenue earner for the airlines is indicated by its progressive development, since initial certification of the Model 747 allowed only eight fare-paying passengers to be carried in that cabin. First, a smoke barrier increased the ▶

Below: Korean Air operates several 747 models, including this 747-300.

limit to 16; then a straight staircase in place of the original spiral allowing seating to increase to 24; then the addition of a second type emergency exit/door made it possible to seat 32 (special staircase) or 45 (straight staircase) and finally extending the upper deck fairing aft made the cabin large enough for 69 seats in the Model 747-300 and later models. The first -300 flew on October 1982, with JT9D-7R4G2 engines, and the second on 10 December 1982 with CF6-50E2 engines. As a further development of the stretched upper deck aircraft, Boeing launched the model 747-400 in July 1985 on the back of an order for 10 aircraft placed by Northwest Airlines. The 747-400 differs greatly from the -300 in incorporating extensive changes to the structure and systems, an advanced two-crew flight deck, extended wing tips plus winglets that increase the wingspan to 64.44m (211ft 5in), and a choice of advanced technology lean burn engines, including the 252.4kN (56,750lb) thrust PW5056 257.7kN (57,900lb) CF6-80C2B1F, 258.1kN (58,000lb) RB.211-524G and 269.7kN (60,600lb) RB.211-524H. Other options are available. The 747-400 first flew on 29 April 1988, obtaining certification (with Pratt & Whitney engines) 10 January 1989. In May 1990, Boeing decided to market only the Model 400, the last of the earlier 'Classic' types, a 747-200F, being delivered to Nippon Cargo Air Lines on 19 November 1991.

VARIANTS

The Model 747-300 was available with engine and gross weight options similar to those of the Model 747-200. The Model 747-300 Combi has a rear side freight door and provision for mixed passenger/freight loads and the Model 747-300SR is a short-range variant designed, like the SR version of the Model 747-100, to operate at lower weights in order to achieve a higher ratio of flights

ght hours. At least one Model 747-300 has been completed in VIP onfiguration for a Middle East head of state and carried the designation Model 7-43 in line with Boeing practice for its corporate aircraft. The basic passenger 47-400 was followed by the 747-400M Combi passenger/freight version, ertificated on 1 September 1989. Demand for a high-density configuration on apan's domestic trunk routes produced the 747-400 Domestic, which was ertificated for 568 passengers on 10 October 1991. An all-freighter, the 747-00F, flew on 7 May 1993. It differs from the other variants in retaining the hort upper deck of the Model 200, and has a strengthened floor and cargo ading facilities. Maximum cargo payload is 113,000kg (249,120lb). erformance improvement packages (PIP) were announced in 1993, including small increase in gross weight and drag reduction. These were applied to new oduction aircraft and were offered as retrofits to existing aircraft. Winglets for further 6-7% drag reduction, for retrofit to the -300 model, were being flight sted in summer 2000.

oeing is developing a family of 747 derivatives to ensure its future place in the rge aircraft category. Three new models are being planned, all having high ommonality with the 747-400 to ease integration into the existing 747-400 eets. The 747-400X is the same size as the existing 747-400, but offers more nge or payload capability, as well as an updated flight deck. Maximum take-f weight is 412,770kg (910,000lb) and range 7,690 nautical miles (14,240km). he 747X incorporates all the enhancements of the 747-400X, plus a modified ▶

elow: French independent UTA operated the 747-300 'Big Boss' until tegrated into Air France in January 1990.

wing, faster speed, new landing gear, an increase in fuel, and a choice
engines from the General Electric-Pratt & Whitney Engine Alliance or Rol
Royce in the 302-311kN (68,000 - 70,000lb) range. A maximum take-off weig
of 473,100kg (1,043,000lb) gives the 747X a range of nearly 9,000 n mil
(16,650km), enabling it to fly non-stop for 18 hours. The 747X Stretch v
become the world's largest 747 with a fuselage 9.60m (31ft 6in) longer than t
747-400 and a high-density seating for 660 passengers. A 747X Stret
Freighter is also planned.

SERVICE USE
The model 747-300 was certificated on 7 March 1963 and entered service w

above: The Boeing 747-400 is seen here in old South African Airways' markings.

wissair on 28 March, with JT9D engines. The first operator with CF6-50E2 ngines was UTA, starting on 1 April 1983, and the first with RB.211-524D4 ngines was Qantas, starting on 25 November 1984. Northwest Airlines ceived its first 747-400 on 29 January 1989 and put the type into service on February. The 747-400F freighter entered service with Luxembourg-based argolux in November 1993. Since ending production of the 747-300 after 81 ad been built, Boeing has received 614 orders for the 747-400, of which 537 ad been delivered by 1 January 2001.

Boeing 757

SPECIFICATION
(Boeing 757-200)

Dimensions: Wingspan 38.05m (124ft 10in); length overall 47.32m (155ft 3in) height overall 134.56m (44ft 6 in), wing area 185.2m² (1,994ft²).

Power Plant: Two Pratt & Whitney PW2037 turbofans rated at 178.4kN (40,100lb) or PW2040 rated at 185.5kN (41,700lb) or Rolls-Royce 535C rated 166.4kN (37,400lb) or 535E4 rated at 178.4kN (40,100lb).

Weights: (with R-R 535E4 engines) Operating weight empty 57,108kg (126,060lb); max take-off 99,790kg (22,000lb); max landing 89,810kg (198,000lb); max payload 24,830kg (54,740lb).

Performance: Max cruising speed 505kts (935km/h); initial cruising altitude 11,880m (38,970ft); take-off field length 2,225m (7,300ft); landing field length 1,494m (4,900ft); range with max fuel 4,270nm (7,900km); range with max payload nm (7,060km).

Accommodation: Flight crew of two with provision for an observer. Mixed-class arrangements mainly six-abreast ranging from 178 to a maximum tourist layout for 239 passengers. Underfloor cargo volume 50.7m³ (1,790ft³).

The Boeing 757, launched in mid-1978, is essentially a 'big brother' for the Model 727 which, up to the mid-1980s, retained its position as the best-seller among the Western world's jetliners. During the 1970s Boeing devoted much time and effort to studying possible stretches of the Model 727, with particular attention to the advantages to be gained from the use of more ▶

Below: The 757-200 has been the major medium-range, single-aisle aircraft on the European charter scene, carrying holiday makers from northern Europe as far as the Canary Islands and to Funchal on Madeira, where this 757-200 of German airline LTU Süd was photographed.

modern engines. In the end, the Model 757 emerged as a wholly new desig
Although attempts were made to retain commonality with the Model 727, th
switch from a configuration using three rear-mounted engines to one with a pa
of engines in underwing pods made this difficult, and with a new wing and
low-mounted tailplane the Model 757 retained little of the Model 727 other tha
the same basic fuselage cross section, which was therefore similar to that als
used in the Models 707 and 737. Even the original intention of using a flig
deck with Model 727 features was eventually abandoned in favour of achievir
the best possible commonality with the Boeing 767, and as finally built, th
Model 757 had more in common with the latter than the former, to the exte
that it is possible for pilots to obtain a single flight rating that allows them to

Above: The Boeing 757 is available with a choice of power plants, including the Pratt & Whitney PW2037 and Rolls-Royce 535C engines. This Caledonian Airways aircraft, operated on lease from British Airways, was fitted out with Rolls-Royce engines.

ther the Model 757 or the Model 767. Of the several advanced high bypass tio turbofans under development, the RB.211-535 was chosen as one of the ost suitable for the Model 757, with the General Electric CF-32C1 rated at 3.7kN (36,500lb) as an alternative. Until the launch of the new aircraft, the first being aircraft to be launched with a foreign engine, on 31 August 1978, two ternative fuselage lengths were on offer, as the Model 757-100 and Model ▶

757-200; the two launch customers, British Airways and Eastern Air Lines, bot chose the -200 with Rolls-Royce engines, and the -100 was eventually droppe as an option. Also dropped, by General Electric's decision not to proceed wit its development, was the CF6-32 engine option, after Pratt & Whitney ha entered the market with the PW2000 family, and a version of the latter ha become the alternative to the RB.211 in the Model 757. Flight testing began o 19 February 1982 at the Boeing factory at Renton, with four more aircraft use in the flight development programme. The first flight with PW2037 engine was made on 14 March 1984.

VARIANTS

The Model 757-200 is available at two different gross weights, and with sever different engine options from Rolls-Royce and Pratt & Whitney. In 1985, th first sale was made of a freighter version, designated Model 757PF (packag freighter), with a large cargo door in the forward fuselage port side, a singl crew entry door and no cabin windows. The same large loading door is used the Model 757M Combi which retains the standard features for passenge carrying and can be used to accommodate mixed cargo/passenger loads varying combinations. The designation Model 77-52 is used to identif corporate/executive versions of the 757. ETOPS (extended twin-engin operations) were certified with Rolls-Royce RB.211-535E4 engines December 1986. In 1992, Pemco Aeroplex developed a 757-200F freight version by converting existing passenger models. This is available in all-carg combi and quick-change configurations. An extended-range version providing 600nm (1,110km) increase in maximum range has been given the suffix EF The 757-300 'stretch' was launched at the 1996 Farnborough air show following receipt of an order for 12 aircraft from German charter airline Condo The -300 is 7.11m (23ft 4in) longer than the standard -200 and is able

ccommodate some 20 per cent more passengers, bringing maximum capacity
) 289. Some strengthening of the wing and landing gear and a retractable tail-
kid are other 757-300 features. The 757-300 made its first flight on 2 August
998. Under an agreement announced on 5 October 1999, Boeing has
urchased a large number of 757-200s from British Airways, which it will
onvert to special freighter configuration for DHL under the designation 757SF.
n extended-range 757-200X version is being studied, which would combine
ie fuselage of the 757-200 with the strengthened wing of the -300 model, and
ave increased fuel for longer range.

ERVICE USE

ollowing its certification by the FAA on 21 December 1982 and the CAA (in the
'K) on 14 January 1983, Boeing 757 deliveries to Eastern Air Lines began on
2 December 1982 and to British Airways on 25 January 1983. These two
rlines started revenue service with the type on 1 January and 9 February 1983
:spectively. The Model 757 with PW2037 engines was certificated in October
984, and deliveries to Delta Air Lines began on 5 November that year, with the
rst service flown on 28 November. The first Model 757 with the uprated
B.211-535E4 engines was delivered to Eastern on 10 October 1984. United
arcel Service (UPS) acquired its first 757-200PF on 17 September 1987, while
ie first extended-range passenger model, suffixed ER, was delivered to Royal
runei Airlines on 6 May 1986. Launch customer Condor Flugdienst took
elivery of the first 757-300 on 10 March 1999, following FAA certification with
20-minute ETOPS approval on 27 January 1999. At 1 January 2001, Boeing
ad orders for 1,027 757s, with 948 delivered.

*elow: Northwest Airlines is a prolific user of the 757-200, shown here in
previous colour scheme. It has 48 in the fleet, with more on order.*

Boeing 767

SPECIFICATION
(Boeing 767-300)
Dimensions: Wingspan 47.57m (156ft 1in), length overall 54.94m (180ft 3 in); height overall 15.85m (52ft 0in), wing area 283,3² (3,050ft²).
Power Plant: Two General Electric CF6-80C2B2F or Pratt & Whitney PW4050 turbofans, each rated at 222.5kN (50,000lb).
Weights: Operating weight empty 86,955kg (191,700lb); max take-off 159,210kg (351,000lb); max landing 136,080kg (300,000lb); max payload 37,470kg (82,605lb).
Performance: Max cruising speed 492kts (910km/h); initial cruise altitude 11,250m (36,910ft); take-off field length 2,652m (8,700ft); landing field length 1,646m (5,400ft); range with typical payload 4,250nm (7,860km).
Accommodation: Flight crew of two. Typical mixed-class configuration seats 250 passengers, with maximum 328 in 8-abreast tourist layout. Hold volume 114.10m³ (4,030ft³).

Boeing conducted many studies during the early and mid seventies with a view to providing a new medium-range aircraft of large capacity, in order to maintain its competitive position vis-à-vis Airbus Industrie, which was at the same time projecting an aircraft of similar size. For much of the time, the project was known as the 7X7, and its precise size and overall configuration remained uncertain until the first airline orders were obtained. As finally launched, the Boeing 767 was a twin-aisle aircraft, breaking away from the constant cabin cross section used by Boeing for the 707/727/737/757 narrow-body series and having a fuselage that was 1.24m (4ft1in) wider. This allowed an eight-abreast layout with two aisles (2+4+2) and no passenger more than one seat away from an aisle. Initially, Boeing planned to use a three-man flight deck, with a two-pilot arrangement offered later as an option, but airline ▶

Below: Spanair, one of Spain's largest scheduled and charter carriers, operates the 767-300ER on long-haul services.

preference led to adoption of the two-man flight deck as standard before deliveries began, although this called for modification of a number of aircraft already completed, Much use was made in the design of advanced materials including new alloys as well as composites, and the avionics included an advanced digital flight management system with electronic flight instrument systems (EFIS) – one of the first to be applied as standard to a commercial transport. Two variants of the basic aircraft were planned at first as the 767-100 and 767-200 with different fuselage lengths, but all early orders were for the larger capacity version and the 767-100 was not continued. The Boeing-owned 767-200 prototype made its first flight at Everett, Washington, on 26 September 1981 with Pratt & Whitney engines, followed by three in United Airlines configuration. The fifth aircraft was the first with General Electric engines, in Delta Air Lines configuration, and was flown on 19 February 1982. A stretched model, the 767-300 was announced in February 1983. Using the same basic airframe as the 767-200ER, the 767-300 incorporates fuselage plugs fore and aft of the wing, with lengths of 3.07m (10ft 1in) and 3.35m (11ft 0in) respectively, providing seating for up to 290 passengers. It also has strengthened main and nose gear legs and some thickening of wing skins. The 767-300 made its first flight on 30 January 1986, powered by the JT9D-7R4D rated at 213.5kN (48,000lb).

VARIANTS

The basic variant is the 767-200 at a max take-off weight of 136,078kg (300,000lb). A medium-range variant operates at 142,991kg (315,000lb). The extended-range 757-200ER with additional wing centre-section tanks and a gross weight of 156,490kg (345,000lb) made its first flight on 6 March 1984. The basic 757-300 is offered with the same take-off weight and engine options as the 767-200ER, but includes heavier models, including a 181,435kg (400,000lb) high gross weight variant. Additional fuel capacity with enlarged wing centre-section tanks and higher weights up to 181,437kg (400,000lb) resulted in the 767-300ER, certificated in December 1987. A specialised 767-200PF package freighter was launched with a UPS order in January 1993, followed later that year by the 767-300F, which differed in having cargo loading and an enhanced environmental system. Engine options for all 767 models include the CF6-80A and JT9D-7RD4 both rated at 213.5kN (48,000lb), and the ▶

Below: Malév Hungarian Airlines was the second Central European carrier to introduce the Boeing 767 (the first was LOT of Poland), which reflected the general trend of replacing old Soviet aircraft with modern Western equipment. Malév operates two Boeing 767-200s on its long-haul North American flights to New York.

CF6-80A2 and JT9D-7R4E and -7R4E4 rated at 222.4kN (50,000lb). Other G and P&W variants, as well as the Rolls-Royce RB211-524G and H are availab for specific versions. The 767-400ER is basically a derivative of the 767-300E with a 6.43m (21ft 1in) fuselage stretch, new main landing gear, and extende wingspan and canted winglets to improve performance; , and a maximum tak off weight 204,120kg (450,000lb); it made its maiden flight on 9 October 200 A 767-400ERX offering 747-400ER size with 737-300ER range, a horizontal ta fuel tank, increased thrust engines and take-off weight of 210,923k (465,000lb) is under consideration.

SERVICE USE

Initial certification of the 767-200 by the FAA was obtained on 30 July 198 (JT9D-7R4D engine) and on 30 September 1982 (CF6-80A engines). Fir: customer delivery with CF6-80A engines, to Delta, was on 25 October 198

nd first service flown 15 December. First 767-200ER, with JT9D-7RE4 ngines, was delivered to Ethiopian Airlines on 18 May 1984 and entered ervice 6 June. First delivery with JT9D-7R4E4 engines (-200 ER) was made CAAC, 8 October 1985. Japan Airlines placed the first order for the 767-00 on 29 September 1983 and put the type into service on domestic utes on 20 October 1986, following certification on 22 September. The 67-300ER entered service with launch customer American Airlines in ebruary 1988. Both freighter variants are now in service, the 767-300PF ith UPS since October 1995 and the 767-300F with Korean airline Asiana nce August 1996. The 767-400ER entered service with Delta Air Lines utumn 2000. At 1 January 2001, Boeing had orders for 901 767s, of which 17 had been delivered.

elow: United Parcel Service operates the 767-300PF 'Package Freighter'.

Boeing 777

SPECIFICATION
(Boeing 777-200)
Dimensions: Wingspan 60.93m (199ft 11in); length overall 63.73m (209ft 1in); height overall 18.51m (60ft 9in), wing area 427.8m² (4,605ft²).
Power Plant: Two General Electric GE90-85B turbofans, each rated at 377kN (84,700lb) or Pratt & Whitney PW4077 or Rolls-Royce Trent 877 both rated at 342kN (76,850lb)
Weights: Operating weight empty 141,340kg (311,600lb); max take-off 247,210kg (545,000lb); max landing 201,850kg (445,000lb); max payload 29,050kg (64,050lb).
Performance: Max cruising speed 499kts (923km/h); service ceiling 13,135m (43,100ft); take-off field length 2,135m (7,000ft); landing field length 1,585m (5,200ft); range with typical payload 7,260nm (13,430km).
Accommodation: Flight crew of two. Twin-aisle cabin layout, seating typically 375-400 passengers in two classes, or up to 440 in 10-abreast tourist configuration.

Responding to airline interest in an aircraft with a capacity between the 767-300 and 747-400, Boeing began an intensive market study in winter 198 which culminated in an authorisation by the board of directors on 8 December 1989 to offer airlines a new aircraft, then known as the 767-X. At the same time, Boeing set up a New Airplane Division in Renton, Washington, to oversee its development. The design was shaped by the input from several airlines an

...e competition from the McDonnell Douglas MD-11 and the Airbus A330/340 ...mily of long-range widebody aircraft, and included initial 'A-Market' and ...nger-range 'B-Market' models. Orders and options for 68 aircraft (34+34) from ...nited Airlines on 15 October 1990 led to the formal launch of the 777 two ...eeks later. All Nippon Airways became the second launch customer on 19 ...ecember with a firm order for 15 aircraft and options for 10 more. Boeing and ...apanese airframe manufacturers signed an agreement, on 21 May 1991, for a ...sk-share programme covering about 20 per cent of the structure. As offered ... the airlines, the A-Market model envisaged 375/400 passengers in a twin-...sle, two-class layout with a standard take-off weight of 229,520kg (506,000lb) ...d a range of 4,050 nm (7,500km), plus two heavier and longer-range options. ...e B-Market 777 was available with weights of up to 267,620kg (590,000lb) ...d a range to 6,600nm (12,250km). The 777 is the first Boeing aircraft to ...ature a fly-by-wire system and other design features include award-winning ...ool' six-across flat panel displays visible in all lighting conditions and from all ...gles, and new lightweight structural materials. A long-span, large area ...ew technology wing with increased thickness was developed for ...proved operating performance, including take-off, climb rate, fast high ...titude cruise and payload/range. The three major engine manufacturers all ...eveloped large new fuel-efficient and quiet high bypass ratio turbofan ...ngines capable of eventually developing thrusts of 445kN (100,000lb). The ▶

elow: Singapore Airlines 777-200ER photographed at Shanghai.

entirely new 777 is undoubtedly a product of the computer age. It was th
first jet airliner to be 100 per cent digitally defined and pre-assembled usir
a powerful Dassault/IBM CATIA CAD/CAM (computer-aided design ar
computer-aided manufacturing) system and made extensive use of fini
element analysis, so that virtually no paper drawings were made. Anothe
innovation was the design/build approach which brought together all desic
and manufacturing disciplines and airlines at an early stage in the design 1
minimise any in-service surprises. The first 777 was rolled out of the Boeir
factory on 9 April 1994 and made its maiden flight at Seattle on 12 Jur
1994. It was joined in the flight-test programme by eight other 777
including two powered by GE90 engines (first flight 2 February 1995) ar
two with Rolls-Royce Trent 800 engines. The first Rolls-Royce-powere
aircraft took to the skies on 26 May 1995. Four days later, the 777 becam
the first aircraft ever to earn FAA approval for extended-range twin-engir
operations (ETOPS) at service entry.

VARIANTS

The 777-200 is the basic medium-range aircraft capable of carrying 375 passengers a distance of up to 4,785nm (8,850km). It is available with three different take-off weights from 229,520kg (506,000lb) to 247,210kg (545,000lb). Longer ranges to 7,335 nm (13,584km) are offered in the 777-200ER (formerly 777-200IGW), with 286,897kg (632,500lb). The 777-300 'stretch' was launched on 26 June 1995 on the strength of 31 commitments by four airlines announced at the Paris air show a few days before. The fuselage has been stretched by 10.13m (33ft 3in) to provide a maximum seating capacity in a high-density layout for 550 passengers. Other features of the 777-300 are a strengthened airframe, inboard wing and landing gear; ground-manoeuvring ▶

Below: The high-capacity Boeing 777 is Boeing's first commercial aircraft with fly-by-wire controls and digitally defined and pre-assembled using a powerful computer system.

cameras and tailskid. Customers have a choice of three engine types whic can be installed on all 777 models. These are the General Electric GE90, Pra & Whitney PW4074/77 and Rolls-Royce Trent 800, rated between 329.17k (74,000lb) and 423kN (95,050lb). All three are in operation. A proposed 777 100X 'shrink' appears to have been put aside in favour of same size ultra lon range derivatives, dubbed the 777-200LR and 777-300ER, launched on 2 February 2000. The 777-200LR (previously 777-200X) will be the longes range aircraft in service, able to carry 301 passengers in a three-class layo a distance of 8,860nm (16,405km). The 777-300ER (formerly 777-300X) w carry 365 passengers over a range of 7,200nm (13,330km). Both will hav overall structural strengthening, greater wingspan with new raked wing tip increased thrust engines, increased wing fuel capacity (plus auxiliary bo tanks in the -200LR only), and a maximum take-off weight of 341,105 (752,000lb). Orders have been placed by Japan Airlines and Korean A

ove: All Nippon Airways was a partner in the development of the
eing 777 as launch customer in the 'Working Together' programme.

rvice entry is anticipated in 2003/2004.

SERVICE

llowing simultaneous FAA and JAA certification with Pratt & Whitney engines
19 April 1995, launch customer United Airlines officially took delivery on 17
ay. The first 777 revenue service was flown on 7 June between London and
ashington, DC. British Airways received the first 777-200IGW on 6 February
97 and initiated revenue services three days later on the London-Boston
ute. Inaugural service of the 777-300 by Cathay Pacific Airways is planned for
ay 1998 following the first flight on 16 October 1997. Firm orders stood at
3 on 1 January 2001, with 316 delivered.

Boeing (McDonnell Douglas) BC-17X

SPECIFICATION

Dimensions: Wingspan (including winglets) 51.74m (169ft 9in); length overall 53.03m (174ft 0m); height overall 16.79m (55ft 1in).
Power Plant: Four 180kN (40,440lb) thrust Pratt & Whitney PW2440 turbofan engines.
Weights: Max take-off weight 265,354kg (585,000lb); max payload 78,063kg (172,0981b).
Performance: Max cruising speed Mach 0.77; service ceiling 13,715m (45,000ft); minimum dry runway length l,165m (3,820ft); range with max paylo. 2,500nm (4,630km).
Accommodation: Flight crew of two, with two observer positions.

The BC-17X Globemaster is based on the successful McDonnell Dougl. C-17 military airlifter which has been in service with the US Air For. since 1993. Formerly referred to as the MD-17, development of the BC-1 is the subject to an agreement between Boeing and the USAF following 18-month Commercial Application of Military Airlift Aircraft (CAMAA), whi predicted a market for 10 such aircraft by 2010. Specifically designed carry heavy and outsize loads to and from paved and unpaved sho runways, the high-wing, T-tailed aircraft features a rear-loading ramp whi allows wheeled items to be rolled on and off~ or towed via a built-in winc with little or no requirement for ground support. The cargo bay is

ctangular cross-section and has a maximum loadable length of 26.82m
8ft), width of 5.28m (17ft 4in) and height of 4. 5m (14ft 9in), giving a total
oacity of 592m³ and a maximum payload of 78,060kg (172,091lb). Range
th maximum payload is 2,500nm (4,630km). The BC-17X would be
uipped with quadruple-redundant digital fly-by-wire flight controls with
echanical back-up, and an advanced integrated avionics system using four
?T multi-function displays and two head-up displays (FIUDs). It has been
signed to operate with a cockpit crew of two and one cargo specialist.
e BC-17X has demonstrated its ability operate from short dirt airfields
ough a combination of thrust reversers, blown-flap technology and
selage shape (steep rake of tail section). The blown-flap system, whereby
gine exhaust flow is directed through large double-slotted flaps, enables
? aircraft to fly steep approaches at relatively low speeds, for routine
idings on airfields of less than 1,200m (4,000ft) length. The four 180kW
),4401b) thrust Pratt & Whitney PW2440 turbofans are equipped with
ected-flow thrust reversers capable of deployment in flight. On the
ound, a fully-loaded aircraft, using reversers, can back up a two per cent
pe. Earliest delivery of the BC-17X is scheduled for 2004.

*low: The Boeing BC-17X, formerly the MD-17, based on the C-17 military
ighter, is targeted at the outsize cargo market, with a payload range of
i00km (2,500nm).*

Boeing (McDonnell Douglas) MD-11

SPECIFICATION
(McDonnell Douglas MD-11)

Dimensions: Wingspan 51.66m (169ft 6in); length overall 61.37m (201ft 4in); height overall 17.60m (57ft 9in), wing area 338.9m² (3,648ft²).

Power Plant: Three 276kN (62,000lb) Pratt & Whitney PW4462, or 267kN (60,000lb) PW4460, or 274kN (61,500lb) General Electric CF6-80C2D1F turbofans.

Weights: Operating weight empty 129,680kg (285,900lb); max take-off 285,990kg (630,500lb); max landing 195,040kg (430,000lb); max payload 51,755kg (114.100lb).

Performance: Max cruising speed 511kts (945km/h); take-off field length 3,185m (10,450ft); landing field length 2,118m (6,950ft); range with typical payload 6,840nm (12,667km).

Accommodation: Flight crew of two. Seating for up to 410 passengers, nine-abreast with twin aisles. Underfloor baggage/cargo volume 194.0m³ (6,850ft³).

or many years, stretched (and in some cases 'shrunk') versions of the DC-10 were studied by the Douglas Aircraft Company under a number of different designations, while production of the DC-10 itself continued in a form little changed from that in which it was launched. As noted in its own entry, the DC-10 was produced in only four principal series, all having fundamentally the same fuselage length and differing primarily in weights, fuel capacities and engine type and power. Almost from the start of the design, however, possible stretched-fuselage versions were being considered and in the early 1970s, for example, a 12.8m (42ft) lengthening was considered a possibility, to allow the DC-10 to carry 365 passengers for 3,600nm (6,680km). Stretched versions of the Srs 10, Srs 30 and Srs 40 continued under study throughout the 1970s but ▶

Below: Swissair was an early operator of the passenger MD-11 and has the largest number of them on its fleet with a total of 15 aircraft. All will be converted to freighters for FedEx.

no market was found for these projects. New power plants, such as the RB.21 535 and PW2037, were then being considered, and two-crew cockpits wi digital instruments and CRT displays were under review. When McDonn Douglas decided, in late 1982, to replace the famous 'DC' series of designation with a new 'MD' series, this project became the MD-100, but was discontinue in November 1983 when all work on projected new commercial aircraft wa temporarily suspended by the parent company. In 1984, work resumed, with high priority, on a stretched derivative of the DC-10 with the designation MD-1 and on 29 December 1986 this was formally launched into production. Based c a close study of the prospective market, the MD-11 evolved between 1984 an 1986 as a very-long-range large-capacity transport, using the basic DC-1 fuselage cross section, with a 5.66m (18ft 7in) stretch. The wing has a 3.05 (10ft) increase in span and outward-canted winglets that add another 1.32m (4 4in), plus other new features such as a smaller tailplane containing fuel that ca be used to assist aircraft trimming, carbon brakes, revised tail cone, greater us of composites and advanced metals, a two-man cockpit and digital FMS and EF on the flight deck. First flight took place on 10 January 1990, powered by thre General Electric CF6-80C2 turbofan engines, while the Pratt & Whitney PW446

owered model made its first flight on 26 April 1990. A total of five aircraft (four
ith GE engines and one with P&W engines) was used in the flight test
ogramme which culminated in FAA certification on 8 November 1990.

ARIANTS

he standard passenger MD-11 failed to meet its design guarantees and from
e outset has been undergoing a Performance Improvement Programme (PIP)
med at weight and drag reductions and range extension. Maximum take-off
eight for all versions is 273,289kg (602,500lb), but an optional 285,990kg
30,500lb) is also available. The MD-11 Combi, certificated in April 1992, is a
ixed passenger/cargo version, capable of carrying four to 10 cargo pallets on
e main deck, in addition to between 168 and 240 passengers. It has a main
rgo door at the rear. A convertible model, the MD-11CF convertible freighter,
as launched in August 1991 with an order from Martinair Holland, and
atures a main deck port side cargo door at the front. A windowless all- ▶

*elow: Federal Express took delivery of the first MD-11F in 1991 and is
s largest operator.*

freighter MD-11F is also in production, as is an extended-range version, th
MD-11ER, launched in February 1994. The MD-11ER carries up to 11,356 litre
(3,000 US gallons) in an auxiliary tank in the lower cargo compartmer
increasing range by up to 480nm (889km). All models can be fitted with
choice of three engines, including the 267kN (60,000lb) thrust PW4460, th
274kN (61,500lb) CF6-80C2D1F, and the 276kN (62,000lb) PW4462.

SERVICE USE

The MD-11 was committed to full-scale development on 29 December 1986,
which time 12 companies had placed orders for 52 aircraft with 40 more (
option. The MD-11 obtained its FAA certification on 8 November 1990. Fir

elivery was made to Finnair on 29 November, entering service on 20
ecember. The first MD-11F freighter went to Federal Express on 11
eptember 1991, followed by the MD-11 Combi, delivered to Alitalia on 27
ovember 1991. Martinair Holland took delivery of the first MD-11CF
onvertible freighter on 2 December 1994. Launch customer World Airways
ccepted the first MD-11ER in March 1996. At 1 January 2001, Boeing had
eceived orders for 200 MD-11s, of which 198 had been delivered. Boeing
as announced that production will cease in 2001 after orders have been
lfilled.

elow: Delta Air Lines operates 15 MD-11s.

Boeing (McDonnell Douglas) MD-80

SPECIFICATION

(McDonnell Douglas MD-88)

Dimensions: Wingspan 32.87m (107ft 10¼in); length overall 45.06m (147ft 10in); height overall 9.19m (30ft 2in), wing area 115.1m² (1,239ft²).

Power Plant: Two 93.4kN (21,000lb) Pratt & Whitney JT8D-219 turbofans.

Weights: Operating weight empty 35,369kg (77,976lb); max take-off 67,810kg (149,500lb); max landing 58,965kg (130,000lb); max payload 19,969kg (44,024lb).

Performance: Max cruising speed 499kts (924km/h); take-off field length 2,552m (8,375ft); landing field length 1,585m (5,200ft); range with max payload 2,502nm (4,635km).

Accommodation: Flight crew of two. Seating for up to 172 passengers, five-abreast with single aisle. Underfloor baggage/cargo volume 35.48m³ (1,253ft³).

From 1975 onwards, Douglas Aircraft Company (a division of McDonnell Douglas) studied a number of possible derivatives of the DC-9 that would take advantage of the refanned versions of the Pratt & Whitney JT8D engine. An early example of this engine, the JT8D-109, was flown on a DC-9 starting on 9 January 1975, to gain data on the new engine, which went into production

the JT8D-209. DC-9 variants identified as the Srs 50RS, Srs 60, Srs 50-17R ⦁d DC-9SC were among those studied with this or other engines and with ⦁ch innovations as a supercritical wing and/or fuselage extensions. Market ⦁rveys eventually led to the launch, in October 1977, of what was then known ⦁ the DC-9 Super 80, with a fuselage 4.34m (14ft 3in) longer than that of the ⦁s 50, JT8D-209 engines and other new features. Swissair, Austrian Airlines ⦁d Southern Airways became the launch customers for what would prove to ⦁ the most successful of all DC-9 variants. Three Super 80s required for ⦁rtification made their first flights on 18 October 1979, 6 December 1979 and ⦁ February 1980.

⦁RIANTS

⦁ree subvariants of the Super 80 were offered, all with the same overall ⦁nensions but with different engine powers, fuel capacities and operating ⦁eights. These were the DC-9 Series 81 as initially deployed; the DC-9 Srs 82 ⦁th 89kN (20,000lb) JT8D-217s (plus emergency thrust reserve) and the same ▶

⦁low: One-time Swiss airline CTA operated the MD-87 on its European ⦁liday charters.

fuel as the Srs 81; and the DC-9 Srs 83 with 93.45kN (21,000lb) JT8D-219s an an extra 4,3901 (966 Imp gal) of fuel in cargo compartments tanks. First flight were made of the series 82 on 8 January 1981 and of the MD-83 on 1 December 1984. In 1984, the designation of the DC-9 Super 80 was change to MD-80 and the three production variants became the MD-81, MD-82 an MD-83. In 1985, the MD-87 was announced, featuring a fuselage reduced length by 5.0m (16ft 5in), 89kN (20,000lb) JT8D-217B engines and a standar fuel capacity of 22,1016 (4,863 Imp gal), plus optional auxiliary tanks. The MI 87 was ordered first by Finnair and Austrian Airlines, and made its first flight c

December 1986. A 25.4cm (10in) extension of the fin above the tailplane was introduced on the MD-87 to balance the shorter moment arm. A fifth member of the family was launched early in 1986 when Delta Air Lines ordered the MD-88, a close relative of the MD-82 with JT8D-217C engines, a 72,575kg (160,000lb) gross weight and a number of systems and equipment refinements including electronic flight instrument system (EFIS) in the cockpit, combined with a flight-management system and an inertial reference system. The MD-88 ▶

Below: Crossair MD-83 carried a special promotional colour scheme.

made its first flight on 15 August 1987. Executive versions were also produce
MD-82s were also built in China.

SERVICE USE

The MD-81 gained FAA certification on 26 August 1980 and entered servi
with Swissair on 5 October 1980. Certificated on 30 July 1981, the MD-
entered service with Republic Airlines in August, followed in 1982 by the high
gross weight option at 67,812kg (149,500lb) with JT8D-217A engines
provide a significant increase in range with maximum payload. The MD-
received FAA certification in 1985 and went into service with Alaska Airlin

Above: The acquisition of MD-81/82 aircraft enabled Adria Airways, now independent Slovenia's national carrier, to expand internationally.

...d Finnair in early 1986. Finnair, together with Austrian Airlines, also became ...e first operator of the MD-87, which was certificated on 21 October 1987. The ...al MD-88 version was granted FAA certification on 9 December 1987 and ...tered service with launch customer Delta on 5 January 1988. Production ...ased after delivery of the last aircraft to Trans World Airlines (TWA) on 21 ...ecember 1999. A total of 1,191 aircraft were built (including 35 by SAIC in ...ina).

Boeing (McDonnell Douglas) MD-90

SPECIFICATION
(McDonnell Douglas MD-90-30)

Dimensions: Wingspan 32.87m (107ft 10in); length overall 46.51m (152ft 7in); height overall 9.33m (30ft 7¼in), wing area 112.3m² (1,209ft²).

Power Plant: Two 111.2kN (25,000lb) IAE V2525-D5 turbofans.

Weights: Operating weight empty 39,916kg (88,000lb); max take-off 70,760kg (156,000lb); max landing 64,410kg (142,000lb); max payload 17,350kg (38,250lb).

Performance: Max cruising speed 437kts (809km/h); take-off field length 2,166m (7,105ft); landing field length 1,600m (5,250ft); range with typical payload 2,275nm (4,216km).

Accommodation: Flight crew of two. Seating for up to 172 passengers, five-abreast with single aisle. Total baggage volume 36.8m³ (1,300ft³).

The MD-90 was designed as a stretched, high-technology follow-on to the successful MD-80 series. The most notable external difference, apart from the 1.45m (4ft 9in) lengthening of the fuselage forward of the wing to provide accommodation for another 10 passengers to a maximum of 172, is the replacement of the Pratt & Whitney JT8D engines by the International Aero Engines (IAE) V2500 turbofans with electronic control. Another external feature is the enlarged tailfin of the MD-87. New characteristics include an improved cabin interior with larger overhead bins, better lighting, handrail at bin level, digital environmental control system and vacuum toilets; Bendix variable-speed constant frequency electrical generation; 421kW (565shp) AlliedSignal GTCP131-9D auxiliary power unit (APU); carbon wheel brakes with digital anti-skid system saving 181kg (400lb) in weight; and powered flight controls to cope with increased pitch-axis inertia caused by heavier engines and longer forward

*bove: Launch customer of the MD-90 in 1995, Delta Air Lines now
perates 16 of the type.*

selage. The flight deck is similar to the MD-88, but an optional Advanced
ommon Flightdeck (ACF) with six flat-panel colour displays will be offered. The
␣D-90 programme was launched on 14 November 1989, with an order from
␣elta Air Lines for 50 firm and 115 options, later revised downwards. The first
␣rcraft flew on 22 February 1993, followed by a second on 27 August. Both
␣ere used in the test programme leading to FAA certification on 15 November
␣994, two months after the first production aircraft took to the air on 20
␣ptember. The MD-90 was built on the same production line as the MD-80,
␣ith major subassemblies provided by Alenia of Italy, AeroSpace Technologies
␣ Australia, Aerospatiale of France, Spain's CASA, and several plants in China. ▶

*elow: US carrier Reno Air operated a large fleet of MD aircraft from its
␣ub at Reno, including two MD-90s.*

VARIANTS

The baseline model, and the only one in service by 1998, is the MD-90-30 powered by two 111.2kN (25,000lb) thrust IAE V2525-D5 turbofans. 2,200nm (4,000km) range is possible with the MD-90-30ER, which also features increased take-off weight of 76,270kg (168,145lb) and additional fuel. The MD-90-50 heavier gross weight version was never built. It had provision for up to 6,738 litres (1,780 US gallons) extra fuel to add 700nm (1,296km) to the range, compared to the MD-90-30. Maximum take-off weight was increased from 70,760kg (156,000lb) to 78,245kg (171,500lb), necessitating reinforcing of the wing, fuselage, tail surfaces, landing gear, wheels and brakes. More powerful 124.5kN (28,000lb) IAE V2528-D engines also distinguished this variant from the MD-90-30. The MD-90-55 was similar to the -50, but had additional emergency doors on each side of the forward fuselage to allow the carriage of up to 187 tourist-class passengers. The MD-90-30T was being built in China to meet a Trunkline requirement for the local market, under an agreement signed on 4 November

994. The programme never really got under way, and only three had been
ompleted by the Shanghai Aviation Industrial Corporation (SIAC) when China
ancelled the agreement in mid-1998. Apart from SAIC as prime contractor,
ne Shanghai Aircraft Manufacturing Factory (SAMF) was responsible for the
ailplane and elevators for assembly by Shenyang Aircraft Corporation (SAC).
hengdu Aircraft Industrial Corporation built the nose section, passenger and
rew doors and airstairs, while Xi'an Aircraft Company (XAC) produced the
orward fuselage and wings.

ERVICE USE
ne first MD-90-30 was delivered to Delta Air Lines on 24 February 1995 and
ntered service between Dallas/Fort Worth and Newark, New Jersey, on 1
pril. Production terminated in 2000 after delivery of the 114th aircraft.

elow: Japan's third-largest airline uses the MD-90 on domestic services,
tted out in a single-class arrangement for 166 passengers.

Bombardier (Canadair) Challenger

SPECIFICATION
(Challenger 604)

Dimensions: Wingspan 19.61m (64ft 4in); length 20.85m (68ft 5in); heigh overall 6.30m (20ft 8in); wing area 48.31m² (520.0ft²).

Power Plant: Two 41.0kN (9,220lb) General Electric CF34-3B1 turbofans.

Weights: Operating weight empty 9,806kg (21,620lb); max take-off 21,863k (48,200lb); max landing 17,236kg (38,000lb); max payload 2,435kg (5,370lb).

Performance: Max cruising speed 476kts (882km/h); service ceiling 12,500 (41,000ft); take-off field length 1,737m (5,700ft); landing field length 846 (2,775ft); range with typical payload 4,077nm (7,550km).

Accommodation: Flight crew of two. Max capacity for 19 passengers.

The Canadair Challenger evolved from a design by Bill Lear for a 14-sea twin-engined executive jet with a 4,325nm (8,000km) range and a to speed of 525kts (970km/h) he dubbed the LearStar 600. In order to mainta the progress made by the Canadian aircraft industry, Canadair struck a de on 2 April 1976, giving it exclusive rights (initially for five months only) f the design, manufacture and marketing of the proposed aircraft. Prelimina design began five days later, and on 29 October, Canadair gave the g ahead on the strength of 28 firm orders, plus a conditional contract for 2 from Federal Express. In March 1977, the aircraft was renamed th Canadair Challenger. The first of three pre-production aircraft made i maiden flight on 8 November 1978, followed by the first production aircra on 21 September 1979. The Avco Lycoming ALF502L-2-powered CL-60 Challenger received its Canadian certification in August 1980. A total of 8 were delivered before the initial version was replaced by the CL-601-1 which first flew on 17 September 1982 and differed largely in having 41.0k (9,220lb) General Electric CF34-1A engines and winglets (later als retrofitted to 78 CL-600s). A total of 66 CL-601-1As were delivered betwee May 1983 and May 1987. On 28 September 1986, Canadair flew the C

Below: The Challenger 601-3R has a non-stop range of 6,640km.

Above: Bombardier Challenger 604 has been fitted with the UltraQuiet cabin.

-601-3A with advanced 'glass' cockpit and improved CF34-3A engines, which remained in production until October 1993, when 134 had been delivered. The extended-range CL-601-3ER (formerly CL-601-3A/ER) flew on 8 November 1988. In this version, the tail fairing was replaced with a conformal fuel tank, which extended the fuselage length by 0.46m (1ft 6in). A total of 92 modification kits for earlier aircraft were supplied between March 1989 and July 1993, when the -3ER became the standard production version. Further range increase, new CF34-3B engines and other improvements produced the Challenger 604, which received FAA certification on 2 November 1995. First customer delivery was made in January 1996. More than 500 of all Challenger models are in service across the world.

Bombardier (Canadair) CRJ

SPECIFICATION
(CRJ Series 200ER)
Dimensions: Wingspan 21.21m (69ft 7in); length overall 27.77m (87ft 10in); height overall 6.22m (20ft 5in), wing area 54.54m² (587.1ft²).
Power Plant: Two 41.0kN (9,220lb) General Electric CF34-3B1 turbofans.
Weights: Operating weight empty 13,740kg (30,292lb); max take-off 23,133kg (51,000lb); max landing 21,319kg (47,000lb); max payload 6,217kg (13,708lb).
Performance: Max cruising speed 464kts (859km/h); service ceiling 12,500m (41,000ft); take-off field length 1,527m (5,010ft); landing field length 1,423m (4,670ft); range with max payload 1,645nm (3,046km).
Accommodation: Flight crew of two. Seating for up to 52 passengers, four-abreast , two seats each side of central aisle. Total baggage volume 13.64m³ (483ft³).

When Canadair designed the CL-600 Challenger business jet, th aircraft was given a wide fuselage cross-section which made suitable for use as a commuter airliner, and soon after Bombardier ha acquired Canadair in 1986, design studies were begun to stretch th Challenger into a 50-seat regional jet. An advanced design phase wa initiated on 16 November 1987 and substantially compeleted by Decembe the following year. Main elements of the design include a 3.25m (10ft 8in fuselage extension forward of the wing and a 2.84m (9ft 4in) insertion af which more than doubled the Challenger's 19-seat capacity to 50 seats additional emergency exits overwing and opposite second passenger doo drop-down air stair; modified tailplane leading-edges; and a 15 per cer increase in wing area to meet the more stringent field length requirements The CRJ wing also differed in having a strengthened box and modifie outboard leading-edges and inboard spoilers, plus new 'fly-by-wire' fligh spoilers and outboard 'spoilerons'. The 38.83kN (8,729lb) thrust Genera

Below: Brit Air of France took delivery of the first CRJ700 in spring 2001

Above: The CRJ-900 is an 86-seat stretch derivative of the CRJ-700.

ectric CF34-3A1 turbofan engine of the Challenger 601-3A was retained in
e CRJ. The go-ahead for the Regional Jet programme was announced on
March 1989, at which point a total of 62 commitments had been
ceived. The prototype was rolled out on 6 May 1991 and the 1 hour 25
inute maiden flight took place four days later.

ARIANTS

e Series 100 is the initial production version with a maximum take-off weight
21,523kg (47,450lb), while the 100ER has a higher weight of 23,133kg
,000lb) and an additional 2,582 litres (681.3 US gallons) of fuel for increased
ge. Certificated in 1994, the Series 100LR (for long range) offered further
creases in maximum take-off weight to 23,995kg (52,900lb) for European ▶

operators and 24,040kg (53,000lb) for the North American market, extendir the range to 2,005nm (3,710km). Product improvements, including Cat II landing capability with HGS, installation of overwater equipment, seatbac telephones, enhanced field performance and more became available on ne aircraft in 1996/1997, some of which can be retrofitted. Canadair also produce the Series 200 and Series 200B hot-and-high version, both fitted with improve CF34-3B1 turbofans. Both models are available in extended-range ER and st longer range LR versions. Corporate Jetliner is an executive version, typica seating 18-30 passengers, and capable of cruising at 458kts (850km/h) ar flying non-stop in excess of 2,000nm (3,700km), and the Canadair Spec Edition (SE) has a 3,000nm (5,550km) trans-Atlantic capability and state-of-th art avionics. In January 1997, Canadair announced the go-ahead of the CRJ now known as the Series 700, a stretched derivative with a 4.72m (15ft 6i longer fuselage to accommodate 70 passengers, a slight increase in wingspa and more powerful 56.4kN (12,670lb) or 61.3kN (13,790lb) CF34-8C1 engine The CRJ700 first flew on 27 May 1999. Bombardier formally launched anoth family member, the 90-seat CRJ-900, at the Farnborough Air Show in July 200 which is due to fly in the first half of 2001, with deliveries to airlines beginnir in the fourth quarter of 2002. Compared to the -700, the CRJ900 feature fuselage plugs of 2.29m (7ft 6in) forward and 1.57m (5ft 2in) after to provid seating for 86 passengers, strengthened main landing gear, two additior overwing exits, and more powerful CF34-8C5 engines. The CRJ900 will also k available in the CRJ900ER extended-range version with a higher take0c weight of 37,421kg (82,500lb).

SERVICE USE

On completion of a 1,400 hour flight test and certification programme, th

Below: French regional airline Brit Air became the launch customer for the stretched 70-seat CRJ700, when it ordered four aircraft in January 1997. It will feature a fuselage stretch, enlarged wing and empennage and more powerful turbofan engines.

*bove: Bombardier Regional Aircraft reached a significant milestone on
 October 1997, when it delivered the 200th Canadair Regional Jet. The
RJ100 was handed over to Lufthansa CityLine, the original launch
stomer for the type which placed firm orders for 32 aircraft.*

egional Jet received Transport Canada type approval on 31 July 1992, but
ropean JAA certification was delayed until 15 January 1993, primarily by a
wly introduced passenger impact safety requirement, from which the
anufacturer had to request a temporary exemption. US FAA approval was
tained on 21 January 1993. In the meantime, Lufthansa CityLine had
ceived its first aircraft on 19 October 1992 and, operating on the Canadian
gister under Transport Canada certification, had inaugurated revenue service
1 November 1992 on routes from Berlin to Cologne/Bonn, Stuttgart and
ockholm. The first 100ER went into service with Lauda Air in Spring 1994.
st delivery of the Corporate Jetliner was made to Xerox in June 1993, and
udi Arabian company TAG Aeronautics is the first customer for the SE. First
liveries of the CRJ-700 will be made to launch customer Brit Air in spring
01. Orders for the CRJ-100/200 regional jet family totalled 798 units at the
d of 2000, of which 460 had been delivered. The order book for the CRJ700
od at 174 units.

Bombardier (de Havilland Canada) Dash 8

SPECIFICATION

(de Havilland Canada DHC-8 Series 300B)

Dimensions: Wingspan 27.43m (90ft 0in); length overall 25.68m (84ft 3in); height overall 7.49m (24ft 7in), wing area 56.21m² (605ft²).

Power Plant: Two 1,864kW (2,500shp) Pratt & Whitney Canada PW123B turboprops with Hamilton Standard four-blade reversible-pitch fully-feathering metal propellers.

Weights: Operating weight empty 11,677kg (25,743lb); max take-off 19,504kg (43,000lb); max landing 19,050kg (42,000lb); max payload 6,240kg (13,757lb).

Performance: Max cruising speed 285kts (528km/h); max rate of climb 9.15m, (1,800ft/min); service ceiling 7,620m (25,000ft); take-off field length 1,177m (3,865ft); landing field length 1,042m (3,420ft); range with typical payload 700nm (1,297km).

Accommodation: Flight crew of two and seating for up to 56 passengers, four abreast with central aisle. Baggage compartment volume 7.93m³ (280ft³).

As interest in commuter aircraft with a capacity of 30-40 seats grew at the end of the 1970s, de Havilland Aircraft of Canada chose this portion of the airline market for its project to follow the Dash 7. The DHC-8, or Dash 8, that resulted from this decision neatly filled the gap between the 19-seat Twin Otter and the 50-seat Dash 7, but it also came into competition with the new aircraft of similar capacity being developed in a similar timescale by CASA/Nurtanio

nbraer, Shorts and Saab-Fairchild. In keeping with DHC policy and experience, e Dash 8 was designed to have particularly good field performance, and its nfiguration was that of a scaled-down Dash 7, with a high wing, a T-tail, a o-element rudder, and powerful single-slotted flaps supplemented by roll ntrol spoilers. Once again, with the Dash 8, de Havilland designers avoided e use of movable leading-edge devices as a means of achieving high lift for od field performance, believing that such devices were prone to damage in e type of operations for which the aircraft was designed. To power the Dash the company selected the newest engine type offered by Pratt & Whitney nada, a turboprop developed under the PT7 designation but put into oduction as the PW100 family. Under a new P&W designating procedure, the lividual variants of this basic engine were identified as to their power by the t two digits in the designation: thus the 2,000shp (1,41kW) model for the tial production version of the Dash 8 became the PW120, and the uprated gine for later variants is the PW123. The decision to launch the Dash 8 was ached during 1980. Four pre-production aircraft were assigned to the test ing and certification programme, the first of these flying on 20 June 1983. e second followed on 26 October 1983, the third in November 1983 and the irth (the first to be fitted with definitive PW120 engines) in early 1984.

low: Tyrolean Airways operates the Dash 8 Q400 alongside other Dash models.

VARIANTS

The initial version was the 36-seat DHC-8-100, or Dash 8 Series 100, availab[l]
with a choice of 1,491kW (2,000shp) Pratt & Whitney Canada PW120A [or]
PW121 engines. A restyled interior with 63.5mm (2.5in) more headroom w[as]
incorporated from 1990 in the Series 100A, and the Series 100B, introduc[ed]
from 1992, provides PW121 engines as standard for enhanced airfield a[nd]
climb performance. A projected Series 200 with higher operating weights w[as]
first overtaken by the Series 300, but re-launched on 16 March 1992 in t[he]

*Below: Team Lufthansa partner Augsburg Airways has an all-Dash 8 fle[et]
including this Dash 8-300.*

Bombardier (de Havilland Canada) Dash 8

ries 200A, which has the same airframe as the 100A/B, but more
mmonality with the Series 300. The Series 200A has 1,603kW (2,150shp)
V123C engines to give a 30kt (56km/h) increase in speed; while the Series
0B with PW123D engines offers full power for better hot-and-high
rformance. The Series 300 was the second model, put in hand in mid-1985,
d continued after Boeing had acquired DHC in January 1986. It differs from
e 100A in having extended wingtips, two fuselage extensions totalling 3.43m
1ft 3in) to bring passenger capacity to 56, and larger cabin facilities, such as
lleys and baggage compartments. Introduced in 1990 was the Series 300A
th improved payload/range, followed in 1992 by the Series 300B, which
roduced the optional higher gross weight and 1,864kW (2,500shp) PW123B ▶

D-BKIM

Above: The Dash 8-400 is the final stretch of the twin-engined regional turboprop, first flying in January 1998.

engines of the 300A as standard. Further increase in operational performan in high ambient temperatures was achieved with the Series 300E, added 1994. Redesigned interior and Noise and Vibration Suppression (NVS) syste became standard from latter half of 1996; aircraft with NVS are suffixed w the letter Q. Multi-mission military derivatives are known as DHC-8 Dash 8M further stretch was launched in June 1995 in the Series 400, which made first flight on 31 January 1998. Major changes include a 6.83m (22ft 5in) lonc fuselage to accommodate up to 78 passengers; revised control surfaces, ne avionics and baggage and service doors. Power plant is the Pratt & Whitn Canada PW150A turboprop with FADEC, flat rated at 3,781kW (5,071shp), ea driving a six-blade Dowty propeller.

ERVICE USE

e Dash 8 was certificated in Canada to the standards of FAR Pts 25 and
, and SFAR No. 27, on 28 September 1984, shortly followed by FAA
proval in the USA. Deliveries began on 23 October 1984, the second
oduction aircraft going to NorOntair, and this company put the type into
venue service on 19 December 1984. The Series 300 first flew on 15 May
87 and received Canadian DoT approval on 14 February 1989, followed
the FAA on 8 June. Canadian airline Time Air took delivery of the first
craft on 27 February 1989. First Series 200 was delivered to launch
stomer National Jet Systems in Australia in January 1996.Following JAA
proval in December 1999, SAS Commuter took delivery of the first Q400
riant on the 20 January 2000, putting the new type into service on 7
bruary. At 1 January 2001, the Dash 8 series had logged a total of 661
ders, with 573 delivered.

Bombardier Continental

SPECIFICATION

(Bombardier BD-100 Continental)

Dimensions: Wingspan 19.46m (63ft 10in); length 20.93m (68ft 8in); heig
overall 6.17m (20ft 3in); wing area 48.49m² (522.0ft²).

Power Plant: Two rear-mounted 35.8kN (8,050lb) thrust Honeywell AS9
turbofans.

Weights: Operating weight empty 10,138kg (22,350lb); max take-off 17,010
(37,500lb); max landing 15,308kg (33,750lb); max payload 1,360kg (3,000lb).

Performance: Max cruising speed 470kts (870km/h); service ceiling 13,715
(45,000ft); take-off field length 1,509m (4,950ft); landing field length 792
(2,600ft); range with typical payload 3,100nm (5,740km).

Accommodation: Flight crew of two. Standard capacity for eight passenge
in a 'double club' arrangement. Baggage volume 3.0m³ (106ft³).

The BD-100 Continental medium-size business jet was first revealed at the Pa
Air Show in June 1997 as the Bombardier Model 70. It was formally announc
at the Las Vegas NBAA convention on 18 October 1998 and launched at t
following year's Paris Air Show. The Continental jet has been designed to provi
US coast-to-coast range with eight passengers in a stand-up cabin, with take-
field length no more than 1,525m (5,000ft). Primarily constructed of light alloy w
some composites, the aircraft has two new rear-mounted Honeywell AS9
turbofans, each with a thermodynamic rating of 35.8kN (8,050lb), and features

*Below: The Continental mid-size business jet has been designed for US
coast-to-coast range.*

bove: The Continental stand-up cabin will provide comfortable seating r eight passengers.

supercritical wing with a 27o sweepback and winglets. Core avionics system is the Rockwell Collins Pro Line 21, with four-tube EFIS and two-tube EICAS instrumentation. The Bombardier Continental is a truly international programme, with many suppliers involved right across the world. AIDC of Taiwan is building the rear fuselage and tail unit; Canadair the cockpit, forward fuselage and primary flight controls; GKN Westland the engine nacelles, Hawker-de Havilland Australia the tailcone and APU installation kit; Honeywell the power plant and APU; Hurel-Dubois the thrust reversers; Intertechnique the fuel system; Liebherr the flap control, environmental control and anti-icing systems; Messier-Dowty the landing gear; Mitsubisahi the wing; Moog the secondary flight controls; Parker Aerospace the hydraulic system, Rockwell Collins the avioincs; and Shorts the centre fuselage. Final assembly of the first aircraft began at the Learjet Wichita facility in September 2000, with the official rollout spring 2001. Interior completion will be undertaken at Tucson, Arizona. The first flight is scheduled for mid-2001, followed by type certification in autumn 2002 and first customer delivery in December that same year. Bombardier has received more than 40 orders for its new Continental jet.

Bombardier Global Express

SPECIFICATION
(Bombardier BD-700 Global Express)

Dimensions: Wingspan 28.65m (94ft 0in); length 30.30m (99ft 5in); heig
overall 7.57m (24ft 10in); wing area 94.95m² (1,022.0ft²).

Power Plant: Two rear-mounted 65.6kN (14,750lb) thrust Rolls-Roy
Deutschland BR 710A2-20 turbofans.

Weights: Operating weight empty 22,135kg (48,800lb); max take-off 43,091
(95,000lb); max landing 35,652kg (78,600lb); max payload 3,265kg (7,200lb).

Performance: Max cruising speed 505kts (935km/h); service ceiling 15,545
(51,000ft); take-off field length 1,713m (5,620ft); landing field length 814
(2,670ft); range with typical payload 6,500nm (12,025km).

Accommodation: Flight crew of two. Typical configuration for eight to
passengers.

The BD-700 Global Express was developed to meet a perceive
requirement for an ultra-long range business jets capable of flying no
stop sectors up to 6,500nm (12,025km). Announced at the NBAA conventio
on 28 October 1991, and formally launched on 20 December 1993 after th
completion of nearly a year of conceptual design work, the Global Expre
drew heavily on the experience gained with the CRJ Regional Jet and the 1
seat Special Edition (SE) corporate version. The Global Express combines t
fuselage cross-section of the Challenger, and the cabin length of th
Regional Jet, and an all-new 'third-generation' supercritical wing with 3!
sweep, featuring leading-edge slats and winglets. It has a fully-powered f
by-wire control system and is optimised for both high-speed and short-fie
operations. The advanced cockpit is built around the Honeywell Prim
2000XP EFIS system. Japan's Mitsubishi is a key partner in the programm

Below: The Global Express has the longest range of any business jet.

bove: The spacious cabin of the Global Express provides flexibility of youts to suit the business travellers needs.

responsible for the wing and centre fuselage, with de Havilland manufacturing the rear fuselage, engine pylons and vertical stabiliser, as well as undertaking final assembly at its Downsview plant. Shorts designed and manufactures the forward fuselage, engine nacelles, horizontal stabiliser and other composites components. Among many other participants are Rolls-Royce Deutschland (65.6kN (14,750lb) BR 710A2-20 turbofan engines), Honeywell (avionics and APU), and Sextant Avionique (flight control system). Bombardier is responsible for interior completion at its Montreal and Tucson, Arizona facilities. The prototype first flew on 13 October 1996, but several delays pushed back Transport Canada certification to 31 July 1998. FAA certification followed on 13 November, and JAA granted its certificate on 7 May 1999. First customer delivery (to Toyota) was made on 8 July 1999. A modified Airliner version for up to 16 business passengers, for use on scheduled long-haul flights from secondary airports, is under consideration. More than 60 Global Express aircraft are in service, the vast majority in North America.

Bombardier Learjet 23/24/25/28/29

SPECIFICATION
(Learjet 25D)

Dimensions: Wingspan 10.84m (35ft 7in); length 14.50m (47ft 4in); height over 3.73m (12ft 3in); wing area 21.53m² (231.8ft²).

Power Plant: Two rear-mounted 13.1kN (2,950lb) thrust General Electric CJ610-8 turbofans.

Weights: Operating weight empty 3,465kg (7,640lb); max take-off 6,804 (15,000lb); max landing 6,033kg (13,300lb); max payload 1,524kg (3,360lb).

Performance: Max cruising speed 464kts (859km/h); service ceiling 15,548 (51,000ft); take-off field length 1,200m (3,940ft); landing field length 686m (2,250 range with typical payload 1,437nm (2,660km).

Accommodation: Flight crew of two. Max seating for eight passengers.

B ill Lear began preliminary development of a new executive jet in 1959 at Gallen in Switzerland, to where he had retired. Initially known as the Swis American Aircraft Corporation (SAAC) Learjet 23, the company moved work Wichita, Kansas, where the aircraft flew for the first time on 7 October 1963. then, the company had been renamed the Lear jet Corporation. Capable to be flo by a single pilot, the new five/seven seat aircraft was powered by a pair of 12.68 (2,850lb) General Electric CJ610-4 turbojets. A total of 104 was built before it bei superseded by the Learjet 24, which could seat eight passengers and cruise higher altitude. First flown on 24 February 1966, it was followed by the mo powerful 24B and longer-range 24D, which was the first without the tradema bullet fin fairing and to introduce square windows. The Learjet 24E and 24F h refined interiors and improved aerodynamics, and, in the 24F increased rang These models superseded the earlier lightweight 24D/A. A total of 259 Learjet 2 were built between 1966 and 1985. In parallel with the 24, Lear developed the 1 seat Learjet 25 stretched by 1.27m (4ft 2in) and first flown on 12 August 1966. T

bove: The 'stretched' Model 25 remains the largest-selling Learjet.

proved 25B and longer-range 25C came next, and in 1976, a new cambered wing oduced the 25D and longer-range 25F models. The Learjet 25D led to the Learjet and Learjet 29 Longhorn, which introduced a much increased wingspan and a percriticial wing with winglets , but proved unsuccessful, with only five and four ilt respectively. The Learjet 25 logged sales of 368 units and remains the largestlling Learjet.

Left: The Model 28/29 Lougham was an unsuccessful attempt at improving performance through the use of a supercritical wing.

Bombardier Learjet 35/36

SPECIFICATION
(Learjet 35A)

Dimensions: Wingspan 12.04m (39ft 6in); length 14.83m (48ft 8in); heig
overall 3.73m (12ft 3in); wing area 23.53m² (253.3ft²).

Power Plant: Two rear-mounted 15.58kN (3,500lb) thrust AlliedSignal (Garre
TFE731-2-2B turbofans.

Weights: Operating weight empty 4,590kg (10.120lb); max take-off 8,300
(18,300lb); max landing 6,940kg (15,300lb); max payload 1,534kg (3,380lb).

Performance: Max cruising speed 471kts (872km/h); service ceiling 12,500
(41,000ft); take-off field length 1,515m (4,970ft); landing field length 937
(3,075ft); range with typical payload 2,200nm (4,070km).

Accommodation: Flight crew of two. Maximum eight passengers. Baggac
volume 1.31m³ (40ft³).

The availability of the new quieter Garrett TFE731 turbofan produced tv
new models, the Learjet 35 and 36 (originally referred to as the 25B-GF ar
25C-GF (Garrett Fan). A single Learjet 26 testbed had been re-engined with or
TFE731-2 in the starboard nacelle and had first flown on 4 January, leading
the announcement of the two production models the following May. Essentia
a Learjet 25 stretched by 0.33m (1ft 0in), the new eight-seat Learjet 35 had
slightly larger wing with a 0.61m (2ft 0in) wingtip extension, while th
complementary Learjet 36 was a six-seat long-range version capable of a no
stop Atlantic crossing. The first production standard Learjet 36 took to the a

*Below: US-based Flight International has been a prolific user of Learjet
including this Learjet 36.*

bove: The Learjet 35A provided performance enhancements over the
arlier 35 model.

on 22 August 1973 and FAA type certification was awarded in July 1974. Development of an improved cambered wing and other aerodynamic changes, and higher standard maximum take-off weight of 8,162kg (18,000lb) produced the Learjet 35A and Learjet 36A versions, which were further improved in subsequent years. These enhancements included the Century III 'Softflite' package which introduced changes to the ailerons, leading edges and wing fences for better handling, and a further optional (later standard) increase in MTOW to 8,300kg (18,300lb). T/R-400 trust reversers were added in 1983, followed two years later by an entirely new interior with more leg and headroom, adjustable seats, stereo and in-flight telephone and enclosed lavatory. The United States Air Force received 84 Learjet C-21A for operational support tasks, and several other special missions aircraft were produced for the military, including the EC-35A for EW training simulation, PC-35A for maritime patrol, RC-35A and RC-36A for reconnaissance, UC-35A for utility transport, and the U-36A, delivered to the Japan Maritime Self-Defense Force (JMSDF) for target towing, anti-ship missile simulation and ECM roles. Production of the 35/36 series ended in 1996, with 676 and 63 built respectively.

Bombardier Learjet 31/45

SPECIFICATION
(Learjet 45)

Dimensions: Wingspan 14.58m (47ft 10in); length 17.81m (58ft 5in); heigh overall 4.37m (14ft 4in); wing area 28.95m² (311.6ft²).

Power Plant: Two rear-mounted 15.58kN (3,500lb) thrust Honeywell TFE73 20 turbofans.

Weights: Operating weight empty 6,146kg (13,550lb); max take-off 9,298k (20,500lb); max landing 8,709kg (19,200lb); max payload 1,111kg (2,450lb).

Performance: Max cruising speed 468kts (867km/h); service ceiling 15,545 (51,000ft); take-off field length 1,326m (4,350ft); landing field length 811 (2,660ft); range with typical payload 2,380nm (4,407km).

Accommodation: Flight crew of two. Max seating for nine passenger Cargo/baggage volume 1.4m³ (50ft³).

The small seven-passenger Learjet 31 was the successor to the popul 35/36 family and was introduced in September 1987 following the first fligh of the prototype, modified from the 35A, on 11 May. The new aircraft combine the fuselage/cabin and power plant with the wing of the Learjet 55. Delta fir (strakes) were added at the rear to eliminate Dutch roll, stabilise the aircraft high airspeeds, and reduce approach speeds and field lengths. The wing tank of previous Learjets were replaced by winglets. FAA certification was obtaine on 12 August 1988, and production continued until July 1991 when 38 Learj 31s had been delivered. This model was then replaced by the current Learj 31A production version, first announced at NBAA in October 1990. The Learj 31A introduced a five-tube AlliedSignal (now Honeywell) EFIS 50 integrate

Below: The Learjet 31A is one of the fastest business jets with a top speed of 858km/h.

bove: The Learjet 45 can carry nine passengers a distance of more than 400km.

gital avionics package with a Universal flight management system (FMS). nother feature is a 4% increase in speed. The 31A/ER is an optional extended nge version with additional fuel tankage, pushing the maximum range out to 1,782nm (3,300km). An improvements package was announced at the NBAA convention at Atlanta in October 1999, which will provide, from c/n 31A-194 onwards, an increased maximum take-off weight of 7,711kg (17,000lb) and maximum landing weight of 7,257kg (16,000lb), the latter available for retrofit to earlier aircraft. Other features include a revised winglet design based on the Learjet 60 for enhanced high-speed/high-altitude performance, and the FMS as standard fitment. Design started in September 1992 on a new, generally similar model known as the Learjet 45. The 10/11-seat 45 has a larger fuselage with a redesigned stand-up cabin, wing and tail unit, Honeywell Primus 2000 integrated avionics package, and is powered by two Honeywell TFE731-20 turbofans. It combines the docile handling characteristics of the 31/31A and 60 with further improved fuel efficiency and good overall performance. The Learjet 45 made its first flight on 7 October 1995 and obtained its FAA certification on 22 September 1997. First customer delivery was made on 28 July 1998. Around 200 Learjet 31/31As are in service, together with 80 Learjet 45s.

Bombardier Learjet 55/60

SPECIFICATION
(Learjet 60)

Dimensions: Wingspan 13.34m (43ft 9in); length 17.88m (58ft 8in); heigh overall 4.47m (14ft 8in); wing area 24.57m² (264.5ft²).

Power Plant: Two 20.46 kN (4,600lb) thrust Pratt & Whitney PW305 turbofans with FADEC.

Weights: Operating weight empty 6,282kg (13,850lb); max take-off 10,660k (23,500lb); max landing 8,845kg (19,500lb); max payload 1,070kg (2,360lb).

Performance: Max cruising speed 464kts (859km/h); service ceiling 15,545 (51,000ft); take-off field length 1,660m (5,450ft); landing field length 1,043 (3,420ft); range with typical payload 2,735nm (5,065km).

Accommodation: Flight crew of two. Typical seating for six to nin passengers.

The small Learjet 29 Longhorn, which had introduced the NASA-designe supercritical wing and was so named because the Whitcomb wingle superficially resembled the horns of Longhorn cattle, had proved an expensiv failure. Learjet, therefore, set about rectifying that situation by mating the ne wing with a new stretched fuselage and stand-up cabin, producing the seve seat Learjet 55 Longhorn. The first flight of the prototype, powered by tw 16.65kN (3,700lb) TFE731-3-300B turbofans, took place on 19 April 197 followed by the first production aircraft on 11 August 1980. Two other projecte versions, the smaller Learjet 54 and larger Learjet 56, were later abandone

AA certification was achieved on 18 March 1981, with first deliveries effected n 30 April. In July 1983 and spring 1984, two improvement packages became vailable, which included the fitting of automatic ground spoilers, long-life brakes nd modified landing gear. An optional higher take-off weight of 9,752kg 1,500lb) was also approved. Additional fuel capacity produced the 55LR and he still longer-range 55XLR. Further all-round performance improvements and a gital flight deck was introduced in the 55B in September 1986, followed a year ter by the 55C, which incorporated delta fins at the rear for enhanced stability, e elimination of Dutch roll, and reduced approach speeds. The 55C/ER xtended-range version had an additional fuel tank in the tailcone baggage ompartment, while a further optional fuel tank could be fitted in the 55C/LR for ven grater range. Production of the Learjet 55 family ended in 1992, with 147 elivered. By that time, a replacement, in the form of the Learjet 60, had already een flown as a proof-of-concept airframe on 18 October 1990. The Pratt & 'hitney Canada PW305 engine with FADEC was preferred over the TFE331-3A, d the first production aircraft flew with the PW305 on 13 June 1991. The earjet 60 is the largest Learjet ever built and features the now standard inglets and delta fins, a stand-up 1.71m (5ft 7$\frac{1}{2}$in) high cabin, thrust reversers, d Rockwell Collins Pro Line 4 all-digital avionics suite. Certification was otained on 15 January 1993. Some 150 Learjet 55s and nearly 200 Learjet 60s e in service.

elow: First flight of the Learjet 60 at Wichita, Kansas.

British Aerospace ATP

The idea of stretching the original Avro/Hawker Siddeley 748 feederline dates back at least to 1961 when an Avro 748E was projected, with a 1.83m (6ft) fuselage extension and the uprated 2,709kW (2,400shp) RDa 10 Da engines. Market forecasts for this project indicated that it was premature and it did not proceed beyond the paper stage. Twenty years or so were to elapse in fact, before the need for an enlarged derivative of the 748 could be clearly demonstrated, and it was not until 1980 that serious work on such a possibility was resumed at the Manchester works of what had by then become British Aerospace. Although conceived in essence as a stretched and modernised 748, the new aircraft became known as the Advanced Turboprop, shortened to ATP, in preference to BAe 846, its official type number in the drawing office. Several possible stretches of the 748 fuselage were considered, and were evaluated alongside a wholly new aircraft. The 'middle-course' that emerged as the best way to go forward was to aim for a capacity of 60-70 seats and to combine the best features of the Super 748 with new fuel-efficient engines. The 'marketing launch' was announced in September 1982 on this basis, the ATP being designed to use PW124 engines on the basic 748 wing, with a lengthened version of the 748 fuselage (retaining the same cross-section) and a swept-back fin and rudder, adopted to give the aircraft a more modern appearance. By the time the full launch decision was made, on 1 March 1984, the original concept of 'minimum change' from the 748 had been modified to one of 'maximum change', in order to give operators the most modern systems and equipment available in the second half of the 1980s. This included a wholly new, variable frequency AC electrical system; a new environmental control system; a revised hydraulic system; carbon brakes; a completely new avionics suite based on a digital data bus; and an advanced flight deck. The latter incorporates a Smith electronic flight instrument system (EFIS) with four cathode ray tube displays (two for each pilot) and a Bendix multi-function display (located centrally between the pilots). First flight of the prototype took place on 6 August 1986 followed by the first production model on 20 February 1987. JAR 2

Below: British Airways was an early operator of the Advanced Turboprop (ATP). Including franchise airlines, 20 are operated in British Airways markings.

Above: Attempts by British Aerospace to restimulate a sluggish market with the Jetstream 61 proved misguided and also put paid to plans for shorter and stretched designs.

ertification was obtained in March 1988, and FAR 25 in August 1988.

VARIANTS

The basic ATP is certificated in accordance with the US FAR Pt25 and the equivalent Joint Airworthiness Requirements (JAR25) in Europe. The latter permits a higher engine operating temperature than FAR Pt25 allows in the emergency power reserve case. Production of the ATP ceased in 1993, but on 6 April the company announced an improved version, the Jetstream 61, to restimulate the market, but this proved ultimately unsuccessful. The Jetstream 61, certificated on 16 June 1995, had more powerful PW127D engines, increased weights and a new interior, including extra wide seats. Two further new derivatives were proposed, the shorter Jetstream 51 and the longer Jetstream 71, but neither plan went beyond the project definition phase. The ATP is now being made available as a freighter, with West Air of Sweden responsible for the manufacture of a freight door and associated modifications.

SERVICE USE

The first revenue service with the ATP was flown by British Midland Airways on 9 August 1988. Total production amounted to 64 aircraft, of which 57 remain in service.

British Aerospace Avro RJ/BAe 146

SPECIFICATION
(Avro RJ85)

Dimensions: Wingspan 26.21m (86ft 0in); length overall 28.60m (93ft 10in); height overall 8.59m (28dr 2 in), wing area 77.29m² (832ft²).

Power Plant: Four AlliedSignal LF507 turbofans, each rated at 31.14kN (7,000lb).

Weights: Operating weight empty 24,267kg (53,500lb); max take off 43,998kg (97,000lb); max landing 38,555kg (85,000lb); max payload 11,566kg (25,500lb).

Performance: Max cruising speed 412kts (763km/h); take-off field length 1,385m (4,545ft); landing field length 1,189m (3,900ft); range with max fuel 1,600nm (2,963km); range with max payload 1,150nm (2,129km).

Accommodation: Flight crew of two. Maximum one-class layout for 112 passengers six-abreast. Underfloor baggage/cargo volume 18.83m³ (645ft³).

The history of the British Aerospace 146 goes back to the 1960s and to th design studies initiated by the then-independent de Havilland Aircra company for a small turboprop engined feederliner designated D.H.123. Th was a twin-engined, high-wing design, but further studies, which continued Hatfield after de Havilland had been absorbed in the Hawker Siddeley Aviatic company, favoured low-wing layouts with turbofan engines mounted on th rear fuselage. These studies culminated in the H.S. 144 project, but lack of suitable engine led the designers in April 1971 to revert to a high-wing layo using four smaller turbofans, such as the Avco Lycoming ALF 502. In this forr as the H.S. 146, the project was formally launched on 29 August 1973, partnership with the British government. But the economic recession 1974–75 resulted in the termination of the programme in October 1974, whe the H.S.146 reverted to project design status. In substantially the same form originally planned, the aircraft was re-launched on 10 July 1978 by Britis Aerospace, into which HSA had meanwhile been nationalized, once again wi government financial assistance, and an initial production batch was put in hai at Hatfied. From the start of development two fuselage lengths were planne for models identified as the Srs 100 and Srs 200, and constructio development and flight testing proceeded in parallel. The first Srs 100 flew 3 September 1981, followed by the first Srs 200 (the fourth airfran completed) on 1 August 1982. To revive the 146 family and at the same tin eliminate particularly the engine reliability problems that dogged the 14 aircraft, British Aerospace developed the updated Avro RJ series, whi approximates in size to the earlier type. Major changes include uprated FADE controlled LF507 engines, all-digital avionics and updated EFIS, digital flig guidance, and a new comfortable wide look 'Spaceliner' interior with overhe luggage bins. The first development aircraft, an RJ85, was flown at Hatfield 23 March 1992, followed by the RJ100 on 13 May and the first RJ70 on 23 Ju Drag improvements and weight savings were announced in September 199 Final assembly is undertaken at Woodford.

VARIANTS

The initial variant was the BAe 146-100, with an overall length of 26.19m (8! 11in), providing for 82 passengers at 840mm (33in) pitch, or up to a maximu of 93. This has the same power plant as the 146-200, but a maximum take-c weight of 38,102kg (84,000lb). The 146-200, developed in parallel with the 14 100, differs only in length of fuselage and operating weights, with associat

Above: The Avro RJ series has a digital flight deck with Cat IIIa all-weather landing capability as standard.

structural and system changes. A freighter version of the 146-200 was developed, with an upward-hinged door in the rear fuselage port side. The 146-200 QT (Quiet Trader) first flew on 21 August 1986, and can accommodate six standard LD3 freight containers. In September 1984 BAe announced that it was launching a 146-300, featuring a further lengthening of the fuselage to increase the standard seating to 122 at 810mm (32in) pitch, or 130 a 740mm (29in) pitch. It first flew on 1 May 1987. The 146 Series was also built in QT Quiet Trader, QC Quick Change, and executive Statesman versions. The shortest fuselage version of the Avro RJ is the RJ70, which provides typical accommodation for ? passengers, while up to 100 passengers can be accommodated in the ▶

2.39m (7ft 10$\frac{1}{4}$in) longer RJ85 which is the best-selling RJ model. Still furth
capacity increases have been achieved in the RJ100, which can carry 11
passengers in a fuselage stretched by another 2.44m (8ft 0in). All three a
powered by the same 31.14kN (7,000lb) thrust Honeywell LF507 turbofa
engines. A fourth model, the RJ115 with accommodation for 128 passenge
is available, but has not yet found a buyer. In addition to passenger layouts, a
versions can be built as freighters, designated QT Quiet Trader, as the QC Qui
Change model, and as a Combi for the carriage of both passengers and freigh
On 21 March 2000, BAE Systems (the new name for British Aerospac
following the merger with GEC Marconi) announced the formal launch of th

llow-on RJX series, with advanced Honeywell AS977 engines and nsiderable improvements in fuel burn, maintenance costs, noise and missions, and operating range. It is proposed in the same variants as the RJ, signated RJX-70, RJX-85 and RJX-100.

ERVICE USE

ertification of the BAe 146-100 was achieved on 20 May 1983, and Dan-Air put ▶

elow: Aegean Airlines operates new Avro RJ-100s on a domestic rvice within Greece.

the type into revenue service on 27 May. The Srs 200 was certificated in June 198
in the UK and USA, allowing Air Wisconsin to become the first operator of the typ
on 27 June. Air Wisconsin also became the first operator of the 146-300, takir
delivery on 28 December 1988, following certification on 6 September. UK CAA ar
US FAA certification of the RJ Series was completed on 1 October 1993 and
June 1994 respectively. The first aircraft, an RJ85, was delivered to Crossair on 2
April 1993, followed by the RJ100 to Turkish Airlines on 22 July 1993. US airlir

usiness Express, operating as a Delta Connection carrier, took delivery of the first
J70 on 11 September. A total of 209 BAe 146s were produced before being
placed by the Avro RJ, which had logged 165 orders and 154 deliveries at 1
nuary 2001. Orders for the RJX totalled two. First delivery of the RJX-85 will be
ade to launch customer Druk Air in September 2002.

low: A line-up of Avro RJs and BAe 146s at London City Airport.

British Aerospace (BAC) One-Eleven

The One-Eleven had its origins in a design known as the Hunting H,10 projected in the mid-1950s by Hunting Aircraft Ltd as a 48-seat (four abreast) short-range jet transport. Proposed engines in the period 1956-5 when wind-tunnel testing and mock-up construction continued, were th Bristol Siddeley Orpheus turbojet, and the BS.61 or BS.75 turbofans, b after Hunting had been acquired by British Aircraft Corporation (BAC) 1960, the design was enlarged to provide five-abreast seating for about passengers, and Rolls-Royce Speys were adopted. In this form, the aircr became the BAC One-Eleven and a decision to put the type into producti was taken in March 1961. A prototype/company demonstrator first flew 20 August 1963, with Spey Mk 505 engines, 33,340kg (73,500lb) gro weight and a maximum of 79 seats. The One-Eleven design followed t fashion of its day in having rear-mounted engines and a T-tail, configuration that led to the loss of the prototype on 22 October 1963 aft it entered a deep stall during high angle of attack investigation. Aft building more than 200 One-Elevens in the variants described, Briti Aerospace (into which BAC had meanwhile merged) concluded in 1979 agreement with the National Centre of the Romania Aircraft Indust (CNIAR), providing for the latter to establish a One-Eleven production line Romania. The first aircraft assembled by Romania flew at Bucharest on September 1982 and deliveries of components from the UK under th agreement ended in 1986.

VARIANTS

The first production version of the One-Eleven was designated Srs 20 with 46kN (10,330lb) RB.168-25 Spey Mk 506 engines and a maximu weight of 35,833kg (79,000lb). The Srs 300 was generally similar but h 50.7kN (11,400lb) Spey Mk 511 engines, increased fuel in centre secti tank and structural modification for a gross weight of 39,462kg (87,000l The Srs 400, first flown on 13 July 1965, was based on the Srs 300 b optimized for US operators. A stretched version, the Srs 500, w developed primarily to meet BEA requirements, and used the Srs 300/4 airframe with a fuselage lengthened by 4.1m (13ft 6in) and span increas

Below: In recent years, the One-Eleven has become a popular entry-lev jet for low-cost airlines in Europe. This Series 500 was operated by AB Airlines between London and Shannon.

*bove: Noise regulations are pushing the One-Eleven out of Europe. The
st British World One-Eleven 500 flew for the last time in December
00 (Glen Sweeney-LBIPP).

" 1.52m (5ft) at the wingtips. More powerful engines matched the higher
eights of this version. The Srs 500 prototype (a converted Srs 400) flew
 30 June 1967. To provide improved field performance and the ability to
erate from unprepared surfaces, the wings and power plant of the Srs
*0 were combined with the fuselage of the Srs 400 to produce the Srs
'5, flown in prototype form on 27 August 1970 and in production guise on
 April 1971. The Srs 670 flew as a prototype only, and had some
rodynamic refinements to the wing to improve the field performance in
e with Japanese requirements. Romanian production versions of the Srs
'5 and 500 were designated Srs 495 and 560 respectively. A forward side
eight-loading door was developed for Srs 475 aircraft in military service.

ERVICE USE

e One-Eleven 200 was certificated on 6 April 1965 and entered service
th the first customer, British United, on 9 April, followed on 25 April by
e first services by Braniff in the USA, where FAA certification was
tained on 20 April. The Srs 400 was approved in the US on 22 November
*65 and by ARB on 10 December 1965, American Airlines being the first
er. The Srs 500 was certificated at the initial BEA gross weight on 18
ugust 1968, but entered revenue service on 17 November. The Srs 475
as certificated in July 1975 and the first example was delivered to Faucett
 Peru during the same month. Production of the One-Eleven totalled 230
the UK, made up of 56 Srs 200, nine Srs 300, 69 Srs 400, nine Srs 475
d 87 Srs 500 aircraft. Nine were built by Romaero in Romania. Some 90
main in service.

British Aerospace (Hawker Siddeley) 748

SPECIFICATION
(British Aerospace Super 748)

Dimensions: Wingspan 31.23m (102ft 5½in); length overall 20.42m (67ft 0in height overall 7.57m (24ft 10in), wing area 77.0m² (828.9ft²).

Power Plant: Two 1,700kW (2,280shp) Rolls-Royce Dart Mk 552-2 turbopro with Dowty Rotol four-blade constant-speed fully-feathering metal propellers.

Weights: Operating weight empty 12,327kg (27,176lb); max take-off 21,092 (46,500lb); max landing 19,504kg (43,000lb); max payload 5,136kg (11,323lb).

Performance: Max cruising speed 244kts (452km/h); max rate of climb 7.2m (1,420ft/min); service ceiling 7,620m (25,000ft); take-off field length 1,134 (3,720ft); landing field length 1,036m (3,400ft); range with max payload 926m (1,715km).

Accommodation: Flight crew of two and seating for up to 58 passengers, for abreast with central aisle. Cargo/baggage compartment volume 9.54m³ (337ft

Seeking to diversify its product line as it was aware that orders for milita aircraft, upon which it was then heavily dependent, were likely to dwind the Avro company began to explore commercial aircraft designs in the la 1950s. Efforts soon after World War II to enter the civil aircraft market with t Tudor had not been successful, and by the mid-1950s all Avro's design a production activity related to defence contracts. Following the 1957 decision re-enter the commercial field, attention was focused upon the small short-ha turboprop category of aircraft, as a replacement for such piston twins as t Douglas DC-3 and Vickers Viking, and as a competitor for the Fokker F27, then already in flight test. Early studies under the Avro 748 designation were f a 20-seat, high-wing, twin-engined aircraft with a gross weight of only 8,165 (18,000lb), but analysis of airline reaction to this proposal, and of other mark studies, led to the development of a new low-wing design with a gross weig of 14,968kg (33,000lb), two Rolls-Royce Darts and 36 seats. Features of th design, which was launched into prototype construction in January 195 included a high-aspect-ratio wing with a novel type of single slotted flap enhance field performance, and the use of fail-safe principles in structu design. Known at first as the Avro 748, this aircraft later became the H.S.7 when Avro was absorbed into the Hawker Siddeley Group, and then as t British Aerospace 748 after HSA's nationalization. The 748 remained production from 1961 to 1986, and provided the basis for development of t British Aerospace ATP, which then succeeded it. The two prototypes enter flight testing on 24 June 1960 and 10 April 1961 respectively.

VARIANTS
The prototype and first production batch, to Srs 1 standard, had 1,402k (1,880shp) Rolls-Royce RDa6 Dart Mk 514 engines. The Srs 2, first flown November 1961, introduced 1,570kW (2,105shp RDa7 Dart Mk 531 engine and was superseded in 1967 by the Srs 2A with uprated Darts, usually t 1,700kW (2,280shp) Mk 535-2 (originally designated Mk 532-2S), but som with the Mk 534-2 (originally Mk 532-2L) and nine special-purpose aircra with RDa8 variants. The Srs 2C, first flown 31 December 1871, was a S 2A fitted with large freight door in rear port fuselage side. The Srs 2 introduced a number of refinements and improvements, including a 1.22 (4ft) span increase with new wingtips, modified tail surfaces and Dart M 536-2 engines, plus a hush-kit option; the first production Srs 2B flew on

above: LIAT operated the 748 on island-hopping flights in the Caribbean from its base in Antigua.

ne 1979. The final variant was the BAe Super 748, similar to the Srs 2B t with a new flight deck, Dart Mk 552 engines with hush kit and tomatic water-methanol injection options, new cabin interior design, and umber of other improvements. The Super 748 first flew on 30 July 1984. ilitary variants of the 748 were also produced, either similar to the Srs 2B t cleared to operate at higher weights, or with a new rear fuselage corporating clamshell doors and a loading ramp; in the latter form, the be was named Andover. The actual name Coastguarder was applied to a riant equipped for maritime patrol and surveillance and first flown on 18 bruary 1977.

RVICE USE

e 748 Srs 1 was certificated on 7 December 1961 and entered service with yways in 1962. The Srs 2 was certificated in October 1962 and entered rvice with BKS Air Transport. Deliveries of the Srs 2B began in January 1980 Air Madagascar. Deliveries of the Super 748 in 1984, to LIAT. The last delivery s made to Makung Airlines in 1989 bringing total production to 379, including rear-loading Andover C.Mk.1 for the Royal Air Force, and 89 licence-built in dia. Some 115 remain in service.

British Aerospace Jetstream

SPECIFICATION
(Jetstream 41)
Dimensions: Wingspan 18.42m (60ft.5in); length overall 19.25m (63ft 2in); height overall 5.74m (18ft 10in), wing area 32.59m² (350.8ft²).
Power Plant: Two AlliedSignal TPE331-14GR/HR turboprops, flat rated at 1,230kW (1,650shp). Five-blade McCauley metal propellers.
Weights: Operating weight empty 6,473kg (14,272lb); max take-off 10,886kg (24,000lb); max landing 10,569kg (23,300lb).
Performance: Max cruising speed 295kts (547km/h); rate of climb 11.2m/s (2,220ft/min); service ceiling 7,925m (26,000ft); take-off field length 1,523m (5,000ft); landing field length 1,280m (4,200ft); max payload range 775nm (1,434km).
Accommodation: Flight crew of two. Two-abreast seating on right hand side of the aisle and single row on left, for maximum 29 passengers. Rear and ventral baggage volume 6.16m³ (217.5ft³).

The Jetstream was launched in 1965, at which time it was a product of Handley Page, designated the HP.137 and destined to be the last aircraft type produced by that company before its demise in 1969. Handley Page flew the first of several Jetstream prototypes on 18 August 1967, at which time the favoured engines were Turboméca Astazou XIV free-shaft turboprops; later prototypes represented the Jetstream Mk2 with Astazou XVIs and Jetstream Mk3 with Garrett TPE331s, which had been specified by the USAF when it ordered 11 Jetstream 3Ms as C-10As. Five prototypes and 35 production Jetstreams (with Astazou engines) had been completed when all work ceased at Radlett on 27 February 1970, and four more were completed from existing components under the initiative of Terravia Trading Service. Rights in the Jetstream were subsequently acquired by Scottish Aviation, which built 26 navigation trainers for the RAF. In the USA some of the original HP built Jetstreams were modified by the Riley company, to have Pratt & Whitney Canada PTA6A-41 engines; others were brought up to Jetstream 200 standard with Astazou XVIs; and still more became Century III Jetstreams with TPE33...

Below: In the USA the 18-seat Jetstream 31 was very popular, with most of the 381 aircraft produced serving with local commuter airlines.

ove: The larger, 29-seat Jetstream 41 is operated on regional routes the UK, but has sold only slowly abroad.

gines retrofitted by Volpar for Apollo Airways. Scottish Aviation was absorbed ⊃ British Aerospace upon the latter's formation and the Jetstream became ⇥t of the BAe civil aircraft product range, but it was not until December 1978 ⇥t the decision to launch an updated version of the Jetstream was ⇥ounced, backed up in January 1981 with a full production commitment. In reincarnation, the aircraft became the Jetstream 31, as a close relative of the ⇥3 that Handley Page had built with Garrett TPE331 engines. These engines, ⇥ some structural changes, allowed the gross weight of the Mk3 to be reased to 6,577kg (14,500lb), compared with 5,670kg (12,500lb) for the ⇥lier version, and this became the starting weight for the Jetstream 31, BAe ⇥oduced new advanced-technology propellers, a DC (in place of AC) electrical ⇥tem, a revised air conditioning system, a changed hydraulic pump, a totally ⇥ised cockpit layout, and a range of new interior options. No significant ⇥nges were made to the external appearance or the structure of the ⇥tstream 31, the prototype of which (modified from Mk1) flew at Prestwick on ⇥ March 1980. A stretched adaptation for up to 29 passengers was announced ⇥ 24 May 1989 and launched on a risk-sharing basis with Field Aircraft, Pilatus ⇥gzeugwerke, ML Slingsby and Gulfstream Aerospace Technologies. ⇥signated Jetstream 41, the new aircraft made its maiden flight on 25 ⇥otember 1991. Four aircraft were used in the certification programme, with ⇥A approval awarded on 23 November 1992.

⇥RIANTS

⇥ Jetstream 31 has benefited from some small increases in operating ⇥ights since being first produced, but there have been no important variations ⇥roduction standard until the introduction of the Jetstream Super 31, also ⇥erred to as the Jetstream 32, which first flew on 13 April 1988. This version ⇥vided significant improvements in performance and passenger comfort, ⇥ieved with the introduction of more powerful 760kW (1,0020shp) Garrett ⇥w AlliedSignal) TPE331-12 turboprop engines, a re-contoured interior ▶

providing greater cabin width at head height, and reduced noise and vibratic In basic airliner configuration, passenger capacity was 18/19, but Corporate a Executive Shuttle versions for 9/10 passengers were also produced. Oth variants had the QC Quick Change and Special Role designation, intended 1 fast passenger/cargo conversion and for specialist application. One of the was a proposed Jetstream 31EZ for offshore patrol in economic exclusi zones, fitted with a 360 degree scan radar, observation windows a searchlight. British Aerospace has completed a performance improveme package for the Super 31 for hot-and-high operations. This comprises flaple take-off flap setting and the fitting of aerodynamic devices to the engi nacelle/wing joint to reduce drag and enhance climb efficiency. A package available enabling an upgrade to J32EP (enhanced performance). Wingspan a fuselage were stretched by 2.44m (8ft 0in) and 4.88m (16ft 0in) respectively produce the 29-seat Jetstream 41, powered by uprated 1,119kW (1500sł TPE331-14 turboprop engines. Other changes include a Honeywell Primus four-tube EFIS, inward-opening rear baggage door, lower mounted wing to cle cabin aisle, ventral baggage hold, increased fuel capacity in the wing a various aerodynamic improvements. The Jetstream 41 was available as a pu passenger aircraft with seating for 29 passengers; Corporate Shuttle for 8- passengers; and in Combi, Quick Change and Special Role variants similar Jetstream 31.

SERVICE USE

The Jetstream 31 was certificated in the UK on 29 June 1982, using t prototype and the first production aircraft, which had flown on 18 Mar 1982. US certification was obtained on 30 November 1982. The fi delivery was made on 15 December 1982 to Contactair in Stuttga followed on 30 December by the first to a UK operator, Peregrine . Services. A Special Role Jetstream 31 was delivered to the Royal Saudi . Force in November 1987 for navigator training. The Jetstream Super 31 w

Above: Australian regional Impulse Airlines was one of the few foreign airlines to order the larger Jetstream 41.

certificated in the UK on 6 September 1988 and by the FAA to Part 23 in the 19-seat commuter category on 7 October and went into service with Big Sky Airlines of the USA in October 1988. First deliveries of the Jetstream 41 were made to Loganair and Manx Airlines on 25 November 1992. FAA approval was given on 9 April 1993 and the first J41 for a US customer was handed over to Atlantic Coast Airlines in June 1993. AlliedSignal accepted the first Corporate Shuttle in Summer 1994. Production of the Jetstream 31 was completed in 1994 with the 381st aircraft and at the end of 1997 with the 106th Jetstream 41. At 1 January 2001, a total of 220 Jetstream 31/32s and 93 Jetstream 41s remained in service.

Left: Love Air operated the Jetstream 31 for a short time to Deauville in northern France.

Britten-Norman Islander

SPECIFICATION
(Pilatus Britten-Norman BN-2T)
Dimensions: Wingspan 16.15m (53ft 0in) with extended wingtips; length over
10.87m (35ft 7¾in); height overall 4.18m (13ft 8½in), wing area 31.31m² (337ft
Power Plant: Two 298kW (400shp) Rolls-Royce Allison 250-B17 turboprops
with Hartzell three-blade constant-speed fully-feathering propellers.
Weights: Operating weight empty 1,832kg (4,040lb); max take-off 3,175kg
(7,000lb); max landing 3,084kg (6,800lb); max payload 1,113kg (2,454lb).
Performance: Max cruising speed 170kts (315km/h); initial rate of climb 5.3m/
(1,050ft/min); service ceiling 7,620m (25,000ft); take-off field length 380m (1,250ft
landing field length 340m (1,115ft); range with max payload 141nm (261km).
Accommodation: Flight crew of one and seating for up to 9 passengers on
individual side-by-side and bench seats with no aisle. Baggage compartment
volume 1.39m³ (49ft³).

The Islander was conceived in the early 1960s by the original Britten-Norm
company founded by John Britten and Desmond Norman, in an effort
produce a very simple, light twin-engined transport for third-level and commut
airlines. The company had a 25 per cent interest in Cameroon Air Transport a
the BN-2, as the new twin was designated, was designed specifically to meet t
needs of that company, which was regarded as typical of many throughout t
world which needed an aircraft with 6-10 seats, good take-off performance, lc
purchase cost, low operating costs and easy maintenance. Featuring a hic
mounted, untapered and strutted wing, fixed landing gear and unusual 'wall-
wall' seating in the fuselage, with three access doors (two to port and one
starboard), the BN-2 prototype was powered by a pair of 157kW (210h
Continental IO-360-B engines and flew on 13 June 1965. With a span of 13.7
(45ft) and gross weight of 2,155kg (4,750lb), it was later fitted with 194k
(260hp) Lycoming O-540-E engines, with which it flew on 17 December 196
the span then being increased to 14.9m (49ft) and gross weight to 2,585
(5,700lb). A production prototype to similar specification flew on 20 August 196

VARIANTS

The first production standard of the Islander, as the BN-2, was similar to the prototype in its modified form, the first aircraft flying on 24 April 1967. In June 1969, the production standard became the BN-2A, with a number of product improvements, a further change to BN-2B being made in 1978 with higher loading weight and improved interior design. Both the BN-2A and BN-2B were made available in a number of subvariants, the most significant options being 224kW (300hp) Lycoming IO-540-K1B5 engines in place of the original standard O-540-E4C5s (first flown on 30 April 1970); Riley-Rajay superchargers on standard O-540 engines; extended-span wing tips containing extra fuel tankage; and a long-nosed BN-2S with two more seats in the cabin, replacing baggage stowage space that was provided, instead, in the nose (first flown 22 August 1972). A series of suffix numbers added to the BN-2A and BN-2B designations indicated these and other options, such as revised wing leading-edge camber to meet US certification requirements, drooped flaps for better single-engined climb, and (the -20 series) a higher gross weight. On 6 April 1977, the BN-2A-3 prototype flew with 448kW (600shp) Lycoming LTP 101 turboprops, but a switch was made to Allison 250 engines for the production BN-2T Turbine Islander. The BN-2T prototype first flew on 2 August 1950 and many of the previously described options are also available on this model. Military derivatives include the BN-2T Defender, and the latest model, the BN-2T-4S Defender 4000.

SERVICE USE

The BN-2 Islander received British certification on 10 August 1967 and first deliveries were made on 13 and 15 August respectively, to Glosair and Loganair. FAA approval on 19 December 1967 was followed by first deliveries in the USA in January 1968. The BN-2T Turbine Islander obtained UK certification in May 1981 and US approval (to FAR Pt 23) on 15 July 1982. A milestone was reached on 7 May 1982 when the 1,000th Islander was delivered. Production of the Islander exceeds 1,220 units.

Left: The piston-engined BN-2A-26 Islander was flown by Police Aviation Services on behalf of the Hampshire police on aerial surveillance and EMS work. Islanders remain in service with several UK police forces.

Britten-Norman Trislander

SPECIFICATION
(BN-2A Mk III Trislander)
Dimensions: Wingspan 16.15m (53ft 0in); length overall 15.01m (49ft 3in);
height overall 4.32m (14ft 2in), wing area 31.3m² (337.0ft²).
Power Plant: Three 194kW (260hp) Avco Lycoming O-540-E4C5 flat-six piston
engines, with Hartzell two-blade constant-speed fully feathering propellers.
Weights: Operating weight empty 2,650kg (5,843lb); max take-off 4,540kg
(10,000lb); max landing 4,540kg (10,000lb); max payload 1,610kg (3,550lb).
Performance: Max cruising speed 265(km/h); initial rate of climb
5.0m/s (980ft/min); service ceiling 4,010m (13,150ft); take-off field length
595m (1,950ft); landing field length 440m (1,445ft); range with max payload
130nm (241km).
Accommodation: Flight crew of one. Seating for up to 17 passengers on
individual side-by-side and bench-type seats. Total baggage vo0lume 1.33m³
(47.0ft³).

The uniquely-configured Trislander resulted from the effort that began in 19
to 'stretch' the Islander to carry more passengers. The first result of th
activity was a long-fuselage Islander (converted from the original BN
production prototype), which first flew on 14 July 1968. Consideration of t
flight test result obtained with this aircraft led the Britten-Norman company
conclude that additional power was needed to match the higher operati
weights that were, in their turn, required to allow the full potential of
stretched aircraft to be achieved. Rather than redesign the wing to acce
engines of greater power, the designers decided to fit a third engine of t
same type as already used in the Islander, and chose to locate this extra pow
plant in a nacelle at the top of the fin. A redesigned, enlarged tailplane w
fitted in line with the propeller of the third engine for maximum effectivenes
the fuselage cross section was unchanged, as was the wing geometry, bu
little strengthening was required for the higher weights. Known as the BN-

*Below: Aurigny Air Services flies the Trislander on its bus-stop services
in the Channel Islands.*

*bove: Inter-Island operated the Trislander successfully on linking some
f the islands in the Seychelles.*

k III, this three-engined derivative of the Islander was sensibly named the
islander and made its first flight at Bembridge on 11 September 1970.
roduction of the Trislander was initiated in 1970. On 5 June 1982, International
viation Corporation in Florida acquired a licence to produce the Trislander in
e USA, under the new name of Tri-Commutair.

ARIANTS

e BN-2A Mk III entered production with a gross weight of 4,245kg (9,350lb),
is being increased in the BN-2A Mk III-1 version to 4,540kg (10,000lb). A

further change was then made by adopting as
standard the long nose (with extra baggage
capacity) that had been developed for the BN-2S
version of the Islander. This first flew on a
Trislander on 18 August 1974 and resulted in the
designation BN-2A Mk III-2. Introduction of an
auto feather system, which put the propeller into
feather in the event of an engine failure at take-
off, without action by the pilot, brought with it the
designation BN-2A Mk III-3.

SERVICE USE

The first production Trislander flew on 6 March
1971, followed by UK certification on 14 May and
US Type Approval (to FAR Pt 23) on 4 August of
the same year. Aurigny Air Services in the Channel
Islands took delivery of the first customer aircraft
on 29 June 1971 and remains the largest operator
with eight in service. Production of the Trislander
amounted to 73 aircraft in the UK and 12 in the
USA as the TriCommutair.

Canadair CL-44

SPECIFICATION
(Canadair CL-44-D4)
Dimensions: Wingspan 43.37m (142ft 3½in); length overall 41.70m (136f
10in); height overall 11.80m (38ft 8in), wing area 192.8m² (2,075ft²).
Power Plant: Four 4,276kW (5,730shp) Rolls-Royce Tyne RTy.12 Mk
515/10 turboprops, with four-blade Hamilton Standard Hydromatic
constant-speed fully-feathering and reversing propellers.
Weights: Operating weight empty 40,348kg (88,952lb); max take-off
95,250kg 210,000(lb); max landing 74,843kg (165,000lb); max payload
29,959kg (66,048lb)
Performance: Max cruising speed 349kts (647km/h); take-off field length
2,255m (7,400ft); landing field length 1,900m (6,230ft); range with max
payload 2,850nm (5,300km).
Accommodation: Flight crew of three or four. Seating for up to 214
passengers, but used primarily for freight, with usable cabin volume
178.2m³ (6,294ft³), plus two underfloor freight holds totalling 31.4m³
(1,109ft³). Rear fuselage, including tail unit, hinged to starboard for straigh
in loading.

The CL-44 was derived in Canada from the original Bristol Britann
initially to meet an RCAF requirement for a long-range troop and freig
transport. Principal changes were a lengthening of the fuselage, increase
wing span and a switch from Bristol Proteus to Rolls-Royce Tyne engine
The first of 12 CL-44D Yukons for the RCAF flew on 15 November 195
The CL-44D-4, first flown on 16 November 1960, was optimized f
commercial operation as a freighter, with a swing tail (at the time uniqu
and 27 were produced with first deliveries made to Flying Tiger on 31 M
1961, to Seaboard on 20 June 1961 and to Slick on 17 January 196
Loftleidir acquired four to use as passenger transports, and for th
company, Canadair developed the CL-44J with a 4.6m (15ft) fusela
stretch to increase seating from 178 to 214. Four aircraft were converted
CL-44J standard (first flight 8 November 1965) and were used by Loftlei
as Canadair 400s. A single CL-44D-4 was modified by Conroy Aircraft

*bove: Seaboard & Western, later Seaboard World Airlines, was a major
rans-Atlantic cargo carrier.*

Guppy' configuration with increased-diameter upper fuselage lobe, and
rst flying (as the CL-44-O) on 26 November 1969. Most of the CAF Yukons
vere sold for commercial use when retired in 1973, but lack the swing-tail
eature. Just six remained operational at beginning of 2001.

*elow: Cargolux Airlines began flying scheduled and charter services
rith CL-44 swing-tail freighters in May 1970.*

CASA C-212 Aviocar

SPECIFICATION
(CASA C-212-300)
Dimensions: Wingspan 19.00m (62ft 4in); length overall 15.16m (49ft 9in); height overall 6.30m (20ft 8in), wing area 40.0m² (430.6ft²).
Power Plant: Two 671kW (900shp) AlliedSignal TPE331-10R-513C turboprops with Dowty four-blade constant-speed feathering and reversing propellers.
Weights: Operating weight empty 3,780kg (8,333lb); max take-off 7,700kg 16,975(lb); max landing 7,450kg (16,424lb); max payload 2,800kg (6,172lb).
Performance: Max cruising speed 191kts (354km/h); max climb rate 8.3m/s (1,630ft/min); service ceiling 7,925m (26,000ft); take-off field length 895m (2,935ft); landing field length 865m (2,840ft); range with max payload 750nm (1,388km).
Accommodation: Flight crew of two. Seating for up to 26 passengers, four-abreast, two seats each side of central aisle. Total baggage volume 3.5m³ (123.6ft³).

Development of the C-212 began in the late 1960s to meet the requirement of the Spanish air force for a small tactical transport and multi-role aircraft Layout and construction followed conventional practice for an aircraft of th type, with a high wing, fixed landing gear with the main units attached on eac side of the fuselage with sponson-type fairings over the mountings, and a rea loading ramp providing straight-in loading to the box-section cabin. Prototype were first flown on 26 March and 23 October 1971, and the Aviocar entere production against Spanish air force orders. The C-212 was subsequent

eveloped for civil use as a 19-seat commuterliner, whose initial sale was made
Pertamina in Indonesia. An agreement was then concluded with P T Nurtanio
ow IPTN) for the licence production (also in Indonesia) of the Aviocar as a
eans, in particular, of providing access to a substantial market for this type of
rcraft in that country and the Pacific Basin generally. The initial production
rcraft were powered by the 579kW (776shp) TPE331-5'251C engine and had
gross weight of 5,675kg (12,500lb) in the first C-212 CA civil variant, increased
6,300kg (13,890lb) in the C-212CB. In 1978 CASA introduced the more
owerful TPE331-10-501C engine, which allowed the gross weight to be
creased again. At this stage, the aircraft with the different engine versions
ere designated as the C-212-5 and C-212-10 respectively, but this
omenclature was quickly changed to C-212 Srs 100 and C-212 Srs 200. In
984, CASA announced the availability of the C-212 Srs 300, with 671kW
00shp) TPE331-10R-512C engines and Dowty Rotol propellers of a more
cent type than those which had replaced Hartzell propellers in Srs 200 aircraft
July 1983. The Srs 300 has redesigned wing tips, a modified nose with larger
aggage compartment, and a gross weight of 16,975lb (7,700kg). It also has, as
option, a rear fuselage fairing in place of the loading ramp, allowing 28
assengers to be carried at the increased seat pitch of 75cm (29.5in). An
proved version, the C-212 Srs 400 obtained its type certificate on 30 March
978. Its main features are re-rated TPE331-12JR engines, EFIS and cabin
furbishment. Both Srs 300 and 400 are also available in M military, ASW anti-
bmarine, and MP maritime patrol versions. At 1 January 2001, some 35 were
commercial service.

Left: The CASA Aviocar was initially developed to meet a Spanish Air Force requirement but found use as a utility transport with commercial operators.

Cessna 208 Caravan

SPECIFICATION
(Cessna Grand Caravan)
Dimensions: Wingspan 15.88m (52ft 1in); length overall 12.67m (41ft 7in); height overall 4.52m (14ft 10in), wing area 25.96m² (279.4ft²).
Power Plant: One 503kW (675shp) Pratt & Whitney Canada PT6A-114A turboprops with McCauley three-blade constant-speed reversible-pitch and feathering metal propeller.
Weights: Operating weight empty 2,064kg (4,550lb); max take-off 3,969kg (8,750lb); max landing 3,856kg (8,500lb); max payload 1,921kg (4,235lb).
Performance: Max cruising speed 184kts (341km/h); max rate of climb 4.7m/ (925ft/min); service ceiling 6,950m (28,800ft); take-off field length 428m (1,405ft); landing field length 279m (915ft); range with typical payload 960nm (1,776km).
Accommodation: Flight crew of one or two. Seating for up to 14 passengers

Cessna launched the Model 208 as a brand-new design in 1981, aimed providing a light general utility aircraft for passengers or cargo-carrying and suitable for adaptation to a variety of other roles. These could include according to Cessna, such activities as parachuting of supplies or personne firefighting, photographic duties, agricultural spraying, casualty evacuation border patrol and so on. Named Caravan I, the Model 208 prototype firs flew on 9 December 1982, and the first production aircraft was rolled out August 1984. FAA type approval was obtained on 23 October 1984, and March 1986 certification of a float-equipped version was completed, usin Wipline floats.

VARIANTS
Model 208 Caravan I is the basic utility version for passengers and carg powered by a single 447kW (600shp) Pratt & Whitney Canada PT6A-11 turboprop with 3-bladed propeller. Also produced as the Caravan Amphibia

ith floats and tailplane finlets, and as the 208A Cargomaster freighter for ederal Express, with increased take-off weight of 3,629kg (8,000lb), endix/King avionics, underfuselage composite cargo pannier, a 152mm (6in) ertical extension of tailfin, and no windows or rear starboard door. Federal xpress also commissioned the stretched 208B as the Super Cargomaster, hich made its first flight on 3 March 1986. Apart from a 1.22m (4ft) longer selage and the corresponding increase in cargo volume, the PT6A-114 engine as replaced from 1991 by the more powerful 503kW (675shp) -114A. The me engine powers the quick-change Grand Caravan, the largest model pable of carrying up to 14 passengers. The Model 208-675, certificated in oril 1998, combines the airframe of the 208 with the fully rated engine of the 08B. The first, in amphibious configuration was delivered on 15 April 1998. On) April that same year, Soloy Corporation flew the prototype of its Pathfinder conversion of the 208B. This is powered by two PT6D-114A turboprops iving a single propeller and has been stretched by 2.00m (6ft 6¹/₂in), with a rge faired-in cargo pannier also added. The U-27A is a military utility/special issions derivative based on the 208 Caravan I.

ERVICE USE

ederal Express was the first customer for both the 208A Cargomaster, elivered following certification in October 1984, and the 208B Super argomaster, which joined the fleet from 31 October 1986. Brasil Central, ready a prolific user of the Caravan I on commuter operations in Brazil, took elivery of the first Grand Caravan in Spring 1996. At 1 January 2001, more than 200 Caravans had been delivered.

elow: The rugged and versatile single-engine Grand Caravan is
perated in a multitude of roles, which tend towards the carriage of
rgo. Several airlines in more remote regions, like Costa Rica's SANSA,
;e the 14-seat aircraft on air taxi and commuter routes.

Cessna 500/550 Citation I/II/Bravo

SPECIFICATION
(Cessna Citation Bravo)
Dimensions: Wingspan 15.90m (52ft 2in); length 14.39m (47ft 2½in); heig overall 4.57m (15ft 0in); wing area 30.00m² (322.9ft²).
Power Plant: Two 12.84kN (2,887lb) thrust Pratt & Whitney Canada PW530 turbofans.
Weights: Operating weight empty 3,992kg (8,800lb); max take-off 6,713k (14,800lb); max 6,123 kg (13,500lb).
Performance: Max cruising speed 402kts (745km/h); service ceiling 13,715 (45,000ft); take-off field length 1,098m (3,600ft); landing field length 970 (3,180ft); range with typical payload 2,000nm (3,704km).
Accommodation: Flight crew of two. Typical seating for seven to ' passengers. Cargo/baggage volume 2.08m³ (73.47ft³).

When Cessna announced on 7 October 1968 that it was developing a eight-seat pressurised executive jet capable of operating from mo airfields, it could not then have imagined that it would spawned the world largest family of small- to medium-sized business jets. The new jet, dubbe Fanjet 500, made its maiden flight on 15 September 1969, but was soon name Citation. Like most contemporary designs, it utilised two pod-mounted engine attached to the rear fuselage. Several key changes were made during th development programme, including lengthening of the front fuselag

positioning of the engine nacelles further aft, and a larger vertical tail, leading
to FAA certification on 9 September 1971. The increase in take-off weight to a
maximum 5,375kg (11,850lb), the use of optional thrust reversers, an increase
in wing span and new JT15D-1A trubofans produced the Citation I, which
became available in December 1976. The 501 Citation I/SP was certified for
single-pilot operation on 7 January 1977. A total of 691 Citation Is had been built
when production ended in 1985. In parallel, Cessna built the stretched 550
Citation II, which had a 1.14m (3ft 9in) longer fuselage to seat 10 passengers
and more powerful JT15D-4 engines. It first flew on 31 January 1977 and was
certificated in March 1978, followed quickly by the II/SP single-pilot version.
Further improvements culminated in the S550 Citation S/II in 1984. A total of
733 Citation IIs, including 15 T-47As for the US Navy were built until replaced
by the Citation Bravo, announced at the Farnborough Air Show in September
1994. The new Bravo was based on the Citation II airframe, but has a new
modified and more efficient wing, new 12.84kN (2,887lb) Pratt & Whitney
W530A turbofans with thrust reversers as standard, an all-new interior design
and fittings, and a Honeywell Primus 1000 avionics suite.   Substantial
performance improvements include a faster cruising speed, better rate of
climb, and a 250nm (463km) increase in range. The Citation Bravo made its first
flight on 25 April 1995 and obtained FAA certification in January 1997.
Deliveries to customers started on 25 February. More than 140 Citation Bravos
are in service.

*Below: The powerful Citation II proved very popular with more than 700
built until replaced by the Bravo.*

Cessna 525/525A
CitationJet/CJ1/CJ2

SPECIFICATION
(Cessna Citation CJ1)

Dimensions: Wingspan 14.26m (46ft 9$\frac{1}{2}$in); length 12.98m (42ft 7in); heig
overall 4.20m (13ft 9$\frac{1}{4}$in); wing area 22.30m² (240.0ft²).

Power Plant: Two 8.45kN (1,900lb) thrust Williams FJ44-1A turbofans.

Weights: Operating weight empty 2,927kg (6,453lb); max take-off 4,808l
(10,600lb); max landing 4,445kg (9,800lb); max payload 306kg (675lb).

Performance: Max cruising speed 380kts (704km/h); service ceiling 12,500
(41,000ft); take-off field length 1,050m (3,450ft); landing field length 966
(3,170ft); range with typical payload 1,250nm (2,315km).

Accommodation: Flight crew of one or two. Typical seating for six/seve
passengers. Baggage volume 1.66m³ (58.6ft³).

When production of the Citation I ended in 1985, Cessna began work on
new entry level jet, which was to be the smallest and most affordable
its jet family and attract a new type of customer. The launch of the five-se
Model 525 CitationJet took place at the 1989 NBAA convention and the new j
took to the air on 29 April 1991. FAA certification for single pilot operation wa
granted on 16 October 1992, with first customer delivery made on 30 Marc
1993. While clearly a member of the Citation family, it incorporated a numb
of significant new design features. The most noteworthy were the adoption
a new supercritical laminar-flow wing with single-slotted flaps, adding some 1
15kts to the cruising speed, and a new T-tail configuration. A pair of innovati
small FJ44 turbofans, developed by Williams and Rolls-Royce, were chosen
power the CitationJet.

A total of 359 CitationJets were delivered up to early 2000, whe
manufacture turned to the replacement Citation CJ1, first announced at th
NBAA convention on 18 October 1998. FAA certification was obtained on
February 2000, followed by the first delivery on 31 March. Generally similar
the CitationJet, the CJ1 is distinguished by an all-new Rockwell Collins Pro Lir
21 digital avionics suite and a 91kg (200lb) increase in take-off weight. At th
1998 NBAA convention, Cessna also announced the stretched Model 525
Citation CJ2, which aimed at improvements in passenger comfort, speed an
range. Design features include a fuselage stretched by 1.30m (4ft 3in) in th
cabin and tailcone areas providing two extra cabin windows, an increased win
span of 0.84m (2ft 9in), swept tailplane with greater span, and more power
FJ44-2C turbofans rated at 10.68kN (2,400lb) static thrust. The first flight of
prototype (a rebuilt CitationJet) was made on 17 April 1999, with FA
certification obtained in 2000. First customer delivery was scheduled f
January 2001. A total of 20 CJ1s were in service at the end of 2000.

*Right: The CitationJet is the smallest of Cessna's jet family. Intended as
an entry level jet, the aircraft has undergone several changes and two I
production models with common type rating.*

Cessna 560 Citation V/Ultra Encore/Excel

SPECIFICATION
(Citation Ultra Encore)

Dimensions: Wingspan 16.61m (54ft 6in); length 14.90m (48ft 10³⁄₄in); heig█ overall 4.57m (15ft 0in).

Power Plant: Two 15.12kN (3,400lb) Pratt & Whitney Canada PW535 turbofans.

Weights: Operating weight empty 4,525kg (9,977lb); max take-off 7,543kg (16,630lb); max landing 6,895kg (15,200lb).

Performance: Max cruising speed 431kts (798km/h); service ceiling 13,715█ (45,000ft); take-off field length 1,085m (3,560ft); landing field length 879m (2,884ft); range with typical payload 2,000nm 3,704(km).

Accommodation: Flight crew of one or two. Maximum seating for seven passengers.

In the mid-1980s, Cessna started work on a stretch of the Citation S/II provide customers with more choice. This resulted in the new Model 6█ Citation V, first announced at the 1987 NBAA convention. The most notal█ external features were a slight fuselage stretch to provide a full eight-seat cal█ and a seventh window. Internally, the cabin was also restyled and enhanc█ with a new enclosed lavatory/vanity area. The baggage compartments we█ also relocated away from the main cabin. The Citation V engineering prototy█ made its first flight in August 1987, and received its type certificate on█ December 1988.

Customer deliveries started in April 1989 and a total of 260 were bu█ (including two SLAR-equipped TR.20s for the Spanish Air Force) before a m█ 1994 change to the Citation Ultra, which received its FAA certification in Ju█ 1994. The first aircraft was handed over to Korean Air on 26 July 1995. T█ Citation Ultra introduced a digital autopilot, Honeywell Primus II EFIS, a█ increased payload and performance through the application of the improv█ JT15D-5 engine. Military derivatives of the Citation Ultra include the OT-4█ tracker aircraft in service with the USAF, and the UC-35A and UC-35C transp█ for the US Army and US Marine Corps respectively. The latter has additio█ communications equipment, including satellite communications (Satcom). T█ Citation Ultra Encore first flew on 9 July 1998 and has been available since la█ 2000. Compared to the Ultra, it incorporates many improvements, amo█ which are an increased wing span, PW535 turbofans offering a 10% increa█ in thrust and lower fuel consumption, boundary layer energisers and s█ fences to improve stall characteristics, and trailing-link landing gear.

Under the same Model 560 designation is the Citation Excel, which flew█ 29 February 1996 and was first delivered on 2 July 1998. The Excel combin█ the wing and tail surfaces of the Ultra with the shortened version of the Citati█ X fusleage, providing a 10-seat cabin with stand-up headroom, and is power█ by a pair of 16.92kN (3,804lb) PW545A turbofans. Nearly 400 Ultra/Ultra Enc█ and Excel models are in service.

Right: Stretching the Citation II/SP produced the Citation V with seati█ for 10 passengers.

Cessna 650 Citation III/VI/VII

SPECIFICATION
(Cessna Citation VII)
Dimensions: Wingspan 16.31m (53ft 6in); length 16.90m (55ft 5¹/₂in); heigh
overall 5.12m (16ft 9¹/₂in); wing area 28.99m² (312.0ft²).
Power Plant: Two 18.15kN (4,080lb) thrust Honeywell TFE731-4R-2S
turbofans.
Weights: Operating weight empty 6,260kg (13,800lb); max take-off 10,432k
(23,000lb); max landing 9,072kg (20,000lb).
Performance: Max cruising speed 476km/h (881km/h); take-off field length
1,478m (4,850ft); landing field length 890m (2,920ft); range with typical
payload 2,180nm (4,037km).
Accommodation: Flight crew of two. Max seating for 13 passengers.
Baggage volume 1.4m³ (51ft³).

The all-new 650 Citation III was designed as a high-performance, mid-s
complement to the Citation II, marking a radical step-up in the compan
portfolio in an attempt to attract the more prosperous customer. It first flew
30 May 1979 and received certification on 30 April 1982. First deliveries
customers were made a year later. The Citation III looked substantially differe
to other Citation models, with the straight wing replaced by the slightly-swe
NASA designed supercritical wing, and the fin altered to a much more swe
configuration capped by a T-tail. The fuselage was also significantly long
providing accommodation for two crew and up to 13 passengers. New Garr
16.24kN (3,650lb) thrust TFE731-3B turbofans gave a maximum cruising spe
of 472kts (874km/h). Production continued until 1992, by which time 1
Citation IIIs had been delivered. Performance improvements were f
proposed in 1989 in the Citation IV, but this was not proceeded with and v

bove: The Cessna Citation VII has more powerful engines for improved
t-and-high performance.

placed by the Citation VI and Citation VII. The Citation VI was offered as a low-
st development of the Citation III with a new Honeywell SPZ-8000 avionics

package and standard interior layout, although customised interiors were available. The Citation VII was essentially similar, but came with more powerful TFE731-4R-2S engines for better hot-and-high performance. Deliveries of both models started in spring 1992, the first of the latter being delivered to golfer Arnold Palmer. The Citation VI's performance was no match for the VII, and production ceased in May 1995 after only 37 had been built, including two for navaid calibration in China. Later that year, Cessna made available the VII Magnum Edition with a choice of Universal UNS-1CP or Honeywell NZ-2000 flight management systems. The Citation VII remains in production and by 1 January 2001 around 120 were in service.

Left: The Citation VI was a low-cost development of the Citation III with a new avionics package.

Cessna 680 Citation Sovereign

SPECIFICATION (provisional)
(Cessna Citation Sovereign)
Dimensions: Wingspan 19.24m (63ft 1½in); length 18.87m (61ft 11in); heigh overall 5.85m (19ft 2½in); wing area 47.94m² (516.0ft²).
Power Plant: Two 25.3kN (5,686lb) thrust Pratt & Whitney Canada PW306C turbofans with FADEC.
Weights: Max payload 1,134kg (2,500lb).
Performance: Max cruising speed 444kts (822km/h); service ceiling 14,326m (47,000ft); take-off field length 1,219m (4,000ft); landing field length 975m (3,200ft); range with typical payload 2,500nm (4,630km).
Accommodation: Flight crew of two. Max seating for 12 passengers. Baggage volume 2.4m³ (83ft³).

The Citation Sovereign is the newest design to emanate from th Wichita, Kansas-based company. Work was started in mid-1998, and t

w model was announced at the NBAA convention later that year. The
tical design review was completed in late 1999, and construction on the
ototype was began in mid-2000. First customer deliveries are anticipated
be made in 2003. The design goals set by Cessna include a large,
mfortable cabin for up to 12 passengers, plus two crew, good short-field
rformance, and US coast-to-coast operation. It will have a new wing with
6° sweepback, and a mid-mounted tailplane with a sharply-swept profile
the leading edge. Podded Pratt & Whitney PW306C turbofans with
DEC will be attached on the rear fuselage shoulders. The Honeywell
mus Epic is at the heart of the avionics package, which also includes a
our weather radar and four-tube EFIS. Carbon brakes and anti-skid
stem is standard. The Citation Sovereign had logged well in excess of 100
ers at 1 January 2001. The biggest customer is Executive Jet Aviation,
ich ordered 50, plus 50 options, on 20 October 1998, for its NetJets
ctional ownership scheme.

Left: The new Citation Sovereign is being designed for comfortable US coast-to-coast operation.

Cessna 750 Citation X

SPECIFICATION
(Citation X)
Dimensions: Wingspan 19.38m (63ft 7in); length 22.05m (72ft 4in); height overall 5.84m (19ft 2in); wing area 48.96m² (527.0ft²).
Power Plant: Two 28.66kN (6,442lb) thrust Rolls-Royce Allison AE 3007C turbofans.
Weights: Operating weight empty 9,730kg (21,450lb); max take-off 16,193k (35,700lb); max landing 14,424kg (31,800lb).
Performance: Max cruising speed Mach 0.91; service ceiling 15,545m (51,000ft); take-off field length 1,615m (5,300ft); landing field length 1,039m (3,410ft); range with typical payload 3,430nm (6,352km).
Accommodation: Flight crew of two on separate flight deck. Max seating f 12 passengers. Baggage volume 2.32m (82ft³).

The Citation X was targeted at the long-range high-speed corporate market, and is the largest and fastest jet built by Cessna to date, as well having the longest-range. Optimised for non-stop US transcontinental a trans-Atlantic operations, and a high maximum Mach number, the Citation X said by the manufacturer to be the fastest commercial aircraft flying, af

ncorde, and is able to save up to one hour's flying time between Los Angeles
d New York. Equipped with two rear-mounted Rolls-Royce Allison AE 3007C
bofans, each rated at 28.66kN (6,442lb) static thrust for take-off, the aircraft
capable of a maximum cruising speed of Mach 0.91, and a range of over
400nm (6,290km). Superficially, the Citation X resembles the Citation VII, but
s greater angles of sweepback on all flying surfaces (wing sweepback is
0), greater wing span, and is of increased size and weight. The Citation X was
anched in October 1990 and the new Allison engines (the Citation X was the
st application) flew on a modified Citation VII in August 1992. First flight of the
ation X prototype followed on 21 December 1993. After an extensive flight
st programme, FAA certification was granted on 3 June 1996, and golfer
nold Palmer accepted the first Citation X the next month. The Citation X
sign team was awarded the prestigious Collier Trophy for aeronautical
hievement in February 1997. Cessna delivered its 3,000th Citation on 19
ovember 1999. By 1 January 2001, more than 120 Citation X models were in
rvice.

*low: The Citation X was targeted at the long-range, high-speed
rporate jet market.*

Cessna 401/402

SPECIFICATION
(Cessna 402C Businessliner)
Dimensions: Wingspan 13.45m (44ft 1½in); length 11.09m (36ft 4½in); height overall 3.49m (11ft 5½in); wing area 20.98m² (225.8ft²).
Power Plant: Two 242kW (325hp) Continental TSIO-520-VB turbocharged engines.
Weights: Operating weight empty 1,849kg (4,077lb); max take-3,107 kg (6,850lb); max landing 3,107kg (6,850lb).
Performance: Max cruising speed 213kts (428km/h); service ceiling 8,200m (26,900ft); take-off field length 537m (1,763ft); landing field length 322m (1,055ft); range with typical payload 420nm (777km).
Accommodation: Flight crew of two. Max seating for 10 passengers.

Having entered the cabin-class twin market in the early 1960s with the Mod 411, Cessna turned its attention to the third-level airline development in t United States, which had begun to link some of the smaller communities w each other, as well as into hub airports. Its answer was the nine-seat Model 4 with a convertible cabin and reinforced floor of bonded crushed honeycom construction, which could quickly be transformed into a light cargo transp when required. In parallel Cessna designed the Model 401 with identi airframe and power plant mainly for the executive transport market with six/eight-seat layout. The Model 401 first flew on 26 August 1965 and the sar prototype was used for the Model 402. The FAA type certificate granted to bo

rcraft on 20 September also covered both types. A low-wing cantilever onoplane with 300hp Continental TSIO-520-E air-cooled engines, the 401 tained the fixed wingtip fuel tanks first introduced in the Model 411. Minor odifications produced the 401A and 401B, but these were superseded itirely by the 402 from 1972. The Model 402A added a 0.74m³ (26ft³) baggage a lengthened nose and optional crew entry door, while a larger, more refined ibin with square windows and a tenth passenger seat produced the Model)2B. On 8 December 1971, Cessna renamed the Model 402B as the Model)2B Utiliner, and introduced the Model 402B Businessliner, making a clear stinction between freight and commuter use. Mk II versions were made vailable on 29 October 1975, including a package of factory-installed quipment as standard, and in 1978, MK III versions with further improvements standard equipment. The Model 402C incorporates many of the nprovements introduced with the 414A Chancellor. These include a new onded 'wet' wing of increased span, eliminating the wingtip tanks, new ndercarriage without wheel well doors, more powerful 242kW (325hp) TSIO-20-VB turbocharged engines, and many other detailed changes. The 402C was so offered in both Utiliner and Businessliner versions, and with Mk II and Mk equipment. Production ceased in 1985 after 545 Model 401s and 1,645 odel 402 variants.

elow: The Cessna 402 has been popular with small commuter airlines d with business flyers.

Cessna 404 Titan/441 Conquest/ Reims F406 Caravan II

SPECIFICATION
(Cessna 404 Titan Ambassador)
Dimensions: Wingspan 14.23m (46ft 8in); length 12.04m (39ft 6in); height overall 4.04m (13ft 3in); wing area 22.48m^2 (242.0ft^2).
Power Plant: Two 280kW (375hp) Continental GTSIO-520-M geared and turbocharged engines.
Weights: Operating weight empty 2,205kg (4,861lb); max take-off 3,810kg (8,400lb); max landing 3,674kg (8,100lb).
Performance: Max cruising speed 217kts (402km/h); service ceiling 9,205m (30,200ft); take-off field length 683m (2,240ft); range with typical payload 1,483nm (2,748km).
Accommodation: Flight crew of two. Max seating for 10 passengers.

In July 1975, Cessna announced that it was developing a new piston tw targeted at the airline, freight and corporate markets. Essentially a stretche 402B with enlarged vertical tail, dihedral tailplane, trailing-link undercarriag and 280kW (375hp) Continental GTSIO-520M geared and turbocharge engines, the unpressurised Model 404 Titan was designed for take off with 1,560kg payload from a 770m (2,530ft) strip. It had first flown on 26 Februa 1975, and production deliveries got under way in October the following yea Cessna offered three major variants, each differing in internal equipment fit suit various operational roles. Baseline aircraft was the Titan Ambassade

Below: The 10-seat 441 Conquest business aircraft was built in parallel with the Titan, sharing the same fuselage.

*above: The Cessna 404 Titan proved popular on commuter routes where
it was flown with up to 14 passengers.*

configured for passenger services with 10 seats and popular on scheduled
commuter routes, while the Titan Courier was fitted out for quick conversion
from passenger (seats were on rails) to freight layouts and
vice versa. The Titan Freighter was a dedicated cargo aircraft
with a cargo door. A total of 396 Titans were built between
1976 and 1982. The turbine-powered six to 10-seat Cessna
441 Conquest shares the same fuselage and was developed
in parallel with the Titan, Cessna announcing the new
business aircraft on 15 November 1974. The first flight took
place on 26 August 1975. Intended to slot in between its
own piston- and trubofan-powered aircraft, the Conquest's
performance benefited greatly from the 474kW (636shp)
Garrett TPE331-8-403S turboprop engines, which were
developed specially to meet the high-speed, high-altitude
requirements set by Cessna. Other performance-enhancing
features were a high aspect ratio bonded wing, and the high
strength trailing-link landing gear. From 1983, the aircraft was
marketed as the Conquest II, but production finished soon
after, with 362 built in total. French company Reims Aviation
builds the F406 Caravan II, a 14-seat development based on
the Conquest/Titan airframe. First flown on 22 September
1983, the Caravan II is powered by a pair of 373kW (500shp)
Pratt & Whitney Canada PT6A-112 turboprops, and has been
adapted for a multitude of missions, from passenger and
freight (with underbelly cargo pod) transport, medevac, aerial
survey, target towing, navaid calibration, and as a maritime
patrol aircraft under the name of Vigilant. It remains in
production.

Cessna 411/414 Chancellor/ 421 Golden Eagle

SPECIFICATION
(Cessna 421C Golden Eagle III)
Dimensions: Wingspan 12.53m (41ft 1¹/₂in); length 11.09m (36ft 4¹/₂in); height overall 3.49m (11ft 5¹/₂in); wing area 19.97m² (215ft²).
Power Plant: Two 280kW (375hp) Continental GTSIO-520-L geared and turbocharged engines.
Weights: Operating weight empty 2,258kg (4,979lb); max take-off 3,379kg (7,450lb); max landing 3,266kg (7,200lb).
Performance: Max cruising speed 241kts (447km/h); service ceiling 9,205m (30,200ft); take-off field length 544m (1,786ft); landing field length 219m (720ft); range with typical payload 955nm (1,770km).
Accommodation: Flight crew of two. Max seating for eight passengers.

Cessna had been a prolific producer of single-engine light aircraft, but o
18 July 1962 it flew the eight-seat Model 411 low-wing cabin busines
twin with retractable tricycle undercarriage, oval cabin windows, airsta
door, tip tanks, and Continental engines. Deliveries commenced in Octob
1964, and Cessna followed up in 1967 with the Model 411A wi
lengthened nose for baggage, optional extra fuel tanks in the engir
nacelles, and lighter and more efficient props. A total of 302 (252 Model 4
and 50 Model 411A) had been built when production was completed
1972. On 14 October 1965, Cessna had flown the Model 421, which wa
basically a pressurised version of the 411A with higher MTOW, broader ta

nd more powerful Continental geared and turbocharged GTSIO-520-C ngines. FAA type approval was received on 1 May 1967, with deliveries tarting soon after. Minor improvements were offered in 1969 in the Model 21A, but a more significant development followed with the 421B Golden agle, announced on 10 December 1969. Principal changes from the earlier nodels comprised a 0.71m (2ft 4in) increase in length, a 0.61m (2ft 0in) xtension of the wing span, higher gross weight, and many other quipment and performance enhancements. The 10-seat 421B Executive ommuter offered from February 1970 was targeted at the third-level airline narket. The final version, available from 1976, was the 421C Golden Eagle vith a bonded 'wet' wing, no tip tanks, higher tail and more efficient props. Iodel 421C Golden Eagle II and 421C Golden Eagle III incorporated varying ypes of standard equipment. Production ceased in 1985 after 1901 Model 21s had been built. Soon after the introduction of the 421, Cessna was ffering a cheaper and lighter model, designated 414, which combined the rframe of the 421 with the Model 402 wing. It entered service in ecember 1969, but was replaced in 1978 by the much improved 414A hancellor, which featured the 'wet' wing and other changes incorporated the 421C Golden Eagle. The 414A also ceased production in 1985 after 070 had been completed.

elow: The Cessna 421 Golden Eagle which followed on from the Model 11 had significant performance enhancement over earlier models.

Convair 540/580/600/640

SPECIFICATION
(Convair 580)
Dimensions: Wingspan 32.12m (105ft 4in); length overall 24.84m (81ft 6in); height overall 8.89m (29ft 2in), wing area 85.5m² (920.0ft²).
Power Plant: Two 2,796kW (3,750shp) Allison 501-D13H turboprops, with Aeroproducts four-blade constant-speed feathering and reversing propellers.
Weights: Operating weight empty 13,732kg (30,275lb); max take-off 26,371kg (58,140lb); max landing 22,985kg (50,670lb); max payload 4,023kg (8,870lb).
Performance: Max cruising speed 297kts (550km/h); initial rate of climb 11.2m/s (2,200ft/min); take-off field length 1,435m (4,700ft); landing field length 1,270m (4,160ft); range with typical payload 1,970nm (3,650km).
Accommodation: Flight crew of two. Seating for up to 56 passengers, four-abreast , two seats each side of central aisle. Total baggage/cargo volume 14.56m³ (514.0ft³).

During the 1950s and early 1960s the Convair 240, 340 and 440 family of twin-engined transports became the subject of several conversion programmes to fit turboprop engines. In all, about 175 of the original airframes were converted in this way, making the Convair the most successful of several contemporary schemes to apply turboprop power to what had been designed as piston-engined transports. The first programme aimed at airline application was initiated by the Napier engine company in the UK in 1954, and a Convair 340 with 2,288kW (3,060shp) Eland NEl.1 turboprops flew on 9 February 1955 as the model 540. Six more of these conversions were made, and the type entered airline service in July 1959. The second turboprop conversion scheme was set up by the Allison company. Either the Model 340 or Model 440 could be converted in this scheme to produce a new variant known as the Convair 580, or sometimes the Super Convair, with Allison 501-D13 engines. The first conversion was flown on 19 January 1960, and this proved to be the most successful of the three turboprop Convair programmes with 130 aircraft being converted eventually, the majority for airline use. The added power of the

*bove: Caribair operated the Convair twin on its scheduled services in
entral America and the Caribbean.*

rboprops required increases in the span and area of the tailplane, and in the
eight and area of the fin, and considerable changes were made internally. Third
id last of the turboprop Convairs introduced a pair of Rolls-Royce RDa10 Dart
k 542-4 engines with Rotol 3.96m (13ft) diameter four-bladed propellers, and
as applicable to all models of the piston-engined transport. When modified,
odel 240s became Model 600s, while Model 340s and 440s became known
; Model 640s with Darts. The first Model 600 flew at San Diego on 20 May
)65, and the first Model 640 later the same year. The Convair 580 was
rtificated on 21 April 1960 and entered service with Frontier Airlines in June
)64, earlier deliveries having been for corporate customers. Service entry of
e 600 with Central Airlines followed on 30 November 1965, and of the 640,
ith Caribair, on 22 December 1965. At 1 January 2001, a total of 105 turbine-
)wered versions remained in service.

*Left: Many Convair
580s have been
converted for freight
use, as shown here in
service with DHL
International.*

Curtiss C-46 Commando

SPECIFICATION
(Curtiss C-46A)

Dimensions: Wingspan 32.92m (108ft 0in); length overall 23.27m (76ft 4in); height overall 6.60m (21ft 8in), wing area 126.15m^2 (1,358ft^2).

Power Plant: Two 1,496kW (2,000shp) Pratt & Whitney R-2800-34 air-cooled 14-cylinder piston engines, with three-blade Hamilton Standard Hydromatic constant-speed fully-feathering propellers.

Weights: Operating weight empty 14,970kg (33,000lb); max take-off 21,772kg (48,000lb); max landing 21,228kg (46,800lb); max payload 5,265kg (11,630lb).

Performance: Normal cruising speed 162kts (301km/h); initial rate of climb 6.6m/s (1,300ft/min); service ceiling 8,410m (27,600ft); range with typical payload 1,000nm (1,850km).

Accommodation: Flight crew of two. Seating for up to 62 passengers, five-abreast with single aisle. Total cabin volume for freight 65.1m3 (2,300ft^3), plus additional underfloor holds totalling 12.9m^3 (455ft^3).

Of the types of aircraft serving the airlines in 1998, the C-46 can claim to be the second oldest, only the Douglas DC-3 having flown earlier. Of similar configuration to the famous Douglas type, the Curtiss transport was conceived in 1937 as the CW-20. Considerably larger than the DC-3, it differed also in having a fuselage of 'double bubble' cross section, to offer the largest possible cabin volume for the smallest drag. First flown on 26 March 1940, the CW-20 appeared too late to capture any part of the pre-war airline market although strangely enough, the prototype was impressed for military service with the USAAF and was passed to the UK, where it joined the war time fleet of BOAC. For the USAAF, Curtiss built 3,141 examples of the CW-20 in military guise

Below: The C-46 found a ready market in Bolivia, being well suited for freight operations via its cargo loading doors.

*bove: The C-46 Commando was used by Delta Airlines on cargo
rvices, but generally took second place behind the DC-3.*

esignated C-46 and named Commando. Major variants in US military service
ere the C-46A with a large port-side cargo door and reinforced floor; the C-
D personnel transport with an additional starboard cargo door; the C-46E,
hich reverted to the single cargo door but had a stepped windshield; and the
46F with the same R-2800-75 engines and two cargo doors. Some C-46As
ere diverted to the US Marine Corps as the R5C-1and used mainly in support
its island-hopping operations in the Pacific. A 36-seat commercial version,
signated CW-20E, was being considered near the end of World War Two but
as not built. After World War II many hundreds of these aircraft were acquired
civilian operators, at first for passenger use but subsequently (and more
rticularly) as freighters, for which their military style cargo-loading doors
ade them particularly suitable. As 'aerial tramps', C-46s became much used
the US and Central and South America, and some 20 can still be found flying
this role, well away from the trunk routes, at the beginning of 2001.

Dassault Falcon 100/200/2000

SPECIFICATION

(Dassault Falcon 2000)

Dimensions: Wingspan 19.33m (63ft 5in); length 20.22m (66ft 4in); heig
overall 7.06m (23ft 2in); wing area 49.02m² (527.6ft²).

Power Plant: Two 26.3kN (5,918lb) thrust GE/Honeywell CFE738-1-1B turbofans

Weights: Operating weight empty 9,405kg (20,735lb); max take-off 16,556k
(36,500lb); max landing 14,970kg (33,000lb); max payload 3,270kg (7,210lb).

Performance: Max cruising speed 481kts (891km/h); service ceiling 14,330
47,000(ft); take-off field length 1,658m (5,440ft); landing field length 1,591
(5,220ft); range with typical payload 3,120nm (5,778km).

Accommodation: Flight crew of two. Max seating for 19 passenger
Cargo/baggage volume 3.8m³ (134ft³).

Designed in association with Sud-Aviation, the 10-seat Dassault Falcon serie
was the French company's attempt to maintain a strong civil production lin
and one of a number of twin-engined business jets that appeared in the ear
1960s. Work started in 1961 and a first prototype, the Mystere XX, flew on

ay 1963 with rear-mounted Pratt & Whitney JT12A-8 turbofans. These were
anged to the General Electric CF700 for the production model, which made
s first flight on 1 January 1965 and received its US and French certification on
June that year. First deliveries were made to launch customer Pan American,
hich dubbed the aircraft as the Fan Jet Falcon in the US (later the Falcon 20),
hough in France the aircraft remained known as the Mystere 20. The baseline
craft was the Falcon 20C, followed by the higher-powered Falcon 20D
ithCF700-2D power plants and an 80 gallon fuel increase. The 20E introduced
higher take-off weight of 13,000kg (28,660lb), revised rudder and modified
arter motor, while the 20F was equipped with full leading edge slats and had
further increase in fuel capacity. The Falcon 20G was a maritime surveillance
rsion. In the intervening years, Dassault had built the scaled-down and more
kish-looking seven- to nine-seat, Garrett TFE731-2-powered Falcon 10, initially
own as the Mini-Falcon, which received its certification on 11 September ▶

elow: The Falcon 2000 became the first business jet to
e certificated for Cat IIIa operation using a head-up display.

1973. The improved Falcon 100 was externally distinguishable by a fourth cab window. On 24 April 1979, Dassault flew the improved 20H, which lat became the Falcon 200 and differed largely through the adoption of ne Garrett ATF-3-6A turbofans and a larger integral fuel tank in the aft fuselag Plans by Dassault to produce 30-seat and 40-seat airliner versions as the Falco 30 and Falcon 40 came to nothing. Total Falcon 10/100 production reached 22 units, including six special mission Falcon 10MERs for the French navy, whe production ceased in 1990. Production of the Falcon 20/200 ended in 198 after 516 had been built.

Announced at the Paris Air Show in June 1989 as the Falcon X, th much larger Falcon 2000 was a follow on to the successful 20/200 serie It was officially launched on 4 October 1990, with Alenia joining as a 25 risk-sharing partner in February 1991, responsible for the rear fuselag section and engine nacelles. As with its predecessors, Dassault retaine the twin-engine configuration, fitting higher-powered CFE738-1-1 tubofans, but drew heavily on the three-engined Falcon 900. This include the use of the same fuselage cross-section, although it is 1.98m (6ft 6i shorter, and the Falcon 900 wing with a modified leading edge and r inboard slats. The cockpit features the Rockwell Collins Pro Line 4 EFI system. A Flight Dynamics head-up display can also be fitted, and in Ju 1997, the Falcon 2000 became the first business jet to be certificated f Cat IIIa operation using a HUD. The Falcon 2000 prototype flew on 4 Ma 1993, and FAA type certification was awarded on 30 November 1994. At January 2001, some 120 Falcon 2000s were in service.

Right: The Falcon 20 has been popular for the transport of small and urgent freight.

Dassault Falcon 50/900

SPECIFICATION
(Dassault Falcon 900EX)
Dimensions: Wingspan 19.33m (63ft 5in); length 20.21m (66ft 3¹/₄in); heig overall 7.55m (24ft 9¹/₄in); wing area 49.00m² (527.4ft²).
Power Plant: Two 21.13kN (4,750lb) thrust Honeywell TFE731-5BR-1 turbofans.
Weights: Operating weight empty 11,204kg (24,700lb); max take-off 22,226 (49,000lb); max landing 19,050kg (42,000lb); max payload 2,796kg (6,164lb).
Performance: Max cruising speed 481kts 891km/h); service ceiling 15,550 (51,000ft); take-off field length 1,590m (5,215ft); landing field length 724 (2,375ft); range with typical payload 4,000nm (7,408km).
Accommodation: Flight crew of two. Max seating for 19 passengers. Bagga volume 3.6m³ (127ft³).

Following the general trend towards longer transcontinental and trans-Atlan range business jets, Dassault added a new member to its family using t fuselage cross-section of the Falcon 20/200, but with an entirely new area-rul fuselage, a supercritical wing, and more internal fuel. A three-engined layo was chosen to permit overflight of oceans and deserts. The resultant aircra was the Falcon 50 (Mystere 50 in France), which made its first flight on November 1976 and received its French type certificate on 17 February 197 followed by FAA approval on 7 March that year. The Falcon 50 used ma

Right: A three-engined layout was chosen for the Falcon 50 to permit overflight of oceans and deserts.

Falcon 20/200 components, but had a strongly waisted rear fuselage sectio
and central engine pod, together with a revised tail, and a wing with
compound leading edge sweepback. It was powered by three 16.5kN (3,700l
Garrett TFE731-3 turbofan engines and could carry 12 passengers. It becam
particularly popular as a presidential transport. In April 1995, Dassau
announced the improved and extended-range Falcon 50EX, powered k
uprated TFE731-40 engines providing an initial 7% improvement in fu
consumption. It made its first flight on 10 April 1996, receiving both DGAC ar
FAA certification before the end of that year. The French Navy ordered tl
Falcon 50 Surmar maritime surveillance version, and there are plans for a Falcc
50 Sigint intelligence variant. Soon after the introduction of the Falcon 5
Dassault announced the development of a new, longer-range business jet, tl
Falcon 900, with a redesigned 'wide-body' fuselage, 12 cabin windows, ar
accommodation for up to 19 passengers. It made its maiden flight on 2

ptember 1994, with deliveries starting immediately after certification in
arch 1986. The improved Falcon 900B was certificated at the end of 1991
th new TFE731-5BR-1C turbofans, higher initial cruise altitude and a 100nm
85km) increase in range. Some earlier aircraft have been retrofitted to 900B
andard. Still more powerful TFE731-60 turbofan engines, more fuel, and a
w Honeywell Primus 2000 EFIS avionics suite, plus INS, GPS, Satcom and
JD, produced the Falcon 900EX, capable of a range of more than 4,000nm
408km). The prototype first flew on 1 June 1995 and first deliveries were
ade on 1 November 1996. Dassault is also offering customers the Falcon
0C, which combines the airframe, engines and cabin of the 900B with the
vanced avionics of the 900EX. At 1 January 2001, in excess of 500 Falcon
/900s were in service.

elow: The Falcon 900B has a wide-body cabin for up to 19 passengers.

De Havilland Canada DHC-6 Twin Otter

SPECIFICATION

(de Havilland Canada DHC-6 Twin Otter 300)

Dimensions: Wingspan 19.81m (65ft 0in); length overall 15.77m (51ft 9in); height overall 5.94m (19ft 6in), wing area 39.02m² (420ft²).

Power Plant: Two 462kW (620shp) Pratt & Whitney Canada PT6A-27 turboprops with Hartzell three-blade reversible-pitch fully-feathering metal propellers.

Weights: Operating weight empty 3,363kg (7,415lb); max take-off 5,670kg (12,500lb); max landing 5,670kg (12,500lb); max payload 1,941kg (4,280lb).

Performance: Max cruising speed 182kts (338km/h); max rate of climb 2.33m, (340ft/min); service ceiling 8,140m (26,700ft); take-off field length 262m (860ft landing field length 290m (950ft); range with typical payload 700nm (1,297km).

Accommodation: One or two pilots and seating for up to 20 passengers, two abreast with central aisle. Total cargo/baggage volume front and rear 3.57m³ (126ft³).

The de Havilland Aircraft of Canada Ltd has had a variety of owners since foundation in 1928 as a subsidiary of the then-independent de Havilla Aircraft company in the UK. The latter eventually became part of the Hawk Siddeley Group, which transferred ownership of the Canadian subsidiary Canada's federal government in 1974. At the end of January 1986, DHC, as t Canadian company was frequently known, was purchased by The Boeing C and operated as a subsidiary of Boeing of Canada Ltd, until being acquired Bombardier and the Province of Ontario on 22 January 1992. Now who owned by Bombardier. Despite these changes of ownership, the DHC produ policy has changed little over the years, with the emphasis upon light transp aircraft with STOL capabilities. After successfully developing the DHC-2 Bea for Canadian 'bush' type operations, and the large but generally similar DHC Otter, the company gained twin-engined experience with the DHC-4 Carib and DHC-5 Buffalo, both of which were intended primarily for milita operations. DHC began in January 1964 to design a twin-engined derivative the Otter. Appropriately named the Twin Otter, this DHC-6 project was intend specifically for the commercial operator, especially in the role of commu airliner with short-field capabilities. The design objective was to use as much the Otter as possible, and the DHC-6 emerged with the same basic fusela cross-section as its single-engined forebear, and the same basic wing secti though of longer span. The cabin length was extended, and new nose and t assemblies were introduced. Fixed tricycle landing gear was adopted, a following experience with the Caribou and Buffalo, STOL performance w achieved solely by aerodynamic means, using double-slotted full-span trailir edge flaps, the outboard portions of which also operated differentially ailerons. In November 1964, DHC put in hand the construction of an initial ba of five Twin Otters, and the first of these flew at the Downsview, Ontario, pla on 20 May 1965.

VARIANTS

The first three Twin Otters were powered by 432kW (579shp) PT6/ turboprops, after which a switch was made to the similarly-rated but improv

Right: The excellent STOL performance of the Twin Otter proved ideal i operation to outlying and difficult airstrips

PTA6A-20 as the definitive power plant. Retrospectively, this initial producti◄ version became known as the Twin Otters Srs 100, superseded after 1 aircraft had been built by the Twin Otter Srs 200. The latter differed in having lengthened nose fairing with increased baggage capacity. Production of the S 200 also totalled 115, after which the Twin Otter Srs 300 became the standa production model, with uprated PT6A-27 engines and increased maximum tak off weight, with corresponding benefit to the payload/range performanc During 1974 six aircraft with the designation Twin Otter Srs 300S were used ◄ the Airtransit experiment conducted by Air Canada for the Canadi government. This was an evaluation of the practicability of using suitab adapted aircraft to operate to and from city-centre STOLports which – in t case at Montreal and Ottawa – comprised 610m (2,000ft) paved strips 3C (100ft) wide. The 11-passenger Twin Otter Srs 300S was equipped with upp wing spoilers to facilitate steep approach angles; high-capacity brakes and anti-skid braking system; emergency brakes; improved fire protection for t engines; a sophisticated instrument flight rules (IFR) avionics package; a other changes. Float and combination wheel/ski landing gear were available ◄ the Twin Otter, and a ventral pod was also developed, with a capacity of up 272kg (600lb) of baggage or freight. Military derivatives of the basic type a designated DHC-6-300M or -300MR.

SERVICE USE

The Twin Otter was first certificated (to FAR 23 Pt 135 standards) in May 196 allowing customer deliveries to start in July to US company Floair. Deliveries the Srs 200 began in April 1968 and of the Srs 300 in the spring of 196 Production totalled 842, including 115 each of Series 100 and 200 and 5 series 300, with the last aircraft delivered in December 1988. Many hundre remain in service. The majority of all variants has been delivered for commerc use, in the designed role of third-level airliner, but about 70 were sold military use in a dozen countries and others have been specially equipped such tasks as photographic and geological surveys, firefighting and oil-s dispersal.

Above: Scenic Airlines operates the Twin Otter 300 on sightseeing flights over and through the Grand Canyon. Its 17 aircraft have been remodelled with large square windows for improved view and are known as Vista Liners.

Below: The vast majority of the Twin Otters were sold in Canada and the United States. Air Inuit, owned by the indigenous Inuit people in Quebec, uses its Twin Otter 300s in the Ungava and Hudson coast regions.

De Havilland Canada DHC-7 (Dash 7)

SPECIFICATION
(de Havilland Canada DHC-7 Series100)
Dimensions: Wingspan 28.35m (93ft 0in); length overall 24.54m (80ft 6in); height overall 7.98m (26ft 2in), wing area 79.9m² (860ft²).
Power Plant: Four 835kW (1,120shp) Pratt & Whitney Canada PT6A-50 turboprops with Hamilton Standard four-blade reversible-pitch constant-speed feathering propellers.
Weights: Operating weight empty 12,560kg (27,690lb); max take-off 19,958kg (44,000lb); max landing 19,958kg (44,000lb); max payload 5,130kg (11,310lb).
Performance: Max cruising speed 213kts (427km/h); rate of climb 6.2m/s (1,220ft/min); service ceiling 6,400m (21,000ft); take-off field length 685m (2,250ft); landing field length 660m (2,160ft); range with typical payload 1,170nm (2,168km).
Accommodation: Two pilots and seating for up to 54 passengers, four-abreast with central aisle. Baggage volume in rear compartment 6.8m³ (240ft³).

In pursuance of its policy of specialising in the production of small/medium capacity transport aircraft with STOL capability, de Havilland Aircraft of Canada conducted an extensive market survey of short-haul transport requirements the early 1970s. Based on the results of this survey, design definition was finalised for a STOL aircraft in the 50-seat category and, with the backing of the Canadian government, prototype construction was put in hand in late 1972. The DHC-7, or Dash 7 as it soon became known, was de Havilland's first four-engined aircraft, but its configuration followed earlier practice, with a high-wing, T-tail layout and an aerodynamic high-lift system. The latter made use of double slotted flaps over some 80 per cent of the wing span, operating in the slipstream from the propellers. The flaps operate mechanically for take-off and hydraulically for landing, and are supplemented by two outboard spoilers each wing that can be operated symmetrically or, to supplement the ailerons differentially. Pratt & Whitney Canada worked with DHC to develop a new

Below: The DHC-7's superb STOL performance was perfect for Norwegian airline Wideroe's needs.

above: Sales of the Dash 7 suffered from the lack of downtown STOLports, leading to its replacement by the twin-engined Dash 8.

riant of the PTA6 turboprop, matched to new slow-running five-blade opellers to achieve the lowest possible noise levels. Special attention was ven to the aircraft's noise characteristics and the noise 'footprint', since it was pected that the type would be applicable to planned intercity services using ose-in downtown airports or STOLports. Such operations developed less pidly than DHC anticipated, however, and sales of the Dash 7 suffered cordingly; many regional airlines requiring an aircraft of Dash 7 size have ntinued (for commercial or regulatory reasons) to use out-of-town airports here STOL performance and ultra-low noise levels are less significant than e lower first costs and operating costs offered by the Dash 7's principal mpetitors. The Dash 7 development programme made use of four airframes: e for static testing, one fatigue test specimen, and two for flight test and rtification, which made their first flights at Downsview on 27 March and 26 ine 1975.

ARIANTS

1e basic production model was the Dash 7 Srs 100. An all-cargo or mixed assenger/cargo variant was designated Dash 7 Srs 101 and incorporates a ge forward freight door in the port side of the fuselage. The Dash 7 Srs 150 is an increased take-off weight of 21,319kg (47,000lb) and provision for an xtra 4,145l (1,094 US gallons) of fuel in the wings. With this extra fuel, the aximum range of the Srs 150 was increased to 2,525 naut mls (4,679km). The -cargo or mixed passenger/cargo version of the Srs 150 is designated Dash 7 s 151 and, like the Srs 101, can carry up to five standard pallets in the all-rgo role. A specialised ice reconnaissance version, the Dash 7 IR Ranger, was oduced for the Canadian Department of the Environment. Projected velopments of the type included the Dash 7 Srs 200 with 981kW (1,230shp) T6A-55 engines and the same weights as the Srs 150, and the Dash 7 Srs 300 ith the fuselage stretched to increase the maximum seating to about 70. oduction, however, ended in December 1988 after the 111th customer elivery.

ERVICE USE

anadian certification of the Dash 7 was obtained (to FAR Pt 25 standards) on May 1977, based on the flight test and development of the two prototypes. 1e first production aircraft flew on 30 May 1977 and the second production rcraft entered service with Rocky Mountain Airways in the USA on 3 February 978. Srs 150 aircraft became available for commercial use in 1986, after the st Dash 7IR had been completed for the Canadian Department of the nvironment. At 1 January 2001, 65 Dash 7s remained in service.

Douglas DC-3

SPECIFICATION
(Douglas DC-3)
Dimensions: Wingspan 28.96m (95ft 0in); length overall 19.66m (64ft 6in); height overall 5.16m (16ft 11½in), wing area 91.69m² (987ft²).
Power Plant: Two 895kW (1,200shp) Pratt & Whitney R-1830-92 Twin Wasp air-cooled radial piston engines with Hamilton Standard Hydromatic three-bla constant-speed feathering propellers.
Weights: Operating weight empty 8,030kg (17,720lb); max take-off 11,430kg (25,200lb); max payload 2,994kg (6,600lb).
Performance: Max cruising speed 187kts (346km/h); initial rate of climb 5.4m/s (1,070ft/min); service ceiling 6,675m (21,900ft); range with max payload 305nm (563km).
Accommodation: Flight crew of two. Seating for up to 32 passengers, four-abreast with central aisle. Baggage compartment volume 3.48m³ (123ft³).

A product of the 1930s, the DC-3 soldiers on with an unequalled record world-wide service to airlines and military operators over more than half century. Evolution of this ubiquitous twin began in 1932, primarily to meet TWA requirement for an aircraft to compete with the Boeing 247 that had new entered service with United Air Lines. Responding to that requirement, Dougl – under the guiding influence of the company's founder, Donald Douglas, Snr produced the DC-1, a twin-engined low-wing monoplane of simil configuration to the Boeing 247, with a retractable landing gear and a numb of 'state-of-the-art' technical innovations. First flown on 1 July 1933, the DC entered production in slightly developed form as the DC-2, which first flew o 11 May 1934. TWA's successful operation of DC-2s led American Airlines to a

Below: This South Coast Airways DC-3C, now flown on sightseeing and corporate hospitality flights, started life in July 1943 with the USAAF.

*bove: With its large picture windows, the DC-3 proved popular on
awaiian inter-island routes.*

ouglas to produce a further improved and somewhat enlarged version, which
merged as the DC-3 (or DST, for Douglas Sleeper Transport) to fly on 17
ecember 1935 – the 27th anniversary of the Wright brothers' first successful
owered flight in 1908. Compared with the DC-2, the DC-3 had a wider
selage, larger wing and tail areas, and increased power and weights. It was
tended to seat 24 passengers or carry 16 sleeping berths – hence the DST
pellation. Up to the time that the USA became involved in World War II some
0 examples of the DC-3 had been built for civil use, including almost 100 for
port; after the war ended in 1945, another 28 were delivered to the
mmercial market. Wartime requirements, however, saw the production of ▶

Modern Commercial Aircraft

about 10,200 of the Douglas twin-engined transports for military use – most under the USAAF designation C-47 Skytrain or the RAF name Dakota. Post-war substantial numbers of these ex-military machines reached the airlines, often being known as C-47s or Dakotas rather than DC-3s. Indeed, in the period from 1945 to the mid-1960s, these aircraft became the true workhorses of the world's airline industry, and few companies operating in that period did not have at least one example in the fleet at some time, while not a few built their business exclusively on the revenues generated by a Dakota or two.

VARIANTS

Initial production versions of the DC-3 were powered by 686kW (920hp) Wright GR-1820-G5 Cyclone engines, but 746kW (1,000hp) Pratt & Whitney R-18 Twin Wasps were soon offered as alternatives in the DST-A and DC-3A, while 820kW (1,100hp) Wright Cyclone G-102s distinguished the DC-3B. Production for and use by the military accounted for numerous other variants (and several different USAAF and USN designations, including C-53, C-117 and R4D). After World War II several schemes were developed, by Douglas and other

mpanies, to improve the performance and standard of passenger comfort. is led to the appearance of some modified airframes in Super DC-3 guise. veral other schemes have involved the replacement of the original piston gines with turboprops of various types, including one three-engined variant. the Soviet Union, the DC-3 was built under a pre-war licensing agreement, th the designation Lisunov Li-2; these had Shvetsov M-62R or M-36R gines and numerous differences from the US version.

RVICE USE

e DC-3 obtained its first civil airworthiness certificate on 21 May 1936 and tered service with American Airlines on 25 June 1936. From total production cluding Soviet versions) of 10,926, several thousand have seen airline use ce 1945. Numbers are now declining steadily but some 300 were still in tive service, primarily in Latin America, in 2001.

low: The UK has always been a major user of the DC-3. Air Atlantique ill has some in service on charter and aerial survey work.

Douglas DC-4

SPECIFICATION
(Douglas DC-4-1009)
Dimensions: Wingspan 35.81m (117ft 6in); length 28.60m (93ft 10in); heig
overall 8.38m (27ft 6in); wing area 135.6m² (1,460ft²).
Power Plant: Four 1,200hp Pratt & Whitney R-2000 Twin Wasp radial engin
Weights: Operating weight empty 19,641kg (43,300lb); max take-off 33,113
(73,000lb); max landing 28,800kg (63,492lb).
Performance: Max cruising speed 244kts (451km/h); service ceiling 5,79C
(19,000ft); range with typical payload 1,897nm (3,510km).
Accommodation: Flight crew of three. Single-aisle cabin layout, seati
typically 44 passengers.

In 1935, shortly before the DC-3 entered service, five US airlines produced
specification for a larger and more advanced model with the US airlin
Douglas' response was the DC-4E (four-engined experimental), a four-engin
pressurised aircraft with a 50-seat capacity, which first flew on 21 July 193
However, the many changes required by the airlines, together with t
deteriorating international situation, forced Douglas to scale back its ideas
produce a lighter and simpler unpressurised version, but still retaini
intercontinental range. The definitive DC-4 first flew on 14 February 1942, a
was to be produced as the DC-4A, but the USAAF hi-jacked the project. By t
end of the war, a total of more than 1,000 C-54s, as the military transp

rsion was known, were built. The DC-4 as originally conceived had a design oss weight of 22,680kg (50,000lb) and could carry 40 passengers by day and 8 at night. It was originally offered with a choice of power plants, but airlines entually settled and ordered the type with 1,450hp Pratt & Whitney R-2000 asp 14-cylinder radial engines. Four auxiliary fuel tanks were incorporated in e C-54 Skymaster to enable the US forces to undertake trans-Atlantic and ans-Pacific flights. When the war ended, Douglas offered two new DC-4s to mmercial customers, incorporating all improvements progressively roduced in the C-54 series. The DC-4-1009 had no cargo door, but provided commodation for 44 passengers, and 22 at night when used as a sleeper nsport. Cabin pressurisation was available. The DC-4-1037 cargo transport tained the large cargo door of the C-54. With the availability of large surplus litary machines, large numbers of which found their way into commercial rvice, production of the DC-4-1009 ceased in 1947 after only 79 had been oduced. In the late 1950s, UK company Aviation Traders, designed a car eighter conversion, which first flew on 21 June 1961. The ATL.98 Carvair had entirely new forward fuselage with a hydraulically-operated sideways-ening nose door, to permit the loading of five cars, and an elevated flight ck. None of these remain in active service, but many C-54/DC-4s are still erated as freighters, firefighters and tanker aircraft.

low: The DC-4 has found a niche in the Bolivian freight market.

Douglas DC-6 and DC-7

SPECIFICATION
(Douglas DC-6B)
Dimensions: Wingspan 35.81m (117ft 6in); length overall 32.18m (105ft 7in);
height overall 8.92m (29ft 3in), wing area 135.9m² (1,463ft²).
Power Plant: Four 1,864kW (2,500hp) Pratt & Whitney R-2800-CB17 Double
Wasp 18-cylinder air-cooled radial piston engines, with Hamilton Standard
Hydromatic three-blade constant-speed and feathering propellers.
Weights: Operating weight empty 28,123kg (62,000lb); max take-off 48,534kg
(107,000lb); max landing 40,000kg (88,200lb); max payload 11,143kg (24,565lb).
Performance: Max cruising speed 275kts 509(km/h); initial rate of climb
6.2m/s (1,120ft/min); take-off field length 1,875m (6,150ft); landing field length
1,525m (5,000ft); range with max payload 1,650nm (3,058km).
Accommodation: Flight crew of four. Seating for up to 102 passengers. Total
baggage volume 25.1m³ (886.0ft³).

Prevented by wartime exigencies from exploiting fully the commercial
potential of its first four-engined airliner, the DC-4, Douglas embarked in the
early 1940s upon the design of an enlarged successor to the DC-4. Future
military needs, as well as prospective airline demand, were kept in mind as the
DC-6 took shape, and prototype construction was in fact launched on the basis
of a USAAF contract for a single example designated XC-112. Using
substantially the same wing as the DC-4, the DC-6, as the type became known
in civil guise, had a fuselage lengthened by 2.06m (81in) to increase the basic
passenger capacity to 52. The fuselage was pressurised, and more powerful
engines and improved systems were introduced. The XC-112 first flew on
February 1946. Orders from American Airlines and United Airlines established
the DC-6 in production, however, as the Douglas company's first significant
post-war commercial aircraft, a total of 174 being built by 1951. Subsequent

*Below: Greenlandair operated two Douglas DC-6A/B on charter flights,
mainly to Scandinavia and nearby Canada.*

*bove: The Douglas DC-7 added trans-Atlantic capability to the famous
'C' piston-engined range of airliners.*

olution of the type brought a further lengthening of the fuselage to produce
e all-cargo DC-6A (74 built) and passenger-carrying DC-6B (288 built). When
other redesign of the fuselage was undertaken, coupled with the introduction
Wright R-3350 Cyclone engines in place of the DC-6B's Pratt & Whitney
uble Wasps, the designation was changed to DC-7. The wing of the DC-4
mained little changed in the DC-7 and DC-7B until the DC-7C emerged in
ecember 1955, with wing-root extensions adding 3.05m (10ft) to the span.
oduction of all DC-7 variants totalled 336 and brought the piston-engined era
the 'Douglas Commercial' series to an end. Deliveries of the DC-6 began in
ovember 1946 with the first service flown on 27 April 1947. The DC-6 became
dely used on US trunk routes, while the DC-7 added trans-Atlantic capability.
veral DC-6s survive as freighters, fire-fighting and tanker aircraft.

Embraer EMB-110 Bandeirante

SPECIFICATION
(Embraer EMB-110P2/41 Bandeirante)
Dimensions: Wingspan 15.32m (50ft 3in); length overall 15.10m (49ft 6½in); height overall 4.92m (16ft 2in), wing area 29.1m² (313.2ft²).
Power Plant: Two 559kW (750shp) Pratt & Whitney Canada PT6A-34turboprops with Hartzell three-blade reversible-pitch autofeathering metal propellers.
Weights: Operating weight empty 3,833kg (8,450lb); max take-off 5,900kg (13,007lb); max landing 5,700kg (12,566lb); max payload 1,561kg (3,443lb).
Performance: Max cruising speed 248kts (459km/h); max rate of climb 9.4m (1,787ft/min); service ceiling 6,860m (22,500ft); take-off field length 431m (1,414ft); landing field length 565m (1,854ft); range with typical payload 1,060nm (1,964km).
Accommodation: Two pilots and seating for 19 passengers, two-abreast with single aisle. Total cargo/baggage volume front and rear 2.0m³ (70.6ft³).

The EMB-110 Bandeirante (pioneer) has played a key role in the success foundation of a Brazilian aircraft industry of international status and t development of regional air services in this huge country. Development of t

andeirante began in the late 1960s at the Institute of Research and evelopment under the direction of French engineer Max Holste, and to meet specific requirement of the Brazilian air force for a multi-role transport/trainer. nree prototypes were built by the IRD, making their first flights on 26 October 968, 19 October 1969 and 26 June 1970 respectively, these aircraft being ightly smaller than the later production type and having circular 'port hole' type windows and PT6A-20 engines. To handle production of the aircraft, primarily or the Brazilian air force in the first instance, Embraer (Empresa Brasilièra de eronáutica SA) was founded in August 1969, and from the new facilities set o near São Paulo, the first production Bandeirante flew on 9 August 1972 with T6A-27 engines, slightly lengthened fuselage with 'square' windows and edesigned nacelles. A domestic requirement for a version of the Bandeirante pidly emerged, and Embraer set about meeting this need as soon as the initial emands of the air force had been met. This gave the company, which was still ▶

elow: Although the Bandeirante was developed specifically to open up he interior of Brazil, it has seen prolific use in the UK, including xtensive night postal service for the Royal Mail; shown here is an nproved EMB-110P1A.

a largely unknown quantity outside Brazil, an opportunity to build up it experience of civil operations and the confidence subsequently to launch int the export business, in which it has enjoyed substantial success.

VARIANTS

After production of the EMB-110, EMB-110A and EMB-110B versions for th Brazilian Air Force, the first version of the Bandeirante intended specifically fc commercial use, as a 15-passenger feeder-liner operated by Brazilian third-leve airlines, was the EMB-110C. It was followed by the EMB-110P, developed mor specifically for export markets, with PT6A-27 engines and accommodation fc up to 18 passengers; the maximum weight of this version was 5,600k (12,345lb). After a lengthened version of the Bandeirante had been develope for military use as a cargo carrier (the EMB-110K1) with a 0.85m (2ft 9 1/2i fuselage plug and upward-opening freight-loading door aft of the wing, th same longer fuselage was adopted for the EMB-110P1 and EMB-120F commercial versions, the former being for mixed or all-cargo operations wit the same door as the K1 and quick-change facilities, and the latter being dedicated airliner with up to 21 seats. The EMB-110P2, which became th major civil variant, first flew on 3 May 1977, and in 1981 was joined by the EMI 110P2/41, which was certificated at a maximum take-off weight of 5,900k (13,010lb), an increase of 230kg (510lb), in accordance with the provisions c the US SFAR Pt 41 regulations. The EMB-110P1/41 was the equivalent quic change version. In 1983, after 438 Bandeirantes had been delivered, a series c changes was introduced to improve passenger comfort and handling; the mos obvious external change concerned the tailplane which acquired 10 degrees c

hedral. The commercial versions previously described, but with these new features, were then designated EMB-110PA, EMB-110P2 and EMB-110P2A-41. The designation EMB-110E(J) applied to a seven-seat corporate transport version of the Bandeirante, and the EMB-110S1 was a geophysical survey version, with provision for wing-tip tanks similar to those developed for the EMB-111, a maritime patrol version. Embraer projected in the early 1980s a pressurised version of the Bandeirante, the EMB-110P3, but it was discontinued before a prototype had flown.

SERVICE USE

The original EMB-110 military transport version was certificated to FAR Pt 23 standards, providing a basis for the subsequent approval of individual variants. The civil EMB-110C entered airline service on 16 April 1973, with Transbrasil, and the EMB-110P entered service with TABA, also in Brazil, early in 1976. The first EMB-110P1/41 was delivered to Provincetown-Boston Airlines in the USA during the spring of 1981, and this operator was also the first to receive the EMB-110P1A variant, in December 1983. When production ended in 1995, a total of 494 aircraft had been built, with the last being delivered to the Brazilian Air Force. At 1 January 2001, some 200 Bandeirantes remained in active service.

Below: Based on the outskirts of Paris, Aigle Azur was one of the many French third-level airlines which found the 18-seat aircraft comfortable and economical to operate. This EMB-110P1 was operates cross-Channel from Rouen to London.

Embraer EMB-120 Brasilia

SPECIFICATION
(Embraer EMB-120ER Advanced)

Dimensions: Wingspan 19.78m (64ft 10¾in); length overall 20.00m (65ft 7½in); height overall 6.35m (20ft 10in), wing area 39.43m² (424.4ft²).

Power Plant: Two 1,342kW (1,800shp) Pratt & Whitney Canada PW118 or PW118A turboprops with Hamilton Standard four-blade reversible-pitch fully-feathering propellers with aluminium spars and glassfibre blades.

Weights: Operating weight empty 7,580kg (16,711lb); max take-off 11,990kg (26,433lb); max landing 11,700kg (25,794lb); max payload 3,320kg (7,319lb).

Performance: Max cruising speed 298kts (552km/h); max rate of climb 10.2m/s (2,000ft/min); service ceiling 9,145m (30,000ft); take-off field length 1,560m (5,118ft); landing field length 1,380m (4,528ft); range with typical payload 800nm (1,480km).

Accommodation: Two pilots and seating for up to 30 passengers, three-abreast with single aisle. Total baggage volume in rear compartment 6.4m³ (226ft³).

Very soon after the Bandeirante had been established in production by the newly-founded Embraer organization at Sao José dos Campos near Sao Paulo, a series of related projects was drawn up under EMB-12X designation. These grew out of a wish to produce a pressurised version of the Bandeirante and the three projects shared a common fuselage diameter with different lengths; the smallest was the EMB-121 Xingu, which made use of the Bandeirante's wing (with slightly reduced span) and was intended as a business

ansport. Production of the Xingu eventually proceeded (about 100 being built), ut neither the EMB-120 Araguaia nor the EMB-123 Tapajos were developed in e form projected in 1975, with 20 and 10 seats respectively, a 'Xingu- ameter' fuselage and a new supercritical wing with tip tanks. The concept of pressurised regional airliner somewhat larger than the Bandeirante continued interest the Brazilian design team, however, and by 1979 market surveys had onvinced the company that its next step should be to develop a regional rliner in the 30-seat category. Development was launched officially in eptember 1979. The EMB-120 designation was retained for the new project, hich was named Brasilia in due course, and which retained the same overall onfiguration as the earlier Araguaia: it was thus a twin-engined low-wing onoplane with a circular-section fuselage and a T-tail. To power the Brasilia, mbraer turned once again to Pratt & Whitney in Canada, selecting that ompany's new turboprop that was then being developed as the PT7A-1 and ould enter production as the PW100 series. In the 1,119kW (1,500shp) ersion originally selected for the Brasilia, this engine was designated PW115 nd began flight tests on 27 February 1982 in the nose of Pratt & Whitney's ckers Viscount test-bed in a representative Brasilia nacelle. Metal was cut for e first aircraft on 6 May 1981. Six airframes were put in hand for the evelopment, test and certification of the Brasilia: of these, three were the ▶

elow: Pantanal Linhas Aereas is one of several Brazilian regional airlines *o operate the 30-seat Embraer Brasilia, alongside the smaller* *andeirante aircraft.*

flying prototypes. First flights were made by these three aircraft on 27 Ju 1983, 21 December 1983 and 9 May 1984.

VARIANTS

Initial production models of the basic EMB-120 had 1.118kW (1,500shp) PW11 engines and a maximum take-off weight of 10,800kg (23,810lb), replaced at a early stage with higher output PW115s of 1,193kW (1,600shp). The mor powerful 1,342kW (1,800shp) PW118 was introduced in 1986 in the EMB 120RT (Reduced Take-off) to provide better field performance at a high 11,500kg (25,353lb) weight, and this variant was also available from later the year in hot-and-high specification with PW118As. Since 1994, the standar production version is the EMB-120ER Advanced, previously referred to as EM 120X. In addition to increased range through higher T-O weight, the ER als incorporates aerodynamic improvements, including new leading-edges for flying surfaces, and re-designed cockpit and cabin features to increase comfo levels. The Brasilia has also been produced in all-cargo, Combi and QC (Quic Change) versions; and the Brazilian Air Force has ordered two militar derivatives, the EMB-120SA for airborne early warning (AEW) and EMB-120P for remote sensing. Also operated is the VC-97 VIP transport. An EMB-120 maritime surveillance or ASW version is being proposed.

SERVICE USE

The Brasilia was certificated by the Brazilian CTA on 16 May 1985, followed b FAA approval (to FAR Pt 25) on July 9. British certification was confirmed in Ap 1986. The second prototype was the subject of a formal handover to the fir customer, Atlantic Southeast Airlines of Atlanta, Georgia, on 1 June 198

Below: InterBrasil Star received the 300th Brasilia in September 1995. It operates three EMB-120ER versions in a quick-change (cargo–passengers) configuration.

Above: Although most operate in the Americas, several airlines in Europe have chosen the Brasilia over local aircraft.

ring the Paris air show, but this was for crew training purposes only and e first production aircraft for ASA went into service in October. Two early-andard aircraft were delivered to DLT in Germany in the same month, and 1986 the first 18-seat corporate version of the Brasilia was handed over United Technologies Corporation. The first EMB-120QC was handed over Total Linhas Aéreas of Brazil on 14 May 1993, while the first two oduction EMB-120ER went to Great Lakes Aviation in December 1994. At January 1998, the Brasilia had logged 331 orders, of which 330 had been livered. Since the inroduction of the new ERJ-135 regional jet of similar e, orders for the Brasilia have slowed dramatically. At 1 January 2001, the der book stood at 351 aircraft, with around 245 remaining in commercial rvice.

Embraer ERJ-135/140/145

SPECIFICATION
(Embraer RJ 145ER)

Dimensions: Wingspan 20.04m (65ft 9in); length overall 29.87 m (98ft 0in); height overall 6.75m (22ft 1¾in), wing area 51.18m² (550.9ft²).

Power Plant: Two 31.3kN (7,040lb) Rolls-Royce Allison AE 3007A turbofans with FADEC.

Weights: Operating weight empty 11,585kg (25,540lb); max take-off 20,600k (45,415lb); max landing 18,700kg (41,226lb); max payload 5,515kg (12,158lb).

Performance: Max cruising speed 410kts (760km/h); max rate of climb 12.1m/s (2,380ft/min); service ceiling 11,275m (37,000ft); take-off field length 1,500m (4,925ft); landing field length 1,290m (4,235ft); range with max payload 1,200nm (2,222km).

Accommodation: Flight crew of two. Seating for 50 passengers, three-abreast with single aisle. Total baggage volume 14.75m³ (520.9ft³).

Having established its position in the commuter market with the Bandeiran and Brasilia, Embraer studied a number of projects to enable it to keep foothold in the market by introducing a new type at the appropriate time. A jo development with Shorts, agreed in May 1984, was stillborn, but the CBA-1: of 1986, which involved Fabrica Militar de Aviones (FMA) of Argentina wen great deal further. Using a new supercritical wing, the design was unusual having two pusher turboprops located high on the rear fuselage. First flight w planned for March 1990. However, the general clamour for jet aircr persuaded Embraer to change direction. Original development plans for a tw jet regional aircraft were revealed at the Paris air show on 12 June 1989, whi showed a low-risk 50-seat Brasilia development with wing-mounted turbof

Top: Embraer ERJ-135 on its first flight.

Above: The Legacy is a corporate version of the ERJ-135.

Below: British Regional Airlines operates a growing fleet of ERJ-145s on behalf of British Airways.

engines, but the programme was put in abeyance by company cutbacks Autumn 1990. The following years were spent on a substantial re-design of t wing, landing gear and engine installation, with the latter moved to the rear the fuselage in October 1991. Extensive wind-tunnel testing confirmed, and some cases exceeded, performance predictions, and the first metal for the 145, later ERJ-145, was cut in September 1993. Assembly of the prototy began in October 1994, and this made its first flight on 11 August 1995, ahe of the official roll-out. Three pre-series aircraft were flown on 17 Novemb 1995 and on 14 February and 2 April 1996. The ERJ-145 programme is bei financed by Embraer (34 per cent); four major risk sharing partners comprisi C&D Interiors (USA), Enaer (Chile) Gamesa (Spain) and Sonaca (Belgium); sor 70 risk-sharing suppliers (10 per cent); and Brazilian development fundi institutions (23 per cent).

VARIANTS

Basic initial production version is the RJ 145, which was certificated in 1996 the Brazilian DCA to FAR/JAR 25, FAR Pt.36, ICAO Annex 16 and FAR Pt.1 FAA certification followed in December 1996 and the European type appro was given by the JAA on 15 May 1997. The ERJ-145 is also available as extended-range ERJ-145ER, the longer-range ERJ-145LR, which introduc uprated Rolls-Royce Allison FADEC-equipped AE 3007A1 turbofans a additional fuel to carry a full payload over a distance of 1,640nm (3,037km), extra long-range ERJ-145XR, and the ERJ-145EU customised for Europe operations. On 16 September 1997, Embraer launched the 35-seat ERJ-13 which shares some 90% commonality with the ERJ-145, but has a fusela shortened by 3.53m (11ft 7in). It first flew on 4 July 1998 and received F certification on 16 July 1999. The ERJ-135 is also available in a long-range EF 135LR variant, and as the Legacy corporate aircraft. The 44-seat ERJ-14 which fits between the other two types, was launched on 30 September 19 It made its first flight on 27 June 2000 and was expected to obtain its ty certificate in February 2001. Military multi-mission variants of the ERJ-145 the EMB-145 AEW&C, and EMB-145RS (remote sensing), while an EM 145AGS (airborne ground sensor) version is under consideration.

ove: Continental Express is the largest customer for the ERJ-145.

RVICE USE

liveries of the ERJ-145 began on 19 December 1996 to launch customer ntinental Express, with the first European deliveries to Regional Airlines and rtugalia in May 1997. Continental Express also took delivery of the first ERJ- 5 on 23 July 1999. At 1 January 2001, the firm order book stood at 152 ERJ- 5s, 129 ERJ-140s, and 543 ERJ-140s.

Left: This ERJ145 entered service with Portugalia in June 1997 and achieves a daily utilisation of seven hours. Portugalia was one of the very first European customers for this particular aircraft.

Embraer ERJ-170/190

SPECIFICATION (provisional)
(Embraer ERJ-170)
Dimensions: Wingspan 26.00m (85ft 3¾in); length 29.90m (98ft 1¼in); heig
overall 9.67m (31ft 8¾in).
Power Plant: Two 62.28kN (14,000lb) thrust General Electric CF34-
turbofans with FADEC.
Weights: Operating weight empty 20,150kg (44,423lb); max take-off 35,45(
(78,153lb); max landing 32,450kg (71,540lb); max payload 9,100kg (20,062lb
Performance: Max cruising speed 470kts (870km/h); take-off field len
1,676m (5,500ft); landing field length 1,219m (4,000ft); range with typ
payload 1,800nm (3,334km).
Accommodation: Flight crew of two. Max seating for 70 passengers.

In February 1999, Embraer announced the pre-launch of a new and lar
family of regional jets, the ERJ-170 and ERJ-190 models, receiving its f
order on 14 June 1999 from Crossair and Regional Airlines. The des
specification called for low weight, simplicity, high reliability and economy
maintenance. The programme's joint definition phase (JDF) was concluded
April 2000, which resulted in a basic operating weight increase of 1,50(
(3,307lb), enlargement of the rear passenger door to speed loading a
unloading, and a reinforced cargo floor. A noticeable external change to
ERJ-170 was the addition of winglets, which will enhance the aircra

erating characteristics. First metal was cut on 14 July 2000, for a ojected first flight of the ERJ-170 in late 2001, with certification in ecember 2002. Certification for the ERJ-190 will follow in June 2004. The w family will be built under a risk-share programme, which involves many ternational companies in addition to Embraer. Unlike the smaller Embraer ts, the new family has podded wing-mounted turbofan engines and a mple clean tail. 70-seat ERJ-170 will be powered by twin 62.68kN 4,000lb) General Electric CF34-8E turbofans, while the 90-seat ERJ-190 ll have 82.29kN (18,500lb) CF34-8e-10 turbofans. Both engine types are quipped with FADEC. The ERJ-170 will be available in a standard baseline rsion, a long-range variant to be designated ERJ-170LR, and a corporate odel with additional fuel tanks in the baggage area to extend its range to ore than 4,000nm (7,408km). The longer ERJ-190-100 has a fuselage retch of 6.25m (20ft 6in) to accommodate 98 passengers, a wing span crease of 2.74m (8ft 113/4in), and a strengthened landing gear. A further retch of 2.44m (8ft 0in) to accommodate 108 passengers produces the RJ-190-200. Both ERJ-190 will be offered in baseline and long-range LR rsions. At 1 January 2001, Embraer had firm orders for 90 ERJ-170s and r 30 ERJ-190s.

elow: The ERJ-170 is the smallest of the new Embraer regional jet mily

Fairchild (Swearingen) Metro/Merlin

SPECIFICATION
(Fairchild Metro 23)
Dimensions: Wingspan 17.37m (57ft 0in); length overall 18.10m (59ft 5in) height overall 5.08m (16ft 8in), wing area 28.71m² (309ft²).
Power Plant: Two 776kW (1,000shp) AlliedSignal TPE331-11U-612G turboprops with McCauley four-blade reversible-pitch fully-feathering met propellers.
Weights: Operating weight empty 4,300kg (9,480lb); max take-off 7,484k (16,500lb); max landing 7,110kg (15,675lb); max payload 2,277kg (5,020lb)
Performance: Max cruising speed 290kts (537km/h); max rate of climb 13.7m/s (2,700ft/min); service ceiling 7,620m (25,000ft); take-off field length 1,341m (4,400ft); landing field length 1,273m (4,175ft); range with typical payload 540nm (1,000km).
Accommodation: One or two pilots and seating for up to 20 passengers, two-abreast with single aisle. Total cargo/baggage volume front and rear 5.05m³ (178.5ft³).

The Metro has its origins with the company formed by E Swearingen, which used the Beechcraft Queen Air as the basis of family of business aircraft known as the Merlin I, II and IIB. E continuous refinement and development, Swearingen eventual replaced all major components of the Queen Air to produce the Metr a 19-seat commuter transport, with a parallel version for the corpora market known as the Merlin III. The Metro first flew on 26 August 196 and production was well under way by the time the Swearing company was taken over in November 1971, by the Fairchild Industrie Corporation. As Fairchild Swearingen, the company continued

oduce the Metro at its San Antonio plant, and to develop new variants.
ıe Swearingen name was later dropped, the Texas branch of Fairchild
dustries then becoming the Fairchild Aircraft Corporation.

ARIANTS

ıe original SA-226TC Metro was followed in 1974 by the Metro II, which
troduced some internal changes, 'square' cabin windows and the
ptional installation of a small rocket unit in the tail to improve take-off
erformance in hot-and-high conditions as encountered in many areas
here the Metro was likely to operate. Like the initial model, the Metro II
as restricted to a gross weight of 5,670kg (12,500lb) to comply with US
egulations for commuter airliners. When this restriction was lifted, by
pecial Federal Aviation Regulation (SFAR) 41, Fairchild introduced in 1980
ıe Metro IIA at a gross weight of 5,941kg (13,100lb), and followed this
ith further improvements in the SA-227AC Metro III at 6,350kg
4,000lb). Structural changes and uprated engines made the increased
perating weights possible, and the standard aircraft was subsequently
pproved for 6,577kg (14,500lb), with an option at 7,257kg (16,000lb).
ther changes distinguishing the Metro III from the Metro II included an
xtension of 3.05m (10ft) in wing span, with conical cambered wing tips to
educe drag; new landing gear doors; more streamlined nacelle cowlings;
ıd Dowty Rotol four-blade propellers. Large loading doors in the rear ▶

*elow: The Fairchild Metro III was first introduced into service 1980 but
emains in service in large numbers, providing feeder services to the
rge airport hubs. The particular aircraft depicted was flown by Mesaba
irlines, operating as a feeder carrier, for Northwest Airlink.*

fuselage, a reinforced cabin floor, reduced empty weight and the hig weight option allow an all-cargo version of the Metro, known as th Expediter, to carry a cargo payload of 2,268kg (5,000lb). For operato wishing to standardise on the Pratt & Whitney PT6A engine, Fairchi developed the Metro IIIA with 746kW (1,000shp) PT6A-45Rs, first flow on 31 December 1981. Current production model is the high-gross weig Metro 23, certificated in June 1990 to FAR Pt 23 commuter categor which incorporates many of the improvements of the C-26A and C-26 transport versions built for the US National Guard, and is also available a the Expediter 23, which has a rear cargo door and a payload of 2,495k

Below: The sale of the Metro 23 to China's Hainan Airlines was a considerable scoop for Fairchild, having sold only a handful in the Far East. Hainan Airlines utilises the aircraft on services within the large island of Hainan.

,500lb). It replaced the Expediter I from 1991. Each Metro variant was accompanied by respective Merlin corporate versions, and a number of special missions aircraft. Studies were undertaken into a Tall Cabin Metro with a 'stand-up' cabin.

SERVICE USE

The Metro entered service in early 1971, the first major commuter airline operator being Air Wisconsin. The Metro III was certificated to SFAR 41 standard (the first to be so approved by the FAA) on 23 June 1980. First customer was Crossair, which put the type into service in spring 1981, and the Expediter was first operated by SAT-Air on behalf of United Parcel Service. The Metro 23 began commercial operations in 1991. Production of the Metro/Merlin series was discontinued in 1999 after the receipt of more than 1,000 orders. All but a handful had been delivered by 1 January 2001.

Fairchild Dornier 228

SPECIFICATION
(Dornier 228-212)
Dimensions: Wingspan 16.97m (55ft 8in); length overall 16.56m (54ft 4in); height overall 4.86m (15ft 11½in), wing area 32.00m² (344.3ft²).
Power Plant: Two 579kW (776shp) AlliedSignal TPE331-5-252D or TPE331-10 turboprops with Hartzell four-blade reversible-pitch fully-feathering metal propellers.
Weights: Operating weight empty 3,739kg (8,243lb); max take-off 6,400kg (14,110lb); max landing 6,100kg (13,448lb); max payload 2,201kg (4,852lb).
Performance: Max cruising speed 223kts (413km/h); max rate of climb 9.5m/ (1,870ft/min); service ceiling 8,535m (28,000ft); take-off field length 671m (2,200ft); landing field length 450m (1,480ft); range with typical payload 560nn (1,038km). **Accommodation:** One or two pilots and seating for up to 19 passengers, two-abreast with single aisle. Total baggage volume front and rea 3.49m³ (123.2ft³).

Development of the Dornier 228 began with the work the company undertook under a government-funded research contract, to evolve a 'new technolog wing' (*Tragflügels Neuer Technologie*, or TNT). An example of this wing, featurin the Do A-5 supercritical section and unusual planform with raked tips, flew for th first time on a converted Do 28D-2 Skyservant on 14 June 1979. Associated wit the TNT wing was a new power plant installation, two Garrett TPE331-5 turboprop in conventional wing nacelles replacing the Skyservant's sponson-mounted pisto engines. To take full advantage of the performance and economic gains possib with the TNT, Dornier designed a new fuselage to provide an aircraft able to fulfil range of missions, among which commuter passenger operations were to be th most important. Although some of the structural philosophy of the Skyservant wa retained, the aircraft was completely new, a fact that the original designation (D

Below: The success of the 228-200 with Air Guadeloupe has encouraged the airline to increase its fleet to seven of the type, which fly its main schedules to points in the Leeward Islands and Cayenne.

ove: Fairchild Dornier 228 in service on border patrols.

:) did little to emphasize. In 1989, Dornier redesignated its range of light
nsport aircraft and the new type, then still underdevelopment, became the
rnier 228. Two versions, with different fuselage lengths, had already been
posed as the Do 28E-1 and do 28E-2: to carry 15 or 19 passengers respectively,
se became the Dornier 228-100 and 228-200, and work on the pair proceeded in
allel. The new fuselage, in the shorter of its two forms, was some 3.5m (12ft)
ger than that of the Dornier 128-2 (as the Do 28D-2 had meanwhile become),
ilst the 228-200's fuselage was 1.52m (5ft) longer than that of the 228-100. The
totypes made their first flights on 28 March and 9 May 1981 respectively. On 29
vember 1983, Dornier concluded a licence agreement with Hindustan
ronautics Ltd providing for the construction of up to 150 Dornier 228s in India to
et local military and commercial requirements, and the first aircraft assembled in
lia (using components supplied by Dornier) was flown at Kanpur on 31 January
36.

ARIANTS

e Dornier 228-100 and 228-200 differ from each other in fuselage length,
oviding 15 and 19 passengers respectively. The Dornier 228-100 has the
me take-off and landing weights as the 228-200, but can carry approximately
6kg (300lb) more payload, and has more than twice the range of the 228-200
th maximum passenger payload. In 1984, Dornier introduced the 228-101 and
8-201, which differed from earlier models in having a reinforced floor and
w mainwheel tyres to permit higher operating weights and greater range.
ailable from Autumn 1987 was the 228-202, designed to offer further ▶

increases in payload/range performance. Current production model is the 228-2
certificated in August 1989, which introduced among several innovations, grea
engine power in the 579kW (776shp) AlliedSignal (Garrett) TPE331-5-252D
TPE331-10 turboprops, stronger landing gear, carbon brakes, two strakes under
rear fuselage to improve short-field performance and new avionics. Dornier 228 a
produced in troop, paratroop, ambulance, cargo, maritime patrol, maritime pollut
surveillance and fisheries patrol and photogrammetry/geological survey versio
Plans to transfer production to Harbin Aircraft Manufacturing Company in China
an effort to restimulate the market appear to have foundered.

SERVICE USE
The Dornier 228-100 was certificated in West Germany, in accordance with F
Pt 23 requirements, on 18 December 1981 and deliveries began in Februa
1982 to the first commercial operator, Norving Flyservice in Norway. The 22
200 was certificated on 6 September 1982. British and US certification w
obtained on 17 April and 11 May 1984 respectively. Deliveries from
Hindustan Aeronautics assembly line at Kanpur began on 22 March 1986, wh
the Indian domestic airline Vayudoot received the first of a batch of five Indi
built examples. Production in Germany has now been discontinued, but it
understood that Hindustan Aeronautics has orders for a few more. Total aircr
ordered at 1 January 2001 from both production lines amounted to 308 aircra
of which 270 had been delivered.

*Right: The Dornier 228's excellent short field performance opened up th
market in many of the islands of the Caribbean and the South Pacific. A
Moorea utilises a Dornier 228 on its inter-island flight services linking
Tahiti's Faa'a International Airport with the Society Islands.*

Fairchild Dornier 328

SPECIFICATION
(Fairchild-Dornier 328-110)
Dimensions: Wingspan 20.98m (68ft 10in); length overall 21.28m (69ft 9¾in
height overall 7.24m (23ft 9in), wing area 40.0m² (430.6ft²).
Power Plant: Two 1,626kW (2,180shp) Pratt & Whitney Canada PW119B
turboprops with Hartzell 6-B composite propellers.
Weights: Operating weight empty 8,920kg (19,665lb); max take-off 13,990k
(30,842 lb); max landing 13,230kg (29,167lb); max payload 3,690kg (8,135lb).
Performance: Max cruising speed 335kts (620km/h); service ceiling 7,620m
(25,000ft); take-off field length 1,090m (3,570ft); landing field length 1,165m
(3,825ft); range with max payload 900nm (1,666km).
Accommodation: Flight crew of two. Seating for 33 passengers, three-
abreast with single aisle. Total baggage volume 6.30m³ (222.5ft³).

In late 1986, the Dornier Board approved development of a 30-seat grow
version of the 228, but a lack of clear market definition halted the programr
until 3 August 1988, when Dornier decided to resume work. The Model 3
was intended to offer comparable performance to its earlier utility aircra
including the capability to operate from short and unprepared landing strip
while offering a stand-up cabin and airline-style comfort with seats wider th
a typical Boeing 727/737 configuration. Noise levels were also pegged at 78c
for 75 per cent of the cabin. Dornier combined the basic TNT supercritical wi
of the 228 with a new enlarged and pressurised circular fuselage, develop
from the Federal Ministry of Research and Technology's NRT (*Neue Rum
Technologien*) programme, and a new-design T-tail. A new flap system w

bove: ScotAirways is the only UK operator of the 328.

ground and flight spoilers was also introduced. Extensive use was made composite materials, including the entire rear fuselage and tail unit, making some 23 per cent of the structural weight. On 28 October 1988, Dornier select the Pratt & Whitney Canada PW119 turboprop to power the new aircraft, wh made its first flight on 6 December 1991, Two more development aircraft flew o June and 20 October 1992, followed by the first production aircraft on 23 Janu 1993. The Dornier 328 obtained 14-country European certification to JAA 25 on October 1993. The 328 is being built in an international risk-sharing partnersh which includes Aermacchi of Italy, Daewoo Heavy Industries of South Korea, a the UK's Westland Aerostructures. Final assembly takes place at Dornier's m plant at Oberpfaffenhofen in southern Germany.

VARIANTS

The initial production 328-100, with a maximum take-off weight of 13,440 (29,630lb), has been replaced by the 328-110, whose improvements are bei progressively incorporated into existing aircraft. External changes a performance enhancements of the 328-110 include enlarged dorsal fin a reconfigured and repositioned ventral fin, an increase in take-off weight 350kg to 13,990kg (30,842lb) and range by 270 nautical miles to 1,000r (1,850km). Further improvements are offered in the 328-120 through improvement performance kit (IPK), with the main elements being increas thermodynamic power of its PW119C engines; greater propeller diamet optional ground spoilers and enlarged dorsal and ventral fins. Take-off fie length is reduced to 800m (2,625ft). For markets where greater capacity required, it was planned to introduce a four-abreast 328-200 for 37- passengers within the existing airframe. These would have been available al in corresponding 328-210 and 328-220 configurations, but has been abandone

Below: This Tyrolean Fairchild Dornier 328 ambulance airliner operates from Innesbruck, Austria. It has a cruising speed of 340 knots and a ran; of 1700 nautical miles. When fully loaded it can carry 4 intensive care o up to 12 non-intensive care patients.

above: A large early order from Alaska Air carrier Horizon Air for 20 aircraft failed to stimulate the market and sales of the 328 have remained low. Improved performance and a reduction in the high acquisition cost have failed to reverse its fortunes.

so studied was a 48-seat 328 Stretch to meet a requirement by 328 launch customer Horizon Air, but this too was abandoned in favour of a jet programme.

SERVICE USE

Swiss regional, Air Engiadina, received the first 328-100 on 21 October 1993, following European JAA certification six days earlier. FAA type approval was granted on 10 November, after which Horizon Air accepted its first aircraft. German LBA and FAA certification of the 328-110 came a year later, on 4 November 1994, followed in May 1995 by the 328-120. First customer for the latter was Formosa Airlines of Taiwan. The first application on any aircraft type of the Lockheed Martin APALS (autonomous precision approach and landing system) – fitted to Lone Star Airlines' four 328-110 – led to Cat I certification at non-precision airports. Although the German production line remains officially open, no new orders were placed in 2000. The total order book at 1 January 2001 stood at 104 aircraft, all of which had been delivered.

Fairchild Dornier 328JET

SPECIFICATION

(Fairchild Dornier 328JET)

Dimensions: Wingspan 20.98m (68ft 10in); length 21.28m (69ft 9¾in); heigh overall 7.24m (23ft 9in); wing area 40.00m² (430.6ft²).

Power Plant: Two 26.9kN (6,050lb) thrust Pratt & Whitney Canada PW306/9 turbofans with FADEC.

Weights: Operating weight empty 9,344kg (20,600lb); max take-off 15,200k (33,510lb); max landing 14,090kg (31,063lb); max payload 3,266kg (7,200lb).

Performance: Max cruising speed 405kts (750km/h); service ceiling 10,670r (35,000ft); take-off field length 1,359m (4,460ft); landing field length 1,291m (4,235ft); range with typical payload 900nm (1,666km).

Accommodation: Flight crew of two. Single-aisle cabin layout, seating typically 32-34 passengers in a two-class configuration. Cargo/baggage volume 6.4m³ (226ft³).

Fairchild Dornier completed the critical design review into a new 32-seat regional jet at the company's German plant at Oberpfaffenhofen in June 1997 and a few days later at the Paris air show announced launch orders for six aircraft from French regional, Proteus Airlines, and four from US company Aspen Mountain Air/Lone Star. The 328JET, which started life as an offshoot of feasibility studies into the stretched 328S, is a derivative of the 328 turboprop aircraft and was the first turbofan aircraft in the new 30-plus seat jet category. It closely resembles the turboprop model, but features the Pratt & Whitney Canada PW306/9 high by-pass ratio turbofan, each generating a static thrust of 26.9kN (6,050lb). The additional fuel required is incorporated in a modified wing structure. The only other structural changes are a 20 per cent increase in the length of the rudder trim tab, to maintain minimum speed, and a strengthened ▶

Below: Wanair Fairchild Dornier 328JET flying over Cook's Bay, Moorea.

undercarriage to handle the heavier weights and landing speeds. Th
Honeywell 36-150(DD) auxiliary power unit, an option on the turboprop, is
standard item on the 328JET. The first 328JET, converted from the secon
328 turboprop aircraft, was rolled out in December 1997, with the first fligh
of the prototype taking place on 20 January 1998. Three further prototype
were built and JAA certification was granted on 8 July 1999 after th
completion of 1,560 hours of flight testing. FAA approval followed on 1
July. Aermacchi of Italy in partnership with OGMA of Portugal build th
fuselage, and other main suppliers are Honeywell (avionics based on th
Primus 2000 suite), and Messier-Dowty (landing gear). Final assembly take
place at Oberpfaffenhofen in Germany.

VARIANTS
The baseline aircraft is the 32-seat 328JET, with a 34-seat high-densit
configuration is referred to as the Corporate Shuttle. Also available is the Envo

executive transport version launched at the 1997 NBAA convention in Dallas, Texas. Typical executive configuration provides 12-14 seats with forward galley and wardrobe, and aft galley and toilet facilities. An optional long-range fuel tank extends the maximum range to 2,000nm (3,704km). Proposed is a an all-cargo variant with a large cargo door in the rear fuselage to permit loading of pallets and containers. A 44-seat 428JET project has been abandoned because of high development cost, compounded by the company's inability to attract risk-sharing partners.

SERVICE USE

US regional airline Skyway Airlines took delivery of the first 328JET in July 1999. At 1 January 2001, the firm order book stood at 149 aircraft, of which 57 had been delivered.

Below: 328JET in Envoy 3 executive configuration.

Fairchild Dornier 528/728/928JET

SPECIFICATION (provisional)
(Fairchild Dornier 728JET)
Dimensions: Wingspan 26.62m (87ft 4in); length 26.52m (87ft 0in); height overall 9.04m (29ft 8in); wing area 75.00m² (807.3ft²).
Power Plant: Two 60.39kN (13,575lb) thrust General Electric CF34-8D3 turbofans.
Weights: Max take-off 34,860kg (76,853lb); max landing 32,40kg (71,473lb); max payload 8,210kg (18,100lb).
Performance: Max cruising speed Mach 0.82; service ceiling 12,495m (41,000ft); take-off field length 1,539m (5,050ft); landing field length 1,420m (4,660ft); range with typical payload 1,800nm (3,333km).
Accommodation: Flight crew of two. Single-aisle cabin layout, seating typically 70 passengers five-abreast. Max high-density seating for 85 passengers. Cargo/baggage volume 25.65m³ (906ft³).

A study into a Lufthansa requirement for a 70-seat aircraft was firs announced at the Dubai Air Show in 1997. Initially designated X28JET, th baseline 728JET that emerged was officially launched at the ILA Berl Aerospace Show on 19 May 1999, on the back of a large commitment from Lufthansa CityLine with 60 firm orders, plus 60 options. The baseline five abreast design with General Electric CF34 turbofan engines was frozen December 1999. It is a conventional low-wing design with a 23o 30 sweepback, with two podded wing-mounted turbofan engines. Flying contro are fly-by-wire. The advanced avionics suite is based around the Honeywe Primus Epic with flat-panel liquid crystal displays. Great emphasis has bee placed on passenger comfort, with a 3.25m (10ft 8in) fuselage cross-sectic

Below: The proposed 928JET will carry up to 110 passengers.

bove: Artist's impression of the Fairchild Dornier 728JET.

nd a full standing heigh of 2.06m (6ft 9in), as well as ample baggage space ɔtalling 25.65m³ (906ft³). The standard 728JET provides flexible seating layouts ɔr 70-85 passengers. It was due to make its first flight in march 2001, with ɛrvice entry expected in May 2002. At the NBAA convention in Las Vegas in ɪctober 1998, Fairchild announced the Envoy 7 corporate version of the 28JET, which offers more range and generous seating for up to 18 assengers. Flight Options ordered 25 Envoy 7s at the Paris Air Show in 1999 ɔr its fractional ownership programme, with deliveries starting in late 2002. ne new family also includes the 85-110 seta 928JETwith a fuselage extended y 4.47m (14ft 8in) and uprated 75.6kN (17,000lb) CF34-10D engines, and the nortened 55-63 seat 528JET with derated engines. The 928JET is due to enter ɛrvice in mid-2003, followed by the 528JET in mid-2004. Proposed corporate nodels for the two types are the Envoy 5 and Envoy 9 models. A possible ırther stretch with a minimum of 110 seats, the 1128JET, is believed under :udy. At 1 January 2001, the 728JET (including the Envoy 7) had won firm ʳders for 138 aircraft, and the 928JET for four.

Fokker F27 Friendship/Fairchild F-27/FH-227

SPECIFICATION
(Fokker F27-500 Friendship)

Dimensions: Wingspan 29.00m (95ft 1¾in); length overall 25.06m (82ft 2¼in), height overall 8.71m (28ft 7¼in), wing area 70.0m² (753.5ft²).

Power Plant: Two 1,648kW (2,210shp) Rolls-Royce Dart Mk 552 turboprops with Dowty Rotol constant-speed four-blade propellers.

Weights: Operating weight empty 12,701kg (28,000lb); max take-off 20,820kg (45,900lb); max landing 19,731kg (43,500lb); max payload 5,896kg (13,000lb).

Performance: Normal cruising speed 259kts (480km/h); max rate of climb 7.5m/s (1,480ft/min); service ceiling 8,990m (29,500ft); take-off field length 988m (3,240ft); landing field length 1,003m (3,290ft); range with typical payload 935nm (1,741km).

Accommodation: Two flight crew and seating for up to 60 passengers, four-abreast with central aisle. Total cargo/baggage volume front and rear 8.41m³ (297ft³).

Europe's best-selling turboprop transport emerged as Fokker's first post-war commercial aircraft, designed at the beginning of the 1950s to provide airlines with a 'DC-3 replacement'. Among several project studies, the P.27 of August 1950 became the basis for further development, taking shape by the end of 1952 as a high-wing monoplane with a pressurised circular-section fuselage, two Rolls-Royce Dart turboprops and accommodation for up to 40 passengers. The full payload range was to be only 260 naut mls (482km), restricting the aircraft to the short-haul market, and attention was given to providing good field performance. With Netherlands government backing, two prototypes of the F27, as the project became known, were launched in 1953 and these made their first flights on 24 November 1955 and 29 January 1957 respectively, the second having a lengthened fuselage to increase basic seating from 32 to 36. Increases in fuel capacity were made later to give the F27 greater operational flexibility. Production of the F27, for which the name Friendship was later adopted, was initiated both by Fokker in the Netherlands and, under licence agreements, by Fairchild in the USA. The first production

Below: The 50-seat Fokker F27 Friendship was in production for nearly 30 years and has served in large numbers in all parts of the world. Some 20 still serve in the United Kingdom, including this Jersey European Airways Mk.500, although now with a new owner.

ove: BAC Express Airlines operates the F27-500 on both passenger and ight contracts.

craft flew at Schiphol, Amsterdam, on 23 March 1958 and at Hagerstown, aryland, USA, on 12 April 1958, and a Fairchild-built example became the st to operate revenue services by the type.

RIANTS

e first Fokker production variant was the F27 Mk 100 with Dart Mk 511 (RDa6) gines, matched by the Fairchild F27. The F27 Mk 200, first flown on 20 otember 1962, and F27A introduced uprated Dart RDa7 engines; associated with ese engines were progressive increases in gross weight. The F27 Mk 300 mbiplane and F27B had RDa6 engines and a side-loading freight door in the ward fuselage for mixed passenger/freight operations. The F27 Mk 400 (and milar F27M Troopship) first flown on 24 April 1965, combined the freight door and ght floor with RDa7 engines, while the Mk 600, flown on 28 November 1968, s similar but lacked the former's special all-metal watertight freight door. The Mk 0 was a true quick-change version, its roller floor enabling rapid reconfiguration of e interior. In addition to the Mk 400 Troopship other military versions were also lt, including a maritime patrol aircraft. All these were suffixed with the letter M. rchild's F27F was an F27A with Dart Mk.529s for corporate users, while the F27J d F27M had Dart Mk 532-7 and Mk 532-7N engines respectively. In all, Fairchild lt 128 of its F27 variants, ending in 1970. Fairchild also developed a stretched- elage variant, the FH-227, with a 1.83m (6ft) plug, and built several subvariants h different weights and Dart ratings. The first FH-227 flew on 27 January 1966 d production totalled 79. Fokker's stretched F27 Mk 500, in the project stage for veral years, flew on 15 November 1967, and remained in production, with the F27 200, through 1986. By the time production of these variants was phased out in our of the Fokker 50, sales of the F27 had totalled 579 from the Dutch production e. The last was delivered in 1987.

RVICE USE

e Fairchild F27 was certificated on 16 July 1958 and entered service on 27 vember 1958 with West Coast Airlines. The first Fokker-built F27 entered service h Aer Lingus in December 1958. The Fairchild F27B was certificated 25 October 58 and first entered service with Northern Consolidated. The F27F was tificated on 24 February 1961, and F27J on 3 August 1965 and the F27M on 12 ne 1969. Production ended in June 1986, at which time a total of 581 aircraft had en completed in the Netherlands, with another 108 in the United States. At uary 2001, some 240 Dutch-built and 50 US-built models remained in mmercial service.

Fokker F28 Fellowship

SPECIFICATION
(Fokker F28-4000 Fellowship)
Dimensions: Wingspan 25.07m (82ft 3in); length overall 29.61m (97ft 1¾in); height overall 8.47m (27ft 9½in), wing area 79.0m² (850ft²).
Power Plant: Two 44kN (9,900lb) Rolls-Royce Spey Mk 555-15P turbofans.
Weights: Operating weight empty 17,645kg (38,900lb); max take-off 33,110 (73,000lb); max landing 31,524kg (69,500lb); max payload 10,478kg (23,100lb
Performance: Max cruising speed 455kts (843km/h); service ceiling 10,675m (35,000ft); take-off field length 1,585m (5,200ft); landing field length 1,065m (3,495ft); range with typical payload 1,025nm (1,900km).
Accommodation: Flight crew of two. Seating for up to 85 passengers, five-abreast with single aisle. Total cargo/baggage volume forward and rear 15.84m³ (559.5ft³).

Plans to develop a short/medium-haul jet transport partner for its F turboprop twin were made by Fokker at the beginning of the 1960s, the fi details of this F28 Fellowship being published in April 1962. Projected to ca about 50 passengers over 1,000 naut mls (1,850km), the F28 was at fi studied with Bristol Siddeley BS.75 engines, but the eventual selection wa

ntened and simplified version of the Rolls-Royce Spey, known at first as the ey Junior. In configuration, the F28 was similar to the BAC One-Eleven and uglas DC-9, with a moderately swept wing, engines mounted on the sides the rear fuselage and a T-tail, but it was smaller than either of those types, hough the basic capacity of the initial version grew to 60 and eventually to . To help establish production of the F28, Fokker concluded risk-sharing reements with several companies, including Shorts in the UK (for the wings), d HFB and VFW (later MBB) in West Germany for fuselage sub-assemblies. ree prototypes of the F28 were built, making their first flights on 9 May, 3 gust and 20 October 1967 respectively, and production went ahead on the sis of a launch order placed by LTU, a German inclusive-tour charter operator, November 1965. The first production F28, the fourth aircraft completed, flew 21 May 1968. ▶

RIANTS
low: Iran's government-owned regional airline Iran Asseman has been erating the twin-jet Fokker F28 since 1981 on government flights and heduled domestic services. It operates the F28-4000, fitted out for 85 ssengers, and the smaller F28-1000 for 65 passengers.

Modern Commercial Aircraft

The initial production version of the F28 became known as the F28 Mk 10[00] after a stretched-fuselage variant was introduced as the F28 Mk 2000 in 197[1]. The Mk 1000 is basically a 65-seater (one-class) aircraft, the gross weight [of] which was initially 28,123kg (62,000lb), but subject to subsequent increase[s]. With a side-loading freight door and provision for mixed passenger/freig[ht] loads, the designation is F28 Mk 1000C. The F28 Mk 2000 has a 2.21m (7ft 3[in]) longer fuselage and seats up to 79 passengers in a one-class arrangement [and] first flew on 28 April 1971. In 1972, Fokker introduced the F28 Mk 5000 (sh[ort] fuselage) and F28 Mk 6000 (long fuselage), whose new features were [an] increase of 1.57m (6ft 11½in) in wing span, with leading-edge slats added, a[nd] improved Spey Mk 555-15H engines with additional noise reduction features[. The] Mk 6000 prototype flew on 27 September 1973, but the take-off performan[ce] bestowed by the flaps proved to be an unwanted luxury for most airlines a[nd] the F28 Mk 3000 (short fuselage) and F28 Mk 4000 (long fuselage) became t[he] preferred versions, with the extra span and new engines, but without the sla[ts.]

erior redesign also took the maximum seating up to 85 in the Mk 4000, ich first flew on 20 October 1976.

RVICE USE

e F28 Mk 1000 was certificated by the Dutch authorities on 24 February 69 and entered service with LTU immediately after. The first F28 Mk 00 went to Nigeria Airways in October 1972. The F28 Mk 6000 was rtificated on 27 September 1973, but was not produced. The F28 Mk 00 entered service with Linjeflyg of Sweden late in 1976, and the first erator of the F28 Mk 3000 was Garuda in Indonesia. Sales totalled 241 the end of 1986, when production ended. Of these 160 remained in rvice at January 2001.

low: Argentine carrier American Falcon uses a single F28-1000 on heduled services from Buenos Aires.

Fokker 50/60

SPECIFICATION
(Fokker 50 High Performance)
Dimensions: Wingspan 29.00m (95ft 1¾in); length overall 25.25m (82ft 10in);
height overall 8.32m (27ft 3½in), wing area 70.0m² (753.5ft²).
Power Plant: Two 2,050kW (2,750shp) Pratt & Whitney Canada PW127B
turboprops with Dowty propellers with six composite blades.
Weights: Operating weight empty 12,520kg (27,602lb); max take-off 20,820kg
(45,900lb); max landing 19,730kg (43,500lb); max payload 6,080kg (13,404lb).
Performance: Typical cruising speed 282kts (512km/h); service ceiling 7,620m
(25,000ft); take-off field length 890m (2,920ft); landing field length 1,017m
(3,340ft); range with max payload 1,535nm (2,843km).
Accommodation: Flight crew of two. Seating for up to 58 passengers, four-
abreast with central aisle. Total baggage volume 10.42m³ (368.2ft³).

The Fokker 50 was announced on 24 November 1983 on the occasion of
celebration in Amsterdam of the 25th anniversary of airline service with the
F27 Friendship, which the Fokker 50 was designed to succeed. After prolonged
studies of possible stretched derivatives of the F27, Fokker concluded that the
size of the aircraft was about right for that portion of the regional airline market

*Below: Nakanihon Airline Service (NAL) operates its 56-seat Fokker 50s on
scheduled services in Japan from Nagoya to Toyama, Yonago, Fukushima
and the holiday resort of Hakodate. The size and comfort of the aircraft
allows for an orderly transfer of international passengers at Nagoya.*

above: Belgian regional carrier flies the Fokker 50 into London City Airport.

it sought to fill. Nevertheless, and despite an ongoing programme of product improvement since the F27 had first appeared in 1957, there was much room to introduce the benefits of new technology in the structure and system of the basic aircraft, and this was the keynote of Fokker's approach to the design of the Fokker 50. The most obvious change is in respect of the power plant, a switch being made from the Rolls-Royce Dart of the F27 family to the more modern Pratt & Whitney Canada PW124 with significant gains in fuel economy. Less obvious but more extensive changes have been made under the skin, to the extent that 80 per cent of the Fokker 50's component parts are new or modified by comparison with those of the F27. Thus, apart from the engines with their new nacelles and six-blade propellers, the Fokker 50 has a hydraulic instead of pneumatic system for landing gear and flap operation; a new Hamilton Standard air-conditioning system with a Garrett digital cabin pressure-control system; and Sundstrand integrated drive generators on each engine to supply the electric system. The F27's much-appreciated (by passengers) large cabin windows have given way to a larger number of smaller windows, in the interest of great flexibility of cabin layout, and the cabin itself is wholly redesigned, with large overhead stowage bins and the main passenger access door at the front instead of the rear, with the F27's forward baggage/cargo loading door deleted. ▶

The flight deck was also extensively redesigned, with an all-new avionics including a Honeywell electronic flight instrument system (EFIS) with cathod ray tube (CRT) displays for primary flight and navigation information. A sm airframe change is made with the addition of the wingtips or 'Foklets' variation of the larger winglets that serve a similar purpose) and extensive us is made throughout the airframe of carbon, aramid and glass fibre composite Flight development of the Fokker 50 began on 28 December 1985, using an F2 airframe with the new power plants; a second prototype flown on 30 April 198 had more representative Fokker 50 systems. Both aircraft made use of F2 fuselages, and the first true Fokker 50 flew on 13 February 1987.

VARIANTS
The basic Fokker 50, with 1,864kW (2,500shp) Pratt & Whitney Canad PW125B turboprops, was certificated to JAR 25 by the Dutch RLD on 15 M 1987. It was made available in four-door and three-door configuration providing dedicated access for ground handling services. Maximum capacity 58 passengers. The installation of more powerful PW127Bs, each rated 2,050kW (2,750shp), produced the Fokker 50 High Performance, offering bett airfield performance, especially in hot-and-high locations. The Fokker 50 Util

based on the standard three-door model, with an additional 1.65 x 1.30m (5ft n x 4ft 3¼in) multi-purpose door and heavy-duty floor. There were also a umber of special missions variants for military and government use. Stretched okker 60 and Fokker 60 Utility models for 60 passengers were launched in bruary 1994 and ordered by the Royal Netherlands Air Force. First flight was ade on 2 November 1995.

RVICE USE

erman regional DLT, now Lufthansa CityLine, took delivery of the first Fokker on 7 August 1987. FAA type approval to FAR Pt.25 was achieved on 16 bruary 1989, but no aircraft were delivered new to a US customer. Dutch RLD proval for the Fokker 50 High Performance was won in early 1993, prior to first stomer delivery to Avianca Colombia on 2 April 1993. When production ended 1996 following Fokker's bankruptcy, a total of 232 Fokker 50/60s had been ilt. Some 185 remained in commercial service in January 2001.

elow: The modern Fokker 50 has helped many airlines establish a niche *esence on secondary routes. Air Nostrum operates in the liberalised* *oanish domestic market.*

Fokker 70/100

SPECIFICATION
(Fokker 70)
Dimensions: Wingspan 28.08m (92ft 1½in); length overall 30.91m (101ft 4¾in); height overall 8.51m (27ft 10½in), wing area 93.5m² (1006.4ft²).
Power Plant: Two 61.6kN (13,850lb) Rolls-Royce Tay Mk.620 turbofans.
Weights: Operating weight empty 22,784kg (50,230lb); max take-off 41,730k (92,000lb); max landing 36,740kg (81,000lb); max payload 10,780kg (23,766lb
Performance: Max cruising speed 462kts (856km/h); service ceiling 10,670m (35,000ft); take-off field length 1,665m (5,465ft); landing field length 1,274m (4,180ft); range with max payload 2,015nm (3,731km).
Accommodation: Flight crew of two. Seating for up to 80 passengers, five-abreast with single aisle. Total cargo/baggage volume 21.57m³ (761.9ft³).

(Fokker 100)
Dimensions: Wingspan 28.08m (92ft 1½in); length overall 35.53m (116ft 6¾in); height overall 8.51m (27ft 10½in), wing area 93.50m² (1,006.4ft²).
Power Plant: Two 61.6kN (13,850lb) Rolls-Royce Tay Mk.620 or 67.2kN (15,100lb) Tay Mk.650 turbofans.
Weights: Operating weight empty 24,747kg (54,558lb); max take-off 45,810k (101,000lb); max landing 39,915kg (88,000 lb); max payload 12,013kg (26,486lb).
Performance: Max cruising speed 462kts (856km/h); service ceiling 10,670m (35,000ft); take-off field length 1,825m (5,990ft); landing field length 1,350m (4,420ft); range with max payload 1,680nm (3,111km).
Accommodation: Flight crew of two. Seating for up to 109 passengers, five-abreast with single aisle. Total baggage volume 24.87m³ (878.4ft³).

Above: The Government of Gabon operates a single Fokker 100 on VIP transport duties.

Below: Prototype Fokker 70.

In its search for a programme to maintain its share of the regional airline market through the 1990s, Fokker evaluated a number of possible derivative versions of its F28. These included projects variously identified as the Super F28, the F29 and (in collaboration with McDonnell Douglas) the MDF-100. Finally, on 24 November 1983, the company announced that it was going ahead with a derivative known as the Fokker 100, with backing from the Netherlands government; the designation was chosen to reflect the basic seating capacity (actually 107), in the same way that the improved F27 – announced simultaneously – was renamed the Fokker 50. To achieve the Fokker 100, the original F28 Mk 4000 fuselage was extended by 5.74m (18ft 10in) in two 'plugs', one ahead of and one behind the wing. Although Fokker studied, through extensive wind tunnel testing, the potential of completely new wing aerofoil sections, the final decision favoured retention of the basic F28 wing but unchanged. However, aerodynamic efficiency was improved by changes at the leading and trailing edges, with increased leading-edge chord resulting in the F28's prominent leading-edge 'kink' being virtually eliminated. The changes the aerofoil brought about by the new leading edge resulted, according Fokker, in a 30 per cent improvement in aerodynamics efficiency, an increase in the high-speed buffet limit and a reduction in drag at both high and low speeds. New trailing-edge flaps were adopted, and the landing gear was strengthened for the higher operating weights. Wing span was increased, at the tips, by 3.0m (9ft 9½in), and tailplane span by 1.4m (4ft 7in). Considerable use was made of composites in the structure, for such items as the nosecone, wing/fuselage fairings, cabin floor panels, etc. Cabin redesign gave the Fokker 100 a new look and on the flight deck, digital electronics were introduced to provide a state-of-the-art presentation and equipment fit, with a four-screen electronic flight instrument system (EFIS). The digital autoflight control system provides for Cat II operation, with operators having the option to upgrade to Cat III if autothrottle is fitted. The two Fokker 100 prototypes flew on 30 November 1986 and 25 February 1987. Authorisation for a shortened version for up to passengers was given by the Board in November 1992 and formally launched as the Fokker 70 in June 1993, on the back of 15 firm orders. The second Fokker 100 prototype was modified to Fokker 70 configuration by removing two fuselage plugs (one forward of the wing and one aft), reducing the overall length by 4.62m (15ft 2in). The Fokker 70 retained the same Rolls-Royce T

Below: The Fokker 100 has been the backbone of many fleets, including that of Portugalia.

*ove: The Kenyan Government was the first to acquire the Fokker 70ER
xtended range) version, which is being used on VIP transport. It is
wn by the Kenyan Air Force.*

k 620 turbofans installed on the basic Fokker 100 and made its first flight on
April 1993. Final assembly of the first production aircraft, built alongside the
kker 100, started in February 1994 and was completed with the first flight on
July. Plans for a stretched 137-seat Fokker 130 were abandoned.

RIANTS

e basic Fokker 70 for airline use has typical accommodation for 79
ssengers in five-abreast seating. A VIP/corporate shuttle version with
stomised interior and optional belly tanks, the Fokker Executive Jet 70, was
e first to be delivered. Additional range capability was incorporated in the
kker Executive Jet 70ER, extending range to 3,237nm (6,000km). The
andard Fokker 100, in a typical airline configuration for 107 passengers, was
oduced with optional intermediate take-off weight of 44,450kg (98,000lb) and
gh take-off weight of 45,810kg (101,000lb), higher thrust Tay Mk.650 engines,
ger capacity air conditioning system, and forward toilet. Complementing the
ecutive line of the Fokker 70, the Fokker 100 was also available in Executive
t 100 and Executive Jet 100ER customised versions, but none of these were
er delivered.

RVICE USE

e larger Fokker 100 was the first to be certificated, receiving RLD type
proval to JAR 25 on 20 November 1987. First customer was Swissair, which
ok delivery on 29 February 1988. Eleven days after simultaneous RLD and
A certification on 14 October 1994, the Ford Motor Company accepted the
st Fokker 70, an Executive Jet 70 model. The first airline version went to
mpati Air Transport on 9 March 1995, while the Kenyan Government
ceived an Executive Jet 70ER on 15 December 1995. When the Dutch
anufacturer went into receivership in February 1996, it was agreed that
tstanding orders would be completed, but this was only partially carried out.
al production (unless Fokker is re-activated, which looked unlikely in 1998),
ounted to 282 Fokker 100s and 77 Fokker 70s. Of these, some 43 Fokker
s and 273 Fokker 100s remained in commercial service in January 2001.

GAF Nomad

SPECIFICATION
(GAF Nomad N22B)
Dimensions: Wingspan 16.51m (54ft 2in); length overall 12.57m (41ft 3in); height overall 5.54m (18ft 2in), wing area 30.10m² (324.0ft²).
Power Plant: Two 313kW (420shp) Allison 250-B17C turboprops, with Hartz three-blade
Weights: Operating weight empty 2,446kg (5,432lb); max take-off 3,855kg (8,500lb); max landing 3,855kg (8,500lb); max payload 1,685kg (3,714lb).
Performance: Max cruising speed 169kts (313km/h); initial rate of climb 7.4m/s (1,460ft/min); service ceiling 6,400m (21,000ft); take-off field length 360m (1,180ft); landing field length 410m (1,340ft); max range 580nm (1,074km).
Accommodation: Flight crew of one or two. Seating for up to 12 passenger with central aisle. Total front baggage volume 0.76m³ (27.0ft³).

Development of a small utility transport suitable for military or civil ro begen at Australia's Government Aircraft Factories (GAF) during the m 1960s. As the N2, this project took shape as a strutted high-wing monopla having a slab-sided fuselage of almost square cross section, large side-loadi

Below: The GAF Nomad N22 was among Australia's first attempts to design and produce a transport aircraft. Here, and N22B is displayed o a European demonstration tour.

*bove: Standard (background) and long-fuselage versions of the Nomad
*rmate over an Australian landscape, flying for Northern Territories
edical Services.

*ors and retractable landing gear with stub wings, carrying nacelles into which
*e main wheels retracted. Prototypes of this N2 design flew on 23 July and 5
*ecember 1971, respectively. The name Nomad was adopted for the
*oduction version, and several variants were developed, starting with the N22,
*th a gross weight of 3,629kg (8,000lb). This was later increased to 3,855kg
*500lb) in the N22B, which became the standard short-fuselage variant for
*mmercial use, with up to 12 passengers. Meanwhile, GAF had 'stretched'
*e Nomad's fuselage by 1.14m (3ft 9in) to produce, in 1976, the N24, with
*ating increased from 12 to a maximum of 17. With the same power plant as
*e N22, the N24 was introduced at a gross weight of 3,855kg (8,500lb), but
*is was increased to 4,263kg (9,400lb) in the definitive N24A. In May 1985,
*AF recertificated the N22B at increased gross weight of 4,060kg (8,950lb) as
*e N22C, this version also featuring a force-feed oil filter system. During 1979,
* version of the N22B was certificated as a seaplane, fitted with a pair of
*ipaire (of Minnesota) aluminium floats, and in the following year an
*nphibious variant was also certificated, using Wipaire floats incorporating
*essna wheels and tyres in a retractable installation. Approximately half of the
*tal production of Nomads has been in military versions of the short-fuselage
*22 as the Missionmaster, Searchmaster B and Searchmaster L.

*22 went into service on 18 December 1975 with Aero Pelican, after
*rtification of the production version on 29 April 1975. The N22B was
*rtificated in August 1975. The N22C was approved in May 1985. Certification
* the N24 was obtained in October 1977 and of the N24A in May 1978, with
*R Pt 135 (Appendix A) approval gained in December 1978. Production ended
* late 1984 after the completion of 170 aircraft. Seventeen remained in
*mmercial service in January 2001.

Galaxy Aerospace/IAI Astra/Galaxy

SPECIFICATION
(Galaxy Aerospace (IAI) Galaxy)
Dimensions: Wingspan 17.70m (58ft 1in); length 18.97m (62ft 3in); heig
overall 6.53m (21ft 5in); wing area 34.28m² (369ft²).
Power Plant: Two 26.9kN (6,040lb) thrust Pratt & Whitney Canada
PW306A turbofans with FADEC.
Weights: Operating weight empty 8,709kg (19,200lb); max take-off
15,807kg (34,850lb); max landing 12,701kg (28,000lb); max payload
2,177kg (4,800lb).
Performance: Max cruising speed 494kts (915km/h); service ceiling
13,715m (45,000ft); take-off field length 1,800m (5,900ft); landing field
length 1,037m (3,400ft); range with typical payload 3,620nm (6,704km).
Accommodation: Flight crew of two. Typical seating for four to eight
passengers. Max seating for 10 passengers. Baggage volume 3.7m³
(130ft³).

The Astra and Galaxy mid-size jets are the latest models in a long line
business transports began on 27 January 1963 with the first flight of t

Below: The Galaxy business jet has been designed for transatlantic rang

Above: Galaxy cabin interior provides wide-body comfort for up to 10 passengers.

Aero Commander 1121 Jet Commander. This was acquired by Israel Aircraft Industries (IAI) in 1967 and developed successively as the 1121 Commodore Jet, available in improved 1121A and 1121B versions; 1123 and 1124 Westwind and Westwind 1, the latter with an optional extra fuel tank; and the 1124A Westwind 2 with an all-new wing and winglets, and seating for up to 10 passengers. A total of 441 of these models was built by the end of 1987, when production switched to the 1125 model, launched by IAI at the NBAA convention in October 1979, and renamed Astra in 1981. Although the Astra retained some of the features of the earlier models, it had a low-set and swept back wing, a new standing height cabin, and TFE731-3A-200G turbofan engines. The Astra first flew on 19 March 1984 and a total of 40 were built until replaced by the Astra SP in 1989. This featured various improvements including a digital autopilot and EFIS cockpit. After 37 had been built, it was superseded by the Astra SPX, which flew on 18 August 1994 and was first delivered in 1996. The Astra SPX incorporated substantial performance enhancements, including better payload/range and shorter take-off runs, achieved through more powerful AlliedSignal TFE731-40R-200G turbofans with FADEC and thrust reversers, and the application of winglets. A Rockwell Collins Pro Line 4 avionics suite was standard. Two aircraft are operated by the US Air National Guard on transport and medevac duties with the designation C-38A. Yet another redesigned and improved version, the 1126 Galaxy made its appearance in 1997, taking to the air on 25 December. Powered by twin Pratt & Whitney Canada PW306A engines, the Galaxy has a longer wide-body fuselage and has been designed for non-stop trans-Atlantic range, for example New York-Paris, with a full complement of 10 passengers. The Galaxy was awarded its FAA type certificate on 16 December 1998. First customer delivery took place in January 2000. At 1 January 2001, a total of 120 Astras and 25 Galaxy models were in service.

Grumman G-21 Goose and Turbo-Goose

The Goose amphibian, developed as a four/six-seat business amphibian, first flew in June 1937 and obtained US type approval on 29 September of that year in its initial G-21 form and on 5 February 1938 in improved G-21A form. Produced for USAAF and USN service during the war, numbers of Goose amphibians found applications in airline operation, especially in countries with extensive coastlines and lakes, such as Alaska, Canada, New Zealand and Scandinavia. Starting in 1958, the McKinnon company in the USA and later in Canada developed a number of Goose conversions, and some of these were still in small-scale commercial use in 1998. The G-21C and G-21D had four 254kW (340hp) Lycoming engines in place of the original Wasp Junior, the G-21D also featuring a lengthened bow. The G-21E introduced 432kW (579shp) Pratt & Whitney Canada PT6A-20 turboprops and the G-21G had 534kW (715shp) PT6A-27s, optional retractable wing-tip floats and increased accommodation.

Right: A rare photograph of a British-registered Grumman Goose.

Below: The amphibious Grumman Goose saw extensive service in Canada and with island operators.

Grumman G-73 Mallard and Turbo-Mallard

The G-73 Mallard was developed as one of Grumman's first commerci‌al ventures after World War II, in continuation of the company's pre-w‌ar interest in amphibious transports for the private and business owner. Th‌e Mallard first flew on 30 April 1946, powered by a pair of 448kW (600shp) Pra‌tt & Whitney R-1340-8WH1 Wasp air-cooled radial piston engines. With a gros‌s weight of 5,670kg (12,500lb), the Mallard cruised at 257km/h (139kts) a‌t 2,450m (8,000ft) and had a range of 975nm (1,800km). Production totalled 6‌0 and ended in 1951. Most Mallards were purchased by private owners but a fe‌w reached airline service, and continued in this role, primarily in Canada, Alas‌ka and the Caribbean. In 1964, one Mallard operated by Northern Consolidate‌d Airways in Alaska was fitted with a PT6A-9 turboprop on the starboard win‌g

etaining the R-1340 to port) and used for a 15-hour flight trial. After reverting
o standard, this aircraft returned to NCA service but in 1969 was purchased by
rakes Aviation Inc. in Texas and modified to full Turbo-Mallard configuration as
ie G-73T, considerably boosting performance and operating economy. It first
ew in this guise in September 1969 and after FAA type approval in October
970 several more similar conversions were made by Frakes, for operation by
halks International Airlines on its services in the Bahamas, alongside standard
lallards already used by that company.

*elow: Most Mallards were produced for private use, although a few
ntered airline service.*

Grumman G-111 Albatross

SPECIFICATION

(Grumman G-111 Albatross)

Dimensions: Wingspan 29.46m (96ft 8in); length overall 18.67m (61ft 3in); height overall 7.87m (25ft 10in), wing area 96.2m² (1,035ft²).

Power Plant: Two 1,100kW (1,475hp) Wright R-1820-982C9HE3 air-cooled radial piston engines, with Hamilton Standard three-blade constant-speed feathering and reversing propellers.

Weights: Operating weight empty 10,659kg (23,500lb); max take-off 14,129kg (31,150lb); max landing 14,129kg (31,150lb); max payload 3,630kg (8,000lb).

Performance: Normal cruising speed 206kts (383km/h); initial rate of climb 6.35m/s (1,250ft/min); service ceiling 2,440m (8,000ft); take-off distance on water 1,340m (4,400ft); landing distance on water 965m (3,170ft); range with max payload 405nm (750km).

Accommodation: Flight crew of two. Seating for 28 passengers in single seats with central aisle. Total baggage compartment volume 7.93m³ (280.0ft³)

The G-111 has its origins in the Grumman G-64 Albatross design of the peric immediately after World War II, first flown on 24 October 1947 as th XJR2F-1 utility transport amphibian for the US Navy. Later production batche for the USAF as search and rescue amphibians were designated SA-16, and a variants later received HU-16 designations. During the late 1970s, as Albatros

mphibians became available upon being retired by the USAF and USN, rumman developed a conversion programme, in conjunction with Resorts ternational, for a version of the Albatross to operate in the commuter role. entified as the G-111 (the original Grumman design number for the HU-3B variant), a prototype of this civil conversion first flew on 13 February 979 and FAA type approval was obtained on 29 April 1980. The conversion cluded restoration of the airframe to zero-time standard through a full spection and repair, removal and overhaul of the engines, modernization f the flight deck, installation of passenger seats in the cabin, with rovisions of suitable access doors and emergency hatches, and a ghtweight, solid-state avionics system throughout. Although Grumman urchased 57 Albatrosses for conversions, only 12 were delivered to esorts International by 1986, some of these going into service with esorts subsidiary Chalks International and others being available for sale. variant with Garrett TPE331-15UAR turboprops and Dowty-Rotol four-ade propellers was also studied by Grumman and Resorts International, ut not developed. Plans by Frakes International to re-engine the Albatross ith Pratt & Whitney Canada PT6A turboprops also came to nothing.

elow: The Grumman Albatross was converted to civil use from military irframes and operated successfully by Chalks International Airlines.

Grumman Gulfstream I and I-C

SPECIFICATION
(Gulfstream I-C)
Dimensions: Wingspan 23.88m (78ft 4in); length overall 22.96m (75ft 4in); height overall 7.01m (23ft 0in), wing area 56.7m² (610.3ft²).
Power Plant: Two 1,484kW (1,990shp) Rolls-Royce Dart 529-8X or -8E (RDa.7/2) turboprops, with Rotol four-blade constant-speed propellers.
Weights: Operating weight empty 10,747kg (23,693lb); max take-off 16,329kg (36,000lb); max landing 15,551kg (34,285lb); max payload 3,356kg (7,400lb).
Performance: Max cruising speed 308kts (571km/h); initial rate of climb 9.7m/s (1,900ft/min); service ceiling 9,145m (30,000ft); take-off field length 1,480m (4,850ft); landing field length 845m (2,770ft); range with max payload 434nm (804km).
Accommodation: Flight crew of two. Seating for up to 37 passengers, three-abreast with offset aisle. Total baggage volume front and rear 7.1m³ (251.0ft³)

Design of this long-range, large-capacity corporate transport began in 195 and set the basic circular fuselage cross-section and nose, which has bee carried through all subsequent derivatives, including the latest jet-powere models. Grumman opted for the Rolls-Royce Dart turboprop for high-spee cruise, and an auxiliary power unit to permit independent operation fro remote airfields. The G-159 Gulfstream I first flew on 14 August 1958, an deliveries began soon after the type received FAA certification on 21 May 195 While designed primarily as a corporate aircraft with 10-14 executive seats, th Gulfstream I was also used on commuter airline services in Britain and th United States configured for 24 passengers. The US Coast Guard accepted tw aircraft, designated VC-4A, for VIP duties in the summer of 1963, and the U

Below: Birmingham Executive Aviation used the 24-seat Gulfstream I or scheduled services.

*bove: The Gulfstream I was designed as a long-range corporate
ansport with Rolls-Royce Dart turboprop engines.*

avy ordered nine TC-4s for navigator training in December 1966. Production
talled 200 and ceased in 1969. Ten years later, Gulfstream American
orporation, which had purchased the rights to the Gulfstream I, offered a
onversion for up to 38 passengers three-abreast, with the fuselage stretched
3.25m (10ft 8in). Known as the Gulfstream I-C, this model made its first flight
25 October 1979, and a total of nine were delivered from November 1980.
total of 35 remained in service in January 2001.

Gulfstream II/III

SPECIFICATION
(Gulfstream III)

Dimensions: Wingspan 23.72m (77ft 10in); length 25.32m (83ft 1in); height overall 7.43m (24ft 4½in); wing area 86.83m² (934.6ft²).

Power Plant: Two 50.7kN (11,400lb) thrust Rolls-Royce Spey Mk 511-8 turbofans.

Weights: Operating weight empty 17,236kg (38,000lb); max take-off 31,615kg (69,700lb); max landing 26,535kg (58,500lb).

Performance: Max cruising speed 442kts (818km/h); service ceiling 13,720m (45,000ft); take-off field length 1,554m (5,100ft); landing field length 975m (3,200ft); range with typical payload 3.650nm (6,760km).

Accommodation: Flight crew of two or three. Typical seating for 19 passengers. Baggage volume 4.44m³ (157ft³).

The turboprop-powered Gulfstream, while being more comfortable and having a greater range, could not, however, compete fully with the new crop of business jets. In recognition, studies were begun into a swept-wing aircraft using the same cabin, but Rools-Royce Spey turbofans in place of the Darts. The launch decision was made in May 1965, and the production Gulfstream II (no prototype was built) flew for the first time on 2 October 1966. FAA certification was obtained on 19 October 1967, and the first customer delivery was made on 6 December that year. From July 1971 production aircraft incorporated an engine hush kit, and flight testing began on a Gulfstream II (TT) with wingtip tanks, increasing fuel capacity

,156kg (26,800lb) and maximum take-off weight to 29,711kg (65,500lb). is version, certified in September 1976, provided an IFR range of 80nm (5,893km). Production ended in 1979 after the completion of 256 craft. The Gulfstream II benefited later from Gulfstream III technology, rticularly the new swept wing with winglets, but also involving structural odifications to permit increases in take-off weight, operating speeds and uising altitude. The resulting Gulfstream II-B upgrade was first flown on March 1981 and received its certification on 17 September 1981. More an 50 Gulfstream IIs have been upgraded to date. GIIs with new blended nglets developed by Seattle-based Aviation Partners are designated ulfstream II-SP. The improved and longer-range Gulfstream III, notable for new winglets and a fuselage lengthened by 0.96m (3ft 2in), made its first ght on 2 December 1979, and received its FAA certification on 22 ptember 1980. Military transport versions were procured by the US Air rce as the C-20A and C-20B, and by the US Navy as the C-20D and C-20E. special missions version, the Gulfstream III-SRA-1 flew on 14 August 84. In May 1997, Atlantic Aviation delivered a Gulfstream III refurbished th a new 'wide-inside' interior, which added 0.18m (7in) clearance to the sle, and a cabin entertainment system. Gulfstream III production ended in ptember 1988 after 206 had been built. Some 245 Gulfstream IIs and 195 ulfstream IIIs remained in service in January 2001.

low: The Gulfstream II with Rolls-Royce Spey turbofans replaced the rboprop-powered Gulfstream I model.

Gulfstream IV

SPECIFICATION
(Gulfstream IV-SP)
Dimensions: Wingspan 23.72m (77ft 10in); length 26.92m (88ft 4in); height overall 7.44m (24ft 5in); wing area 88.29m² (950.4ft²).
Power Plant: Two 61.6kN (13,850lb) thrust Rolls-Royce Tay Mk 611-8 turbofans.
Weights: Operating weight empty 19,278kg (42,500lb); max take-off 33,838kg (74,600lb); max landing 29,937kg (66,000lb); max payload 2,948kg (6,500lb).
Performance: Max cruising speed 505kts (936km/h); service ceiling 13,715m (45,000ft); take-off field length 1,662m (5,450ft); landing field length 973m (3,190ft); range with typical payload 4,220nm (7,815km).
Accommodation: Flight crew of two. Typical seating for 12-14 passengers. Max seating for 19 passengers. Baggage volume 4.8m³ (169ft³).

The Gulfstream IV represented another leap forward in capability from t Gulfstream III, which remained in production during its developme Noticeable differences from the GIII include a new wing redesign aerodynamically for reduced cruise drag and also structurally redesigned make it lighter and carry 544kg (1,200lb) more fuel, increased tail span, and 1.37m (4ft 6in) longer fuselage, with a sixth window on each side. New clear and more powerful Rolls-Royce Tay turbofans replaced the smoky Speys. T Gulfstream IV was also fitted with a highly advanced Sperry SPZ-8000 EF avionics suite, including fully-integrated flight management and autothrot systems. Another notable performance improvement was the ability to ca eight passengers over a substantially increased distance of over 4,600r (8,520km). Four production prototypes were built, with the first making maiden flight on 19 September 1985. FAA certification was received on 22 Ap 1987 and the Gulfstream IV went on to accumulate many speed and distan world records. The original baseline aircraft was replaced from September 19

Below: The Gulfstream IV-SP has found a market niche as a special missions aircraft, here in service with the Swedish Government on signals intelligence missions.

ove: The Kingdom of Saudi Arabia operates the Gulfstream IV-SP in ·edevac configuration.

the Gulfstream IV-SP (special performance) model, a higher weight aircraft 'nounced at the NBAA convention in October 1991 and first flown on 24 June 92. The new model had better payload/range capability, and an improved ·neywell SPZ-8400 flight guidance and control system. In September 1994, ·lfstream announced two new variants, the Gulfstream IV-MPA Multipurpose ·craft, and the long-range Gulfstream IV-B. The GIV-MPA features a quick- ·ange interior for up to 26 passengers or 2,177kg (4,800lb) freight (or a ·mbination of both). A large cargo door and larger emergency exits are ·ndard. The IV-B study focused on incorporating the winglets from the ·lfstream V and additional fuel for a 400nm (741km) increase in range, but this ·ject has been postponed. Military special requirements versions are ·signated Gulfstream SRA-4, and include the C-20F for the US Army, C-20G · US Navy and USMC, the C-20G for USAF, and the U-4, selected in late 1994 · the Japan Air Self-Defence Force (JASDF). At 1 January 2001, some 400 ·lfstream IVs were in service.

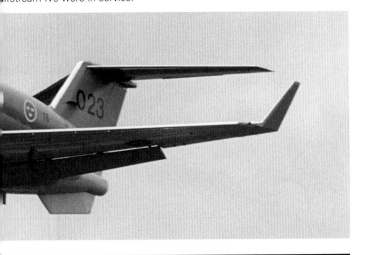

Gulfstream V

SPECIFICATION
(Gulfstream V)

Dimensions: Wingspan 28.50m (93ft 6in); length 29.39m (96ft 5in); height overall 7.87m (25ft 10in); wing area 105.63m² (1,137.0ft²).

Power Plant: Two 65.6kN (14,750lb) thrust Rolls-Royce Deutschland BR710-48 turbofans with FADEC.

Weights: Operating weight empty 21,772kg (48,000lb); max take-off 41,050kg (90,500lb); max landing 34,155kg (75,300lb); max payload 2,948kg (6,500lb).

Performance: Max cruising speed 499kts (924km/h); service ceiling 15,545 (51,000ft); take-off field length 1,826m (5,990ft); landing field length 966m (3,170ft); range with typical payload 6,500nm (12,038km).

Accommodation: Flight crew of two or three. Typical seating for 15 to 19 passengers. Baggage volume 6.4m³ (226ft³).

A study into a very long-range business jet was announced at the NBA convention in October 1991, and firmed up, together with the engi selection, at the Farnborough Air Show the following September. The resulta Gulfstream V is the world's first ultra long-range business jet capable of flyi 6,500nm (12,025km) at speeds up to Mach 0.885 and at a maximum cruis altitude of 15,445m (51,000ft). Its extra-ordinary range capability makes it t only business jet able to fly non-stop from New York to Tokyo. To date, t Gulfstream V has set 65 world and national speed and distance records. Bas on a re-engineered GIV fuselage lengthened by 2.13m (7ft 0in), the Gulfstrea V features a larger and 10% more efficient wing, larger vertical and horizon tail surfaces, bigger flight deck by moving bulkhead 0.30m (1ft 0in) aft provide more space for pilots and to accommodate a full-size jump seat. T airstair doors were also moved aft by 1.52m (5ft 0in). Power is provided in t

Below: The Gulfstream V was the world's first ultra-long-range business jet.

Above: Gulfstream V cabin environment with 100% fresh air ventilation and large oval windows.

ape of two 65.6kn (14,750lb) Rolls-Royce Deutschland BR710-48 turbofans th FADEC, developed especially for the GV. The highly advanced cockpit is ilt around the Honeywell SPZ-8500 avionics suite with digital flight anagement system with six colour LCD EFIS, enhanced ground proximity arning system (EGPWS), and terrain collision avoidance system (TCAS), and oneywell/BAE head-up display (HUD). Flight testing of a Kollsman IR sensor gan in September 1999 to provide an enhanced vision system (EVS) in njunction with the HUD for CAT III approach and landing. The system was rtificated in 2000. Aerodynamic enhancements and engine improvements, :luding reduced specific fuel consumption (sfc), is being incorporated in the w Gulfstream V-SP (special performance) model, which will use less runway d have increased range.

The first Gulfstream V flew on 28 November 1995, and was awarded its full A certification on 11 April 1997. The first customer delivery was made on 1 ly 1997, since when around 100 have been delivered. In addition to the basic ng-range corporate transport, Gulfstream has delivered four C-37A models to e USAF as a VIP transport. Also being offered is a special missions variant, hough none has been delivered.

Handley Page Herald

SPECIFICATION
(Handley Page HPR.7 Herald 200)

Dimensions: Wingspan 28.88m (94ft 9in); length overall 23.01m (75ft 6in); height overall 7.34m (24ft 1in), wing area 82.3m² (886.0ft²).

Power Plant: Two 1,570kW (2,105shp) Rolls-Royce Dart 527 (RDa.7) turboprops, with Rotol four-blade constant-speed fully-feathering propellers.

Weights: Operating weight empty 11,703kg (25,800lb); max take-off 19,505k (43,000lb); max landing 17,915kg (39,500lb); max payload 5,307kg (11,700lb)

Performance: Max cruising speed 239kts 443(km/h); initial rate of climb 9.2m/s (1,805ft/min); service ceiling 8,505m (27,900ft); take-off field length 823m (2,700ft); landing field length 580m (1,900ft); range with max payload 608nm (1,127km).

Accommodation: Flight crew of two. Seating for up to 56 passengers, four-abreast , two seats each side of centrl aisle. Total baggage volume 8.1m³ (286ft³)

The design of a medium-sized, short-range feeder liner with a pressuris‹ fuselage was begun by the Handley Page company in the early 1950s. the HPR 3, the new airliner emerged as a high-wing monoplane of conventior design, powered by four Alvis Leonides Major piston radial engines. Tv prototypes were built in this configuration, with the first flight made on August 1955, but early commitments for the purchase of some 29 aircra

ostly for Australian operators, were not made good and it became clear to andley Page that the HPR 3 could not hold its own in the new era of the rboprop. Consequently, in May 1957, the company announced that a version the Herald would be offered with two Darts in place of the four piston ngines, and the latter variant was subsequently dropped. Both prototypes ere converted to have Dart RDa.7 engines, flying for the first time in this form 11 March and 17 December 1958 respectively. The initial production andard was the Herald Srs 100, with a fuselage length of 21.92m (71ft 11in) d a maximum take-off weight of 17,690kg (39,000lb). The Herald Srs 200 atured a 1.09m (3ft 7in) lengthening of the fuselage to give two more seat ws, and higher weights. After the second prototype HPR 7 had flown in Srs 00 configuration on 8 April 1961, the first production example flew on 13 ecember 1961, and 36 of this variant were delivered. In addition, the company ilt eight Herald Srs 400s as military transports for the Royal Malaysian Air rce. The Herald Srs 300 designation referred to the Srs 200 with small odifications to meet US certification requirements. Series 500, 600, 700 and 00 were projected but never built, the company collapsing in 1968. The Srs 00 Herald entered service with British European Airways, following rtification on 25 November 1959. The Srs 200 was certificated on 1 June 161 and entered service with Jersey Airlines. A total of 48 were produced plus vo prototypes. Less than a handful remain in service.

Left: British European Airways was the first customer to take delivery of the Dart Herald.

Harbin Y-12

SPECIFICATION
(Harbin Y-12 (II))
Dimensions: Wingspan 17.23m (56ft 6½in); length overall 14.86m (48ft 9in); height overall 5.57m (18ft 3½in), wing area 34.27m² (368.9ft²).
Power Plant: Two 462kW (620shp) Pratt & Whitney Canada PT6A-27 turboprops with Hartzell three-blade constant-speed reversible-pitch propellers.
Weights: Max take-off 5,300kg (11,684lb); max landing 5,300kg (11,684lb); max payload 1,700kg (3,748lb).
Performance: Max cruising speed 157kts (292km/h); max rate of climb 8.1m (1,594ft/min); service ceiling 7,000m (22,960ft); take-off field length 425m (1,395ft); landing field length 340m (1,120ft); range with typical payload 723n (1,340km).
Accommodation: Flight crew of two and seating for 17 passengers, three-abreast with single aisle. Baggage compartment volume front and rear 2.66m (93.95ft³).

The Y-12 (Y indicates 'Yunshuji' or Transport aircraft, and the designatic is sometimes rendered as Yun-12) is a product of the Harbin aircra factory in Heilongjiang province, one of the major centres of aerospac activity in China. Known as the Harbin Aircraft Manufacturing Corporatic (HAMC), the factory was set up in 1952, and for six years was concerne only with aircraft repair. It then progressed to the licence production Soviet aircraft, building the Mil Mi-4 helicopter (as the Z-5) and the Ilyush Il-28 light bomber (as the H-5) before building the 7-seat twin-engined Y-1

above: The Y-12 was developed by the Harbin Aircraft Manufacturing Corporation (HAMC) in Heilongjiang Province.

below: The 17-seat utility/commuter Y-12 is operated in China and other countries in Asia/Pacific.

utility aircraft, the first modern aircraft of wholly-Chinese design and construction. From the Y-11, with which it shared the configuration but little else, the Y-12 was developed. The first of three prototypes flew on 14 July 1982. Picking the Pratt & Whitney PT6A to power the Y-12, Harbin adopted such new features (compared with the Y-11) as a NASA GAW supercritical aerofoil section, bonded construction in place of rivets, and integral rather than bag fuel tanks. Two prototypes and a static test airframe (at first known as Y-11T1 but then as Y-12 I) were followed by three Y-12 II (originally Y-11T2) development aircraft, used to obtain certification in compliance with US FAR Pt 23 and Pt 135 standards. The first of the Y-12 II flew on 16 August 1984 and received domestic certification in December 1985. Under an agreement between Harbin and the Hong Kong Aircraft Engineering Co. (HAECO), the latter installed Western avionics and interior in the sixth Y-12 to help 'westernise' the aircraft for export. UK certification was received on 20 June 1990.

Modern Commercial Aircraft

VARIANTS
The initial production version was the Y-12 (I), powered by twin PT6A-
engines, but this was soon replaced by the upgraded Y-12 (II), which diffe
primarily in having uprated 462kW (620shp) PT6A-27s and a smaller vertical fi
Leading-edge slats have also been deleted. The Y-12 (II) remains in productic
but is expected to be replaced by the Y-12 (IV), which made its first flight on
August 1993 and received domestic approval on 3 July 1994. FAA certificatic
to FAR Pt 23 followed on 26 March 1995. The Y-12 (IV) incorporates a numb
of changes to improve performance and make the aircraft more attractive
non-Asian customers, particularly North America. Changes inclu
modifications to wing tips, control surface actuation, main landing gear ar
brakes, and remodelled seating for up to 19 passengers. The PT6A-27 has bee
retained, but in uprated form producing 507kW (680shp). Maximum take-c
weights and payload are increased to 5,670kg (12,500lb) and 1,984kg (4,374
respectively. Installation of EFIS, TCAS, GWPS and flight data recorder is bein
considered. Stretched and pressurised versions are also on the drawing boar
The Y-12 (IV) is also being assembled in Canada under an agreement signe
with Canadian Aerospace Group (CAG). The aircraft, marketed as the Tw
Panda, has Western instrumentation, interiors, wheels and brakes. It
powered by more powerful PT6A-34 engines. Delivery to the first custom
was planned for January 2001.

SERVICE USE
The Y-12 first entered service with local airlines, but is now also operated
airlines in Fiji, Bangladesh, Kiribati, Laos, Malaysia, Mongolia and Nepal, as w
as several governments and military forces in Asia/Pacific, Africa and Sou
America. More than 100 had been delivered by January 2001.

IAI Arava

SPECIFICATION
(IAI-101B Arava)
Dimensions: Wingspan 20.96m (68ft 9in); length overall 13.05m (42ft
9in); height overall 5.21m (17ft 1in), wing area 43.7m² (470.0ft²).
Power Plant: Two 559kW (750shp) Pratt & Whitney Canada PT6A-36
turboprops, with Hartzell three-blade variable-pitch fully-feathering and
reversing propellers.
Weights: Operating weight empty 4,000kg (8,818lb); max take-off
6,800kg (14,991lb); max landing 6,800kg (14,991lb); max payload
2,350kg (5,182lb).
Performance: Max cruising speed 172kts (308km/h); initial rate of
climb 6.5m/s (1,290ft/min); service ceiling 7,620m (25,000ft); take-off
field length 745m (2,450ft); landing field length 655m (2,150ft); range
with max payload 237nm (440km).
Accommodation: Flight crew of one or two. Seating for up to 19
passengers, four-abreast with central aisle. Total baggage compartme
volume 2.60m³ (91.8ft³), plus 3.20m³ (113.0ft³) in tail cone.

The first indigenous design by Israel Aircraft Industries (IAI), the B-101
was for a nine-seat corporate jet transport, and reached the mock-u
stage but proceeded no further, whilst a second design, for a six-se
corporate jet, was also abandoned when IAI acquired the design ar
manufacturing rights for the Rockwell Jet Commander, which it went on
develop and produce as the Westwind. Attention then switched to a lig
STOL transport, for which there seemed to be a large world-wide marke

bove: The latest Y-12(IV) version, seen here at Zhuhai, has been nproved and 'westernised'.

bove: This AIA-202 version had unusual winglets and a lengthened fuselage.

oth military and civil. Design work began in 1965 and led to a project for a gh-wing twin-turboprop transport with STOL performance characteristics. he most unusual feature of the design was the twin-boom layout, ombined with a circular-section fuselage having a hinged tail cone for traight-in loading of vehicles or cargo. Like most other aircraft in its class, he new transport, which took the designation IAI-101, was designed to eet the American FAR Pt 23 regulations; which established the maximum ke-off weight at 5,670kg (12,500lb) for civil operations. The first prototype f the IAI-101 flew on 27 November 1969. The name Arava was adopted ▶

for both civil and military types.

The original Arava was designed around a pair of Turboméca Astazou turboprops, but PT6A-27s were adopted instead for the IAI-101 prototypes, switching to the 584kW (783shp) PT6A-34 for the IAI-101 initial production standard, later identified as the IAI-102. This was matched by the IAI-20 military version, which had a maximum weight of 6,804kg (15,000lb). The IAI-101B has PT6A-36 engines and improved performance in hot and high conditions, as well as a better cabin interior. An all-cargo version, with 2,360kg (5,200lb) payload, was known as the Cargo Commuterliner in the USA. The IAI-202 was a modified version with PT6A-36 engines, winglet

nd a lengthened fuselage. The IAI-102 was type-approved by the Israeli uthorities in April 1976, and was the first commercial version to go into ervice. FAA certification of the IAI-101B was obtained on 17 November 980 to SFAR Pt 41 provision, and in October 1982 to the upgraded SFAR t 41C. Production ceased in January 1986 after delivery of 91 aircraft. ewer than 10 of this STOL transport remain in commercial service in entral and South America.

elow: The Arava is easily distinguished from similar types by its twin- oom configuration and side-hinged rear fuselage cone.

IBIS Ae 270

SPECIFICATION
(Ibis Ae 270P)
Dimensions: Wingspan 13.80m (45ft 3¹/₄in); length 12.24m (40ft 1in); height overall 4.79m (15ft 8¹/₂in); wing area 21.00m² (226.0ft²).
Power Plant: One 634kW (850shp) Pratt & Whitney PT6A-42A turboprop.
Weights: Operating weight empty 1,788kg (3,942lb); max take-off 3,300kg (7,275lb); max landing 3,150kg (6,944lb); max payload 1,200kg (2,645lb).
Performance: Max cruising speed 220kts (408km/h); service ceiling 9,700m (31,820ft); take-off field length 266m (875ft); landing field length 409m (1,345ft); range with typical payload 121nm (225km).
Accommodation: Flight crew of two. Max seating for eight passengers.

The 9/10-seat Ibis Ae 270 has a long history, being first proposed by Aer Vodochody in early 1990, then known as the L-270. Progress was slow, wit various changes being made in design specifications in subsequent years t arrive at the present configuration. Roll-out of the first prototype took place o 10 December 1999, and the Ae 270 Ibis, as it was then known, made it maiden flight in early 2000. Three protoypes are being used in the certificatio

rocess, which is expected to be completed in spring 2001. Production will be
1 the Czech republic, with AIDC building the wings and landing gear in Taiwan.
Designed by chief designer Jan Mikula, the Ae 270 is a pressurised utility
ransport with a high aspect-ratio low wing, sweptback vertical tail, and circular
abin windows. Power plant in the basic passenger version is the 634kW
350shp) Pratt & Whitney Canada PT6A-42A turboprop, driving a four-blade,
onstant-speed, reversible-pitch propeller. Accommodation is for two flight
rew (single-pilot certification is being sought) and up to eight passengers.
:xecutive layouts for fewer passengers permit the inclusion of toilet facilities.
he baseline passenger aircraft is the pressurised Ae 270P with Honeywell
vionics and retractable landing gear, while the Ae 270W (previously known as
\e 270U) is the cheaper utility model with one 580kW (778shp) Walter 601F
urboprop, with optional water injection system, fixed landing gear, and Czech
vionics. Wheeled-float versions of the passenger and utility models
espectively are designated Ae 270FP and Ae 270FW.

*Below: The new Ibis Ae 270 utility and multimission aircraft entered
service in mid-2001.*

Ilyushin Il-14

SPECIFICATION
(Ilyushin Il-14M)

Dimensions: Wingspan 31.69m (104ft 0in); length overall 22.30m (73ft 2in); height overall 7.90m (25ft 11in), wing area 99.7m² (1,075ft²).

Power Plant: Two 1,440kW (1,930hp) Shvetsov ASh-821-7 air-cooled 14-cylinder radial piston engines, with four-blade feathering AV-50 propellers.

Weights: Operating weight empty 12,600kg (27,776lb); max take-off 18,000kg (39,683lb); max landing 17,250kg (38,030lb).

Performance: Max cruising speed 208kts (385km/h); initial rate of climb 6.2m/s (1,220ft/min); service ceiling 6,705m (22,000ft); range with max payload 558nm (1,034km).

Accommodation: Flight crew of three or four. Seating for up to 36 passengers, four-abreast , two seats each side of central aisle.

The Il-14 was an improved derivative of the Il-12, which was itself the first product of the Ilyushin design bureau after World War II to achieve large scale production for non-military use, although it was probably designed primarily as a replacement for the Li-2 in the role of military tactical transport. The Il-14, which flew as a prototype in 1952 differed from the Il-12; but like the Il-12, the Il-14 was built for both military and commercial use, the latter in the hands of Aeroflot and designated Il-14P (*Passazhirskii*) with accommodation for 18-24 passengers. In 1956, a slightly stretched version appeared, with a 1.0m (3ft 4in) section inserted in the forward fuselage, increasing accommodation to a maximum of 36. This was designated Il-14M (*Modifikatsirovanny*). Later, considerable numbers of Il-14Ps and Ms were adapted to serve Aeroflot as freighters under the designation of Il-14T (*Transportny*). Up to 3,500 examples of the Il-14 are reported to have been built in the Soviet Union, and VEB Flugzeugwerke built 80 in East Germany. As the Avia 14, the type was also built in large numbers in Czechoslovakia, in several different versions. These aircraft were

Above: The air forces of the former Soviet states, including Bulgaria, used the Il-14 mostly as VIP transports and troop carriers.

...ed in both civil and military guise by the relevant operators in East ...ermany and Czechoslovakia and were exported to other countries in ...e Soviet sphere of influence, including Albania, Poland, Romania, ...lgaria, Cuba and China. Some 50 are still in use in Russia for various ...ssenger and cargo activities.

Left: CSA Czechoslovak Airlines used a large fleet of mostly Czech-built Avia 14-32A models.

Ilyushin Il-18

SPECIFICATION
(Ilyushin Il-18D)
Dimensions: Wingspan 37.40m (122ft 8½in); length overall 35.90m (117ft 9in); height overall 10.17m (33ft 4in); wing area 140.0m² (1,507ft²).
Power Plant: Four 3,169kW (4,250shp) Ivchenko AI-20M turboprops, with AV-68I four-blade constant-speed feathering and reversing propellers.
Weights: Operating weight empty 35,000kg (77,160lb); max take-off 64,000 (141,100lb); max payload 13,500kg (29,750lb).
Performance: Max cruising speed 364kts (675km/h); service ceiling 10,000m (32,820ft); take-off field length 1,300m (4,265ft); landing field length 850m (2,790ft); range with max payload 1,997nm (3,700km).
Accommodation: Flight crew of five. Seating for up to 122 passengers, six-abreast with central aisle.

Of then new technology including gas turbine engines. Named *Moskva*, the prototype was followed by two pre-production aircraft and a service trials batch of 20, of which some were powered by the Kuznetsov NK-4 engine and others by the AI-20. The latter was adopted as the standard power plant on the basis of early service results and, with maximum take-off weight increased from 57,200kg (126,100lb) to 59,200kg (130,514lb), the Il-18B became the fi

ajor production version, with 84 seats. This was followed in production in
61 by the Il-18V, with AI-20K engines rated at 2,983kW (4,000shp) each, fuel
pacity of 23,700l (6,253 US gal) and standard layouts for 90 or 110
ssengers. In 1964, the more powerful AI-20M engine was introduced. Some
ternal redesign of the cabin, with the deletion of the rear cargo hold and
tension aft of the pressurized section, made it possible to increase
commodation to 110 or, by omitting coat stowage space during summer, a
aximum of 122. With these changes the designation became Il-18E, but this
as swiftly followed by the Il-18D, in which fuel capacity was increased to
arly 27 per cent, with extra bag tanks in the centre section of the aircraft.
me Il-18s were modified as cargo carriers after being retired from passenger
rvice, with a large freight door in the rear fuselage side. The Il-18 entered
rvice with Aeroflot on 20 April 1959, followed by the Il-18V in 1961, and by
e Il-18D and Il-18E in 1965. NATO reporting name is 'Cub'. Production is
lieved to have amounted to around 800 aircraft. Some 50 are still in service,
ainly in the CIS and Eastern Europe, with a few operating in the Far East and
ntral America.

low: LOT Polish Airlines was one of many Eastern Bloc airlines to
erate the Il-18 on medium-to-longhaul flights.

Ilyushin Il-62

SPECIFICATION
(Ilyushin Il-62M)

Dimensions: Wingspan 43.20m (141ft 9in); length overall 53.12m (174ft 3½in); height overall 12.35m (40ft 6¼in); wing area 279.5m² (3,009ft²).

Power Plant: Four 107.9kN (24,250lb) Soloviev D-30KU turbofans.

Weights: Operating weight empty 71,600kg (157,520lb); max take-off 165,000kg (363,760lb); max landing 105,000kg (231,483lb); max payload 23,000kg (50,706lb)

Performance: Max cruising speed 496kts (920km/h); take-off field length 3,300m (10,830ft); landing field length 2,500m (8,200ft); range with max payload 4,210nm (7,800km).

Accommodation: Flight crew of four or five. Seating for up to 186 passengers, six-abreast with central aisle. Total cargo/baggage volume 48.0m (1,695ft³).

The Il-62 was first unveiled in September 1962 and made its first flight January 1963, having been developed to provide Aeroflot with a long-range jet transport comparable in comfort and performance to the equipment already in service with Western airlines. Soviet design bureaux matched Western products in most categories of airliner, both turboprop and turbojet, with the notable exception of a four-jet design featuring podded engines on the wing, exemplified by the Boeing 707/Douglas DC-8/Convair 880 generation. Instead when the first Soviet four-jet design was developed by the Ilyushin bureau rear-engined, high-tail layout was chosen, closely matching the configuration

Vickers VC-10. In common with Western designs of similar layout, the Il-62 quired lengthy flight development to overcome the tendency of this type to ter a deep stall from which recovery was impossible. An additional mplication resulted from the tardy development of an engine suitable for the 52, the first example(s) of which flew with 73.6kN (16,535lb) Lyulka AL-7 rbojets. The 103kN (23,150lb) Kuznetsov NK-8-4 turbofans were introduced er in the programme, which involved two prototypes and three pre- oduction aircraft. The Il-62 has the NATO reporting name 'Classic'.

ARIANTS

e Il-62 entered production with NK-8-4 turbofans, and was normally furnished accommodate 168 passengers in a single-class layout, although up to 186 uld be carried. This version had cascade-type thrust-reversers on the outer gines only. By 1971 Ilyushin had produced the Il-62M, in which Soloviev D- KU engines replaced the Kuznetsov engines. The improved specific fuel nsumption of this new engine was combined with increased fuel capacity rough the introduction of a tank in the fin) to give the Il-62M considerably tter payload/range performance, thus overcoming one of the failings of the ▶

elow: Like many other commercial aircraft types produced in the old oviet Union, the Ilyushin Il-62 enabled the USSR's satellite states to aintain their air connections with headquarters in Moscow. Cubana is e largest user left outside what is now Russia, still operating a dozen the improved Ilyushin Il-62Ms on its long-haul flights.

original version. A number of internal changes were made, with a revised layout
the flight deck, new avionics to allow routine operation in Cat II conditions (w
provision to extend to Cat III), and a change in the wing spoiler control system
permit the spoilers to be used differentially for better roll control. A further varia
appeared in 1978 as the Il-62MK, with the same engines as the Il-62M, but w
structural, landing gear and control system changes to permit operation at t
higher take-off and landing weights of 167,000kg (368,170lb) and 110,000
(242,500lb) respectively. Maximum accommodation increased to 195, with
interior redesign featuring a 'widebody' look and enclosed overhead bagga
lockers. Clamshell-type thrust reversers were used on the D-30KU engines.

SERVICE USE

The Il-62 entered service with Aeroflot on 15 September 1967, on the Mosco
Montreal route, after a period of proving flights within the Soviet Union.
replaced the Tu-114 on the Moscow-New York route in July 1968 a
subsequently became standard equipment on most of Aeroflot's long-distan
routes, internationally and domestically. The Il-62M entered service on t
Moscow-Havana route in 1974. Production of the Il-62 in all versions is thoug
to have exceeded 300, of which about 150 have been for Aeroflot, with t
balance going to nations in the Soviet sphere of influence, for airline use
CAAC (China), Interflug (East Germany), Balkan Bulgarian, LOT (Poland), Tarc
(Romania), CSA (Czechoslovakia), Cubana, LA Mozambique and Chos
Minhang (North Vietnam). Around 105 were still in service in January 2001, t
vast majority in Russia and other CIS countries.

*Right: The Ilyushin Il-62 has been front-line long-haul equipment for
Aeroflot since it entered service in 1967.*

Ilyushin Il-76

SPECIFICATION
(Ilyushin Il-76T)
Dimensions: Wingspan 50.50m (165ft 8in); length overall 46.59m (152ft
10in); height overall 14.76m (48ft 5in), wing area 300.0m² (3,229.2ft²).
Power Plant: Four 117.7kN (26,455lb) Aviadvigatel D-30KP turbofans.
Weights: Operating weight empty 89,000kg (196,211lb); max take-off
170,000kg (374,785lb); max landing 140,000kg (308,640lb); max payload
40,000kg (88,185lb).
Performance: Max cruising speed 432kts (800km/h); service ceiling
15,500m (50,850ft); take-off field length 850m (2,790ft); landing field
length 450m (1,475ft); range with max payload 3,600nm (6,660km).
Accommodation: Flight crew of five. Cabin volume 235.5m³ (8,310ft³) fo
cargo. Also available passenger modules for 30 passengers each.

The design of the Il-76 began in the late 1960s to provide a hea
transport for both military and civil use, primarily as a replacement
the Antonov An-12. Key design requirements were the ability
accommodate and lift specific items of military equipment and ci
engineering hardware, but also included a rough-field capability and faciliti
for operation in extreme climatic conditions as encountered in Siberia a
elsewhere. The prototype Il-76 first flew on 25 March 1971, and w
demonstrated at that year's Paris air show. It was joined by two mo
prototypes and three static test airframes. Series production started in 19
and continues at the Chkalov Plant in Tashkent, Uzbekistan. The NAT
reporting name for the Il-76 is 'Candid'.

VARIANTS

The original unarmed Il-76 military version was followed by the Il-76T for civil use, featuring an additional fuel tank in the wing centre-section and higher operating weights. Further increases in fuel capacity and weights, strengthened wings and centre-fuselage, as well as improved Aviadvigatel (Soloviev) D-30KP-1 turbofans produced the generally unarmed Il-76TD. The Il-76M and Il-76MD are armed military variants with rear gun turret, based on the -T and -TD models respectively. First flight of the stretched and ▶

Below: Ilyushin's Il-76 also found its way to many of the Soviet Union's strongest allies, including Syria, whose national airline operates it mainly on government flights. It can carry 50 tonnes of cargo, loaded through the rear clamshell doors, or passengers in specially built 30-seat modules.

modernised military Il-76MF, powered by 156.9kN (35,275lb) PS-90A turbofans, was made on 1 August 1995, and this model is also bei offered in civilianised Il-76TF configuration. The Il-76 was also produced many other specialised military versions, and a new version with CFM turbofans, designated IL-76MF-100, is being considered.

SERVICE USE
Many Il-76s were used by Aeroflot and are now in service with

ccessor airlines in the cargo role and can be seen all over the world. It is lieved that total production has exceeded 850, although many of these ere built for military purposes. Some 295 were in airline service in January 01.

low: The Il-76 typically has a seven-man crew plus provision for a vigator in the nose.

Ilyushin Il-86

SPECIFICATION
(Ilyushin Il-86)
Dimensions: Wingspan 48.06m (157ft 8¼in); length overall 59.54m (195ft 4in); height overall 15.81m (50ft 10½in), wing area 320.0m² (3,444ft²).
Power Plant: Four 127.5kN (28,660lb) Kutznetsov NK-86 turbofans.
Weights: Max take-off 206,000kg (454,150lb); max landing 175,000kg (385,810lb); max payload 42,000kg (92,593lb).
Performance: Max cruising speed 512kts (950km/h); service ceiling 11,000m (36,090ft); take-off field length 2,600m (8,530ft); landing field length 1,980m (6,500ft); range with max payload 1,945nm (3,600km).
Accommodation: Flight crew of three. Seating for up to 300 passengers, nine-abreast with twin aisles.

Intended as a successor to the Ilyushin Il-62 and developed in response to t Boeing 747 to give Aeroflot a chance to compete effectively on long-ha routes, the Il-86 was the first to provide a 'widebody' cabin and the first to ha its engines in wing-mounted pods, all previous Soviet jet transports eith having their engines rear-mounted on the fuselage or buried in the wing roo Even so, it is interesting to record that the first published illustration of the Il-design showed a rear-engined configuration. The Il-86 design dates back to t

ly 1970s, the first of two prototypes having made its initial flight from a
oscow airfield on 22 December 1976. To power the Soviet 'airbus', the
znetsov bureau developed a new engine, the NK-86, although it is believed
at Soloviev turbofans were in view from the outset, and these have now been
opted in the Il-96 derivative. Flight development of the Il-86 appears to have
oceeded relatively smoothly, and the third aircraft, described as the first
oduction example, flew on 24 October 1977 at Voronezh, where the final
sembly line was set up. A substantial contribution to Il-86 production was
de by the Polish aircraft industry, which manufactured the fin and tailplane,
gine pylons and wing slats at the PZL Mielec plant. One of the interesting
atures of the Il-86, and related to the limited support facilities available at
ny airports served by Aeroflot, is that entry to the cabin is by way of airstairs
orporated in three doors at ground level in the lower fuselage. From the
wer deck vestibules, where heavy winter overcoats can be stowed, stairs
d up to the main cabin, making the aircraft independent of airport loading ▶

low: The Soviet Union's first wide-body passenger aircraft was
ended to replace the Il-62 on long-haul flights but proved seriously
ficient in range and had limited international exposure. Few are seen
road; AJT serves within Russia and the CIS.

stairs. The type has the NATO reporting name 'Camber'.

VARIANTS

After going into production, the Il-86 underwent routine improvement a
updating, in the course of which the gross weight was increased to
maximum permitted 208,000kg (458,560lb). As early as 1981 reports we
appearing that a longer-range derivative of the Il-86 was und
development, and by 1986 this was known to have been redesignated Il-9
Production terminated after 103 civil examples had been built, including t
two prototypes. Re-engining with CFM56 engines is being considered
increase its range, which had always been insufficient for intercontinen
routes, but it is unlikely to proceed, given the shortage of cash among t
CIS airlines.

SERVICE USE

The Il-86 entered service on 26 December 1980, operating between Mosco
and Tashkent. Many other domestic destinations were added to the Il-
network during 1981, and the first international service, between Moscow a
East Berlin, was flown on 3 July 1981. Some 95 remain in service, all in Rus
and other CIS countries, with the exception of three flown by China Xinjia
Airlines. The two largest users are Aeroflot and Vnukovo Airlines a
Uzbekistan Airways.

*Right: Aeroflot initially operated virtually all of the 100 Il-86s built, but
these have now been dispersed among the new airlines which emerge
from the old Aeroflot directorates. Only 16 remain in the fleet of Aerofl
Russian International Airlines (ARIA). Two are shown here at Tashkent.*

Ilyushin Il-96

SPECIFICATION
(Ilyushin Il-96M)
Dimensions: Wingspan 60.11m (197ft 2½in); length overall 63.94m (209ft
9in); height overall 15.72m (51ft 7in), wing area 391.6m² (4,215ft²).
Power Plant: Four 156.9kN (35,275lb) Aviadvigatel PS-90A turbofans.
Weights: Operating weight empty 132,400kg (257,940lb); max take-off
270,000kg (595,238lb); max landing 175,000kg (385,810lb); max payload
58,000kg (127,866lb).
Performance: Max cruising speed 469kts (870km/h); service ceiling 11,000r
(36,090ft); take-off field length 3,350m (11,000ft); landing field length 2,250n
(7,385ft); range with max payload 6,195nm (11,482km).
Accommodation: Flight crew of two. Seating for up to 386 passengers, nin
abreast with twin aisles.

The Il-96 (also known as the Il-96-300 in its basic 300-seat form) is an obvic
derivative of the Il-86, although described as an almost wholly new desig
Compared with its predecessor, the Il-96 has a shorter fuselage, though of t
same cross-section, and a new supercritical wing of greater span and area t
reduced sweepback (30 deg), with the addition of large winglets at the tir
Fuel capacity is almost double that of the Il-86, giving the type a substantia
increased range capability. Structurally, the Il-96 makes use of newer materi
to reduce weight, and systems have been modernised, with the introduction

*Right: The Il-96T freighter has no windows fitted. This new version is
flown by Aeroflot and may have export potential.*

a triplex fly-by-wire control system and 'glass' cockpit featuring six displa (three for each pilot) for presentation of all performance and system stat information. Equipment is of a standard to allow operation in Cat III weath minima, but modernisation has not been taken so far as to allow two-cre operation and a flight engineer's position is retained on the flight dec Accommodation for 300 passengers is provided on an upper deck, with tl lower deck reserved for cargo and baggage. The first of five prototypes flew 28 September 1988. A further two airframes were built for static and fatigi testing. Production was started in 1991 and a total of nine aircraft were flyii by the time the new type received certification on 29 December 1992.

VARIANTS

The initial production version is designated II-96-300, alluding to its maximu passenger capacity, although a more normal mixed configuration provides f 235 passengers. It is powered by four Aviadvigatel PS-90A turbofans ea generating 156.9kN (35,275lb) static thrust and has a take-off weight 216,000kg and typical range of 4,860nm (9,000km). A westernised version w 164.6kN (37,000lb) Pratt & Whitney PW2337 turbofans and Rockwell Colli digital avionics, for Cat IIIb fully automatic landing capability, was first project as the II-96-350, but this was changed to II-96M in 1990. A prototyp designated II-96MO first flew on 6 April 1996. The II-96M has a fusela

ngthened to 63.94m (209ft 9in) to provide accommodation for up to 386 ssengers, and an increased take-off weight of 270,000kg (595,238lb). A cargo rsion, the Il-96T, has a 4.85m x 2.87m (15ft 11in x 9ft 5in) cargo door on the rt side forward of the wing, and a maximum payload of 92,000kg (202,820lb). first flew on 16 May 1997 and was expected to receive certification at the end the year. An extended-range Il-96-300V has been ordered by Vnukovo rlines, while the Russian president operates one Il-96PU with VIP interior, ditional communications, and a medical centre. The Il-96MK and Il-96MR are ojected developments with high by-pass ratio ducted Samara NK-93 and iadvigatel PS-90A or Samara NK-92 engines respectively. A proposed twin-gined version is designated Il-98.

RVICE USE

eroflot took delivery of the first Il-96-300 aircraft in early 1993, operating a nall number. These were to be supplemented by the Il-96M from 1998, but e programme has slipped and the first aircraft was not due to be delivered til January 2001. Only 10 Il-96s had been delivered in total.

elow: The Ilyushin Il-96M, powered by four Pratt & Whitney PW2337 rbofans, each generating a static thrust of 164.6kN (37,000lb), goes rough its paces at the 1997 Paris air show.

Ilyushin Il-114

SPECIFICATION
(Ilyushin Il-114)

Dimensions: Wingspan 30.00m (98ft 5¼in); length overall 26.88m (88ft 2in); height overall 9.32m (30ft 7in), wing area 81.9m² (881.6ft²).

Power Plant: Two 1,839kW (2,466shp) Klimov TV7-117 turboprops, with six-blade SV-34 CFRP propellers.

Weights: Operating weight empty 15,000kg (33,070lb); max take-off 22,700kg (50,045lb); max payload 6,500kg (14,330lb).

Performance: Normal cruising speed 270kts (500km/h); service ceiling 7,200m (23,625ft); take-off field length 1,550m (5,085ft); landing field length 1,300m (4,265ft); range with max payload 540nm (1,000km).

Accommodation: Flight crew of two. Seating for up to 64 passengers, four-abreast , two seats each side of central aisle.

Designed as a successor to the Antonov An-24 on Aeroflot routes with ranges of up to 540nm (1,000km), the basic design parameters and configuration was established as long ago as 1986. Equipped to operate weather minima down to ICAO Cat II standard, the Il-114 is a conventional pressurised low-wing monoplane with swept fin and rudder and slight dihedral on the wing centre-section. Extensive use is made of composite materials and advanced metal alloys, including titanium, making up about 10 per cent structural weight. In configuration, it has a striking resemblance to the British Aerospace ATP, also typically seating 64 passengers. Two 1,839kW (2,466shp) Klimov TV7-117 turboprop engines drive low-noise six-bladed CFRP propellers. The Il-114 has built-in airstairs and can operate from unpaved airfields with little ground support. The prototype first flew at the Zhukovsky flight test centre on 29 March 1990. Two more flying prototypes and two for static tests were used in the certification programme which was completed in 1993. The first production aircraft flew on 7 August 1992 at Tashkent in Uzbekistan, where the aircraft is built. Some components are produced by Polish, Romanian and Bulgarian aerospace companies. The loss of the second prototype delayed certification until 26 April 1997.

VARIANTS
The basic production version is the Il-114 with the Klimov TV7-117 turboprops and a maximum tak-off weight of 22,700kg (50,045lb). With higher-rated TV7M-117 engines, increased take-off weight and 500kg (1,102lb) more payload, the aircraft is known as the Il-114M. The Il-114MA is powered by Pratt & Whitney Canada PW127C turboprops and made its maiden flight in 1996. For the export market, TAPO is offering the Il-114-100 (passenger) and Il-114-100T (cargo) versions (formerly known as the Il-114PC) with 2,051kW (2,750shp) PW127H turboprops, and

vanced Sextant avionics. A 40-seat, high-wing development is the Il-112, which is currently in design. Passenger, freight and military utility versions e under consideration. Also being offered are the Il-114P maritime patrol rsion, and the Il-114T Cargo model, featuring a maximum take-off weight 23,500kg (51,808lb) and a 3.31m x 1.78m (10ft 10in x 5ft 10in) cargo or in the rear fuselage. The Il-114T was developed specifically for bekistan Airways. First flight of production aircraft took place on 14 ptember 1996. The Il-114FK is a military reconnaissance/cartographic rsion with a glazed nose, small undernose radome, large observation ster below flight deck windows and container for side-looking airborne dar (SLAR) on portside. Cabin windows have been deleted. A stretch for -75 passengers is planned.

RVICE USE

st delivery made to Uzbekistan Airways, which operated the first commercial ght with the new type on 27 August 1998. Only two aircraft are believed to ve been delivered by January 2001.

low: The Il-114T freighter demonstrated at the Paris air show in 1997. its circular fuselage it can carry up to 6,500kg (14,300lb) of cargo a stance of some 1,000km (620 miles). The propellers are carbon-fibre inforced plastic.

Indonesian Aerospace N-250

SPECIFICATION

(IPTN N-250-100)

Dimensions: Wingspan 28.00m (91ft 10¼in); length overall 28.15m (92ft 4½in); height overall 8.78m (28ft 9¾in), wing area 65.00m² (699.7ft²).

Power Plant: Two 2,386kW (3,200shp) Allison AE 2100C turboprops, wit Dowty six-blade propellers.

Weights: Operating weight empty 15,700kg (34,612lb); max take-off 24,800kg (54,674lb); max landing 24,600kg (54,233lb); max payload 6,200kg (13,668lb).

Performance: Max cruising speed 330kts (611km/h); max rate of climb 10.0m/s (1,968ft/min); service ceiling 7,620m (25,000ft); take-off field length 1,220m (4,000ft); landing field length 1,220m (4,000ft); range with max payload 686nm (1,270km).

Accommodation: Flight crew of two. Seating for up to 68 passengers, four-abreast with central aisle. Total baggage volume 11.65m³ (411.4ft³).

The first fully indigenous aircraft design project of Indonesia's fledglin aerospace industry was announced at the Paris air show on 15 June 19⁇ by Indonesia's technology minister and IPTN's president director Prof Dr Ing J Habibie. Indonesia's most ambitious programme to date, while conventional high-wing configuration and non-swept T-tailplane, neverthele features latest technology, including fully-powered fly-by-wire contro electronic flight instrumentation system (EFIS) and engine indication and cre alerting system (EICAS) with six CRT colour displays. The sixth CRT is for an optional global positioning system (GPS). The structure includes 10 per cent composites, primarily for control surfaces. Allison AE 2100C turboprops with low-noise six-bladed propellers were chosen in July 1990. Prototype construction began in 1992, but it soon became evident that for a 50-seater, the aircraft would be overweight and plans were made the following year to stretch the airframe to provide a 64-68 passenger capacity. The prototype rolled out in the original configuration on 10 November 1994 and made its maiden flight on 10 August 1995. Four more development aircraft and two static/fatigue test airframes participated in the certification programme, with the first N-250-100 flown on 13 December 1996. Domestic certification and FAA/IAA approval not received by January 2001.

VARIANTS

The initial production version will be the N-250-100 with a fuselage 1.525m (5ft 0in) longer than the prototype and shorter engine nacelles. It is to be made available in passenger, cargo and combi models. Based on the short fuselage prototype for 50/54 passengers, the N-250-50 will have a lower-mounted wing box, to reduce weight and drag, and a larger diameter to increase cabin nd baggage volume. An AEW version is under consideration for the future, with a planned in-service date of 2004. A stretched 76-seat version is proposed as the N-250-200. The N-270 is a stretched 70-seat and uprated derivative of the N250-100 optimised for the US market, and is to be assembled at a new plant in Mobile, Alabama, by American Regional Aircraft Industry (AMRAI), owned 40 per cent by IPTN although this has been frozen. Principal changes include the same AE 2100C engines uprated to 2,983kW (4,000shp), six additional fuselage frames to produce a 3.05m (10ft 0in) stretch to accommodate typically 70 passengers, higher gross weight and additional cargo and baggage compartments. IPTN also wants to extend further the market for the N250 with plans to set up a European production line in Germany.

SERVICE USE

At 1 January 2001, orders and options, mostly from Indonesian airlines, totalled 227 aircraft, just 46 short of the company's stated break-even figure. IPTN expects to sell at least 400 to local carriers.

Below: The N-250, shown here on its Paris debut in June 1997, is the embodiment of the bold ambitions of Indonesia's technology minister to develop an aircraft manufacturing industry in his country. But while the aircraft may find a role with Indonesia's domestic operators, the trend towards jet aircraft may limit its appeal elsewhere in the world.

Indonesian Aerospace N-2130

PRELIMINARY SPECIFICATION
(N2130-100IGW)
Dimensions: Wingspan 29.90m (98ft 1¼in); length overall 31.25m (102ft 6½in); wing area 107.4m² (1,150ft²).
Power Plant: Two 85.9kN (19,300lb) turbofans.
Weights: Max take-off 51,500kg (113,537lb); max landing 46,350kg (102,183lb); max payload 11,400kg (25,132lb).
Performance: Max cruise speed Mach 0.80;
take-off and landing field length 1,750m (5,740ft); max range 1,850nm (3,420km).
Accommodation: Flight crew of two. Seating for up to 114 passengers.

The initial NTP study (N-2130 Technology Program) into a 100-seat regiona jet was started in October 1994, but the decision to proceed has yet to b made. The present timetable projects a first flight by mid-2002, wit certification and first deliveries expected in early 2004. The N-2130 is c conventional low-wing design with underwing podded engines, sweptbac wings and tail unit. It features an advanced digital fly-by-wire control system based on the N-250, and integrated avionics computer which provides dat processing and distribution functions. Three candidates have been identified fc

he power plant: the CFM International CFM56-9, BMW Rolls-Royce BR 715-6, and the Pratt & Whitney PW6000. Required static thrust is in the area of 2kN (18,500lb) each. The circular fuselage cross-section incorporates assenger service units (PSU) to permit easy changes in business and conomy class arrangements, choice of a normal or wider aisle width, and large apacity overhead luggage bins per passenger. The proposed family comprises he baseline N-2130-100 for up to 114 passengers and the stretched N-2130-00, which can accommodate 132 passengers in an all-tourist layout. Each ersion will be available with the option of basic and increased grossweight GW). The N-2130 will be able to take off and land on 1,750m (5,740ft) unways and cruise at Mach 0.8 up to 39,000ft. Maximum range is 1,850nm 3,420km). IPTN projects a market for 100-130 seat aircraft of more than 3,200 etween 2005 and 2025, but will find the competition tough. The programme as been put on the backburner as a result of the financial crisis and difficult olitical situation in Indonesia.

Below: The N-2130 represents the enormous ambition of Indonesia's manufacturing industry, although the project appears to have been put on the backburner.

Let L-410 Turbolet

SPECIFICATION
(Let L-410UVP-E)
Dimensions: Wingspan 19.98m (65ft 6½in); length overall 14.43m (47ft 4in); height overall 5.83m (19ft 1½in), wing area 35.18m² (378.7ft²).
Power Plant: Two 559kW (750shp) Motorlet Walter M 601E turboprops, driving Avia V 510 five-blade constant-speed reversible-pitch metal propellers.
Weights: Operating weight empty 3,985kg (8,785lb); max take-off 6,400kg (14,110lb); max landing 6,200kg (13,668lb); max payload 1,615kg (3,560lb).
Performance: Max cruising speed 168kts (311km/h); max rate of climb 7.4m/s (1,455ft/min); service ceiling 7,050m (23,125ft); take-off field length 445m (1,460ft); landing field length 240m (787ft); range with max payload 294nm (546km).
Accommodation: Flight crew of one or two. Seating for 19 passengers, two seats on one side of the aisle, one on the other. Total baggage volume front and rear 1.37m³ (48.4ft³).

After some years of licence-production of Soviet types, the Let Kunovice works began in 1966 the design and development of a small twin-engine light transport intended to meet the needs of East European nations in general (including the Soviet Union) as well as Czechoslovakia in particular. A high wing monoplane of conventional appearance, this aircraft emerged as the XL-410 in 1969, making its first flight on 16 April 1969. New turboprop engines under development by Motorlet at the Walter works were not ready, so prototype and early production aircraft were fitted with imported Pratt & Whitney engines.

VARIANTS
The initial production version of the Turbolet, as the aircraft came to be known

Below: Estonian regional airline ELK operates two Let L-410UVP-E aircraft on scheduled and charter services across the Baltic. Note the prominent external tip tanks.

Above: This L-410UVP-E20 aircraft registered in Finland is the executive version, normally seating a maximum of 13 passengers and first certificated in 1990. It introduced emergency exits, separate baggage hold and Bendix/King avionics including autopilot.

vas the L-410A, with 533kW (715shp) PT6A-27 engines. Thirty-one were built, ncluding four prototypes, one of which later became L-410AB when test flown vith Hartzell four-blade (in place of the original three-blade) propellers. One L-410AF was built (for Hungary) with a revised, glazed nose compartment and vas equipped for the aerial survey role. The L-410AS was equipped with a Soviet avionics fit. In 1973 the Motorlet M 601 engine became available, and he L-410M entered production with the 410kW (550shp) M 601A, soon uperseded by the L-410MA with the more powerful M 601B. The L-410MU ncluded equipment specified by Aeroflot, and production of all 'M' variants totalled 110.

To overcome Soviet criticism of handling characteristics, the L-410UVP, first flown on 1 November 1977, introduced increased wing span and vertical tail area, dihedral on the tailplane, spoilers, automatic bank control flaps and numerous other systems and equipment changes. Soviet certification of the L-410UVP was obtained in 1980. Generally similar to this variant, the L-410UVP-E first flew on 30 December 1984 and introduced five-blade propellers, tip tanks and more powerful engines. It replaced the UVP from early 1985 onwards. Other suffixes were used for specialised versions. The L-420 is an improved L-410UVP-E20 with Walter M601F engines, western avionics and several detail changes. A stretched L-430 with Pratt & Whitney Canada PT6 turboprops is under study.

SERVICE USE

The L-410A entered service on Czech domestic routes operated by Slov-Air in late 1971. The L-410M began deliveries in 1976, followed by the L-410 UVP after certification in 1979. Aeroflot took delivery of its 500th L-410 in March 1985. A total of 1001 were produced, of which 872 were delivered to the then Soviet Union.

Let L-610

SPECIFICATION
(Let L-610G)
Dimensions: Wingspan 25.60m (84ft 0in); length overall 21.72m (71ft 3in); height overall 8.19m (26ft 10½in), wing area 56.0m² (602.8ft²).
Power Plant: Two 1,305kW (1,750shp) General Electric CT7-9D turboprops, with Hamilton Standard HS-14RF-23 four-blade fully feathering reversible-pitch metal propellers.
Weights: Operating weight empty 9,220kg (20,326lb); max take-off 14,500kg (31,967lb); max landing 14,200kg 31,305(lb); max payload 4,200kg (9,259lb).
Performance: Max cruising speed 237kts (438km/h); max rate of climb 8.5m/s (1,673ft/min); service ceiling 8,400m (27,560ft); take-off field length 1,090m (3,577ft) landing field length 645m (2,117ft); range with max payload 302nm (560km).
Accommodation: Flight crew of two. Seating for 40 passengers, four-abreast, two seats each side of central aisle.

The Let National Corporation, based at Kunovice, began development of the L-610 in the mid-1980s, primarily in response to a Soviet specification for a regional airliner with about 40 seats, to operate over stage lengths of 400 600km. Similar in configuration to the smaller L-410, the L-610 is, nevertheless an entirely new design, incorporating a two-spar high wing with single-slotted Fowler flaps and spoilers and integrated fuel tanks, fixed-incidence tailplane high on the fin, auxiliary power unit, and retractable tricycle landing gear. The first L-610M prototype flew on 28 December 1988, but development of this model was suspended in 1996 in favour of the L-610G with .. General Electric CT7-9D turboprops with Hamilton Standard 4-blade propellers, and Rockwell Collins digital avionics including EFIS, weather radar and autopilot. The firs

Lockheed L100 Hercules

SPECIFICATION
(Lockheed L100-30)
Dimensions: Wingspan 40.41m (132ft 7in); length overall 34.37m (112ft 9in); height overall 11.66m (38ft 3in), wing area 162.12m² (1,745ft²).
Power Plant: Four 3,490kW (4,680shp) Allison 501-D22A turboprops, driving four-blade Hamilton Standard constant-speed feathering and reversing propellers.
Weights: Operating weight empty 35,325kg (77,680lb); max take-off 70,308kg (155,000lb); max landing 61,235kg (135,000lb); max payload 23,183kg (51,110lb).
Performance: Max cruising speed 315kts (583km/h); initial rate of climb 8.64m/s (1,700ft/min); take-off field length 1,890m (6,200ft); landing field length 1,480m (4,850ft); range with max payload 1,363nm (2,526km).
Accommodation: Flight crew of four. Seating for up to 128 passengers.

The commercial L100 originated as a 'civilianised' version of the C-130 Hercules military tactical transport, and was first flown in the form of a Model 382 company demonstrator on 21 April 1964. FAA type approval was obtained on 16 February 1965. The origin of the Hercules goes back to an US Air Force specification of 1951 for a tactical transport and multi-mission aircraft

Right: Indonesian airline Merpati Nusantara operated the Hercules on passenger and freight flights.

p: More than 1,000 L-410s were built, with the vast majority delivered the former Soviet Union.

ove: The Let L-610 looks like a larger L-410, but it is a new design, th the tailplane mounted high on the fin.

ht of this version, took place on 18 December 1993. Total orders and options ve been obtained for 20 aircraft, but none had been delivered by January 01. Since the acquisition of Let by US company Ayres, the aircraft has also en marketed as the Ayres 7000.

capable of carrying up to 128 troops. The first YC-130A Hercules flew on August 1954 and went on to become the definitive tactical military airlift From the outset, Lockheed had targeted the civil market, and in 19 announced the sale the GL-207 Super Hercules to Pan American and Sl Airways for delivery in 1962. Powered by four Allison T61 turboprop engine the Super Hercules was to be 7.11m (23ft 4in) longer than the standard milita C-130B. Alternative power plants and even a jet version was proposed, but t project was cancelled, giving way to the L100.

VARIANTS
Small numbers of Model 382B Hercules (some also known as L100s) we built for commercial use from 1965 onwards. These early models had t same 29.79m (97ft 9in) overall length as the basic C-130B. The project L100-10, with D22A engines replacing the 3,022kW (4,050shp) 501-D22 was followed by the L100-20 with the same uprated engines and a 2.54 (8ft 4in) lengthening of the fuselage. The original demonstrator w converted to Model 382E (L100-20) form and first flew on 19 April 196 gaining type approval on 4 October that year. The L100-30 had anoth 2.03m (6ft 8in) fuselage stretch and first flew on 14 August 1970, ty approval being gained on 7 October.

SERVICE USE
Around 110 civil Hercules have been delivered, just over half being L100-30 Almost all were for cargo transport by airlines and government agencie although Indonesia's oil company Pelita Air Services has used the aircraft passenger configuration, seating 128 passengers. Others have be fitted with modules to enable the carrying of passengers. A total of more th 2,150 Hercules had been built by January 2001, and military production continuing. Some 40 civil models remain in active airline service.

Above: Outsize cargo specialist HeavyLift uses the Lockheed Hercules to supplement its larger Russian and Ukrainian aircraft on worldwide ad hoc and contract charter flights.

Below: The Hercules is unsurpassed as a medium-capacity civil and military freihter.

Lockheed L188 Electra

SPECIFICATION
(Lockheed L-188A Electra)
Dimensions: Wingspan 30.1 8m (9ft 0m); length overall 31.81m (1 04ft 6in); height overall 10.0m (32ft l0in), wing area 120.8m² (1,300ft²).
Power Plant: Four 2,800kW (3,750shp) Ailison 501-D13 turboprops, with four blade reversing and feathering propellers.
Weights: Operating weight empty 27,895kg (61,500lb); max take-off 52,664kg (116,000lb); max landing 43,385kg (95,650lb); max payload 12,020kg (26,500lb).
Performance: Max cruising speed 352kts (652km/h); initial rate of climb 8.5m/s (1,670ft/min); service ceiling 8,230m (27,000ft); take-off field length 1,440m (4,720ft); landing field length 1,310m (4,300ft); range with max payload 1,910nm (3,540km). **Accommodation:** Flight crew of three. Seating for up to 98 passengers, six-abreast with central aisle. Underfloor baggage/cargo volume 14.95m³ (528.0ft³).

The trigger for initial design activity by Lockheed's Burbank, Californi company was a 1954 specification produced by American Airlines for short/medium-range transport to operate on its US domestic routes. Broac the design was for a 100-seater with a range of some 2,000nm (3,700kr grossing about 49,900kg (1100,000lb). It was the first US-originating airliner feature turboprop power, and was destined to be the only such aircraft achieve production status in the USA. The first of four prototype/flight te Electras flew on 6 December 1957 and the fifth, which was to be the fi delivered for airline service, flew on 19 May 1958. After the launch orders American Airlines and Eastern Air Lines for 75 aircraft, orders quic accumulated, but evaporated just as rapidly, as the new turbojets proved th

Below: The Electra is popular with UK freight operators, including Atlantis Airlines.

bove: Channel Express operates the Electra on freight Flights.

ility to compete. Confidence in the Electra was also shaken within the
st 15 months of service by two fatal accidents that were traced, after
instaking research, to structural failures occuring in an unforeseen chain
action after damage to the power plant mounting, for example in a heavy
iding. A major structural modification programme was put in hand by
ockheed after the FAA imposed strict flight limitations in March 1960, and
modified aircraft was granted an unrestricted airworthiness certificate on
January 1961. The problem has not occurred since. The initial L-188A
rsion, which accounted for most of the production, was followed by the
nger-range L-188C, which provided extra fuel and operated at higher
eights. From 1967, five years after the end of production, Lockheed
nverted 41 aircraft to freighters or convertible cargo/passenger aircraft,
fitting a large port cargo door forward of the wing and strengthened floor.
rcraft thus modified have been designated L-188AF and L-188CF
spectively. The L-188A obtained FAA certification on 22 August 1958 and
tered service with Eastern Air Lines on 12 January 1959, followed by
merican Airlines 11 days later. The L-188C went into service with KLM
at same year. The commercial production run totalled 170, but the Electra
as also evolved into the highly successful P-3 Orion, which has passed the
0 mark. Around 50 Electras remain in service with cargo operators in
rica, Europe and the Americas.

Above: The Lockheed Electra entered service in 1959 with Eastern Air Lines, but it achieved only limited commercial success.

Below: Many Electras were modified for cargo-carrying, with a large side-loading door and reinforced floor.

Lockheed L1011 TriStar

SPECIFICATION
(Lockheed L1011-500)
Dimensions: Wingspan 50.09m (164ft 4in); length overall 50.05m (164ft 2½in); height overall 16.87m (55ft 4in), wing area 329.0m² (3,541ft²).
Power Plant: Three 222.4kN (50,000lb) Rolls-Royce RB211-524B4 turbofans. Weights: Operating weight empty 111,312kg (245,400lb); max take-off 231,330kg (510,000lb); max landing 166,920kg (368,000lb); max payload 42,003kg (92,600lb).
Performance: Max cruising speed 525kts (973km/h); max rate of climb 14.3m/s (2,820ft/min); service ceiling 13,100m (43,000ft); take-off field length 2,800m (9,200ft); landing field length 2,065m (6,770ft); range with max payload 5,345nm (9,905km).
Accommodation: Flight crew of three. Seating for up to 330 passengers, nine-abreast with twin aisles. Total baggage/cargo volume 118.9m³ (4,200ft³).

ike the Electra, Lockheed's TriStar owes its origins to an American Airlines specification – but contrary to the case of the Electra, this airline did not in e end become a launch customer for the Lockheed jetliner. The 1966 ecification was for a short/medium-range large-capacity transport, and to eet it Lockheed and Douglas produced very similar project designs, the most table feature of which was the combination of podded engines on the wing th a third at the rear of the aircraft. Lockheed obtained launch orders for its 011 design on 29 March 1968, from TWA and Eastern Airlines, after merican had opted for the Douglas competitor. From the big new turbofan gines offered by Pratt & Whitney, General Electric and Rolls-Royce, ▶

elow: British Airways operated the TriStar on scheduled services before ansferring them to charter work.

*Above: Bahrain-based four-nations airline Gulf Air bought four TriStar 1,
in 1976, later supplemented by eight more. They entered service on its
prestige routes, linking Bahrain, Doha, Abu Dhabi, Dubai and Muscat to
London, Cairo, Karachi and Bombay.*

Lockheed chose – with the full approval of its initial customers – the RB.211,
decision that committed Rolls-Royce to a programme of development an
production that led it into bankruptcy in February 1971, placing not only th
TriStar but the whole of the Lockheed company in jeopardy. The first L1011 ha
flown, meanwhile, on 17 November 1970, with four more required for th
certification programme following by 2 December 1971. With the future
Rolls-Royce assured through its nationalisation, Lockheed was able to procee
with the TriStar, using the RB.211-22 at its initial rating of 186.9kN (42,000lb
the first flight with engines of this standard being made on 8 September 197
Production and development proceeded throughout the 1970s, but sales of th
Lockheed TriStar failed to match market projections and production was ende
by Lockheed in 1984, leaving the company without a commercial jet transpc
programme.

VARIANTS

The original TriStar, with a fuselage length of 54.17m (177ft 8½in) and up
400 seats, was the L1011-1, with a gross weight of 195,045kg (430,000lt
This was followed in 1974 by the L1011-200 with RB.211-524 engines rate
at 213.6kN-222.4kN (48,000-50,000lb) and maximum take-off weight of u
to 216,363kg (477,000lb) depending on fuel capacity. With the same high
operating weights and increased fuel capacities but the lower-rated -22

ngines the aircraft was designated L1011-100. The first flight of a TriStar
th -524 engines was made on 12 August 1976. In 1976 Lockheed
unched the L1011-500, which combined higher weights and enlarged fuel
pacity with a shorter fuselage to achieve very long ranges. Advanced
rodynamic features were also introduced in the L1011-500, including
tive controls, resulting in a 2.74m (9ft) increase in wing span and a
duction in tailplane area. The first L1011-500 flew in October 1978, with
2.4kN (50,000lb) 524B engines but without the extended wingtips, which
ere first flown in November 1979. The designation L1011-250 applies to
nversions of the L1011-1 to have the same 524B4 engines as used in the
011-500, allowing maximum take-off weight to be increased to
4,985kg (496,000lb). Fuel capacity is also increased. Conversion of six
011-1s to -250 standard for Delta Air Lines began in 1986. Other L1011-
conversions included the L1011-50, increasing maximum weight from
5,047kg (430,000lb) to 204,119kg (450,000lb), and the L1011-150, with a
) per cent increase in range.

ERVICE USE

e L1011-1 was certificated on 14 April 1972, and Eastern Airlines flew the
st revenue service on 26 April, with TWA flying its first service on 25 June
172. The L1011-200 was certificated on 26 April 1977 and entered service
th Saudia. The L1011-500 entered service with British Airways on 7 May
179 and, with extended wings and active controls, was introduced by Pan
merican in 1980. Production of the TriStar totalled 250 of all versions of which
me 140 remained in active service in 1998. The vast majority are now flown
charter airlines in Europe and North America.

Above: Delta Air Lines is the largest airline still operating the TriStar on mainline services. It was one of the first to order the type when it

ontracted to buy 24 in April 1968 and eventually operated 54 of all ariants. The first entered Delta service in December 1973.

Lockheed L1329 JetStar

SPECIFICATION
(Lockheed L1329-25 JetStar II)
Dimensions: Wingspan 16.60m (54ft 5½in); length 18.42m (60ft 5¼in); heig
overall 6.23m (20ft 5¼in); wing area 50.40m² (542.5ft²).
Power Plant: Four 16.5kN (3,700lb) thrust Garrett AiResearch TFE731
turbofans.
Weights: Operating weight empty 11,226kg (24,750lb); max take-off 20,185
(44,500lb); max landing 16,330kg (36,000lb); max payload 1,280kg (2,820lb).
Performance: Max cruising speed 476kts (880km/h); service ceiling 13,10E
(43,000ft); take-off field length 1,600m (5,250ft); landing field length 1,19C
(3,905ft); range with typical payload 2,605nm (4,820km).
Accommodation: Flight crew of two. Standard seating for 10 passengers.

The four-engined Lockheed L1329 JetStar was one of the first purpose-bu
business jets to be developed. It had its origins in a USAF requirement for a hig
speed transport and training aircraft, and was intended to carry eight to
passengers. Launched as a private venture in March 1957, the prototype first fle
on 4 September that year. The expected large orders from the military did n
however, materialise, although Lockheed eventually build a small number for t
USAF, although it proved far less successful than the competing Sabreliner. T
prototypes were powered by four Bristol Siddeley turbojets, but these we
replaced by the less powerful Pratt & Whitney JT12A-6 turbojets in the producti

rsion, which flew in summer 1960 and obtained FAA type approval in June 1961. e initial production version was known as the L1329-6 JetStar 6, and the USAF ok five early production aircraft as the C-140A for the inspection of military vaids, and 11 VC-140B transport aircraft for use by the special air missions wing Military Air Command (MAC). In summer 1963, the JT12A-6s were replaced by rated 11.43kN (2,570lb) JT12A-6As. A new version, the L1329-8 JetStar 8 was roduced in January 1967. This featured more powerful 14.7kN (3,300lb) JT12A-8 bojets, higher gross weight, improved anti-skid brakes, and an emergency eumatic extension system for the landing gear. A major upgrade was initiated in tober 1972, when Lockheed re-engined the JetStar with higher-thrust, more icient and quieter Garrett TFE731-3 turbofans, which significantly improved the erall performance of the aircraft. Known as the L1329-25 JetStar II, this new craft flew on 18 August 1976 and was certified on 14 December that year. It oved, however, a final fling, with Lockheed suspending JetStar production in 79. A total of 202 JetStars (plus 2 prototypes) were built. In parallel with new-ild JetStar IIs, the AiResearch Aviation Company re-engined existing JetStar 6s d 8s with the TFE731s, and these were known as the JetStar 731. The first of ese made its maiden flight on 10 July 1974. Some 100 JetStars remained in rvice in January 2001.

elow: The four-engined Lockheed JetStar was one of the first purpose-ilt business jets to enter service.

Martin 4-0-4

SPECIFICATION
(Martin 4-0-4)

Dimensions: Wingspan 28.44m (93ft 3¹/₂in); length overall 22.75m (74ft 7in); height overall 8.61m (28ft 2in), wing area 79.9m² (864.0ft²).

Power Plant: Two 1,791kW (2,400hp) Pratt & Whitney R-2800-CB16 Double Wasp air-cooled radial piston engines, with Hamilton Standard Hydromatic three-blade fully-feathering and reversing constant-speed propellers.

Weights: Operating weight empty 14,107kg (31,100lb); max take-off 20,385k (44,900lb); max landing 19,522kg (43,000lb); max payload 4,491kg (9,900lb).

Performance: Max cruising speed 271kts (502km/h); initial rate of climb 9.6m/s (1,905ft/min); service ceiling 8,845m (29,000ft); take-off field length 1,330m (4,360ft); landing field length 1,250m (4,100ft); range with max payload 270nm (499km).

Accommodation: Flight crew of two or three. Seating for up to 52 passengers, four-abreast, two seats each side of central aisle. Total baggage volume 6.7m³ (237.0ft³).

Turning from its military activities in World War II and seeking to re-establish pre-war reputation as a manufacturer of commercial aircraft, the Glenn L Mar Co of Baltimore, Maryland, announced in November 1945 its plan to produce twin-engined 40-seat transport of modern design, offering a substant performance advance over the pre-war types such as the Douglas DC-3 a Curtiss CW-20 (C-46) on which the world's airlines were heavily dependent. T US domestic airlines made up the market of most immediate interest to Martin a early success in meeting the needs of this market appeared to have been achiev when Martin recorded large orders for its Model 2-0-2 (as the new design w styled) from several other operators. Powered by 2,400hp (1,790kW) Double Wa

2800-CA18 engines, the first 2-0-2 flew on 23 November 1946 and was a nventional low-wing monoplane of stressed-skin light-alloy construction, having unpressurized fuselage and a relatively high aspect ratio (10.0:1) wing that was table for its considerable dihedral angle and large double-slotted flaps. Featuring cycle landing gear, the 2-0-2 had several design innovations aimed at the needs airlines with short stage lengths and quick turnarounds. In particular, passenger cess to the cabin was by way of a ventral airstair under the tail so that engines uld remain at ground idle during short stops; and a door in the front fuselage side as intended for galley and cabin servicing, but not for passenger use. An accident iich was attributed to structural failure in the wing grounded the aircraft in 1948 d it returned to service only in 1950 after modification to 2-0-2A standard. The cond 2-0-2 served as the vehicle for development of the 2-0-2A, and first flew as ch in July 1950. On 20 June 1947, a Martin 3-0-3 prototype was flown, this being effect a pressurized version of the 2-0-2, but the difficulties encountered with e original model led to the cancellation of production plans for the 3-0-3. Instead, artin proceeded to develop a more extensively modified and improved variant as e 4-0-4, whose first flight was made on 21 October 1950. The Martin 2-0-2 was arded its US Approved Type Certificate (ATC No. 795) on 13 August 1947, nine onths after first flight, and flew its first revenue service in October 1947 with AN Chile, the first US operator, Northwest, following in November. After odification, the first 2-0-2A entered service with TWA on 1 September 1950, and s same airline put the 4-0-4 into service on 5 October 1951. Martin built 43 of e Model 2-0-2s and 103 of the Model 4-0-4s. A handful remained in active service 2001.

elow: The US domestic airlines, including Easter Air Lines, provided the ain market for the Martin Liners.

McDonnell Douglas DC-8

SPECIFICATION

(Douglas DC-8-73)

Dimensions: Wingspan 45.20m (148ft 5in); length overall 57.12m (187ft 5in) height overall 13.11m (43ft 0in), wing area 271.9m² (2,927ft²).

Power Plant: Four CFM International CFM56-2-C5 turbofans, each rated at 97.9kN (22,000lb) or 106.8kN (24,000lb) static thrust.

Weights: Operating weight empty 75,500kg (166,500lb); max take-off 161,025kg (355,000lb); max landing 117,000kg (258,000lb); max payload 29,257kg (64,500lb).

Performance: Max cruising speed 479kts (887km/h); service ceiling 10,000m (32,800ft); take-off field length 3,050m (10,000ft); range with max payload 4,830nm (8,950km).

Accommodation: Flight crew of three. Seating for up to 269 passengers, six abreast with central aisle. Underfloor cargo/baggage volume 70.80m³ (2,500ft³).

The decision to launch development of a four-jet medium/long range jetlin was taken by Douglas Aircraft Company in June 1955, almost a year aft Boeing had flown its Dash 80 prototype from which the Model 707 fam emerged. As the DC-8, the new aircraft was the first Douglas commercial j and a successor for the DC-7C. It also closely resembled the Boeing 707 overall configuration, although with slightly less sweepback on the wir

Below: After the DC-8 was withdrawn from mainline passenger service, the stretched and re-engined DC-8-70 Series became sought after for th carriage of cargo. Long-established Southern Air Transport operates fou DC-8-73F.

Above: Emery Worldwide has a large fleet of DC-8 freighters, including this DC-8-73CF.

Subject of a launch order from Pan American on 13 October 1955, the DC-8 quickly attracted further orders from US and foreign airlines, and 142 were on order by the time the prototype made its first flight on 30 May 1958. Powered by JT3C turbojets, the prototype represented the medium-range domestic version; other variants were already in production, as detailed below under the Variants heading.

VARIANTS

Subsequent to its introduction, the initial version of the DC-8 was designated the DC-8 Srs 10, distinguishing it from the long-range DC-8 Srs 30 which, with JT4A engines, first flew on 21 February 1959. For airlines requiring enhanced take-off performance in the domestic variant, the DC-8 Srs 20 had the JT4A engines, but operated at the lower Srs 10 weights, and was first flown on 29 November 1958 (being the second DC-8 to fly). As an alternative to the Pratt & Whitney JT4As, Douglas offered to fit Rolls-Royce Conways in the DC-8 Srs 40, first flown on 23 July 1959. During the DC-8's production life, several different versions of the JT4A were fitted in the airliner, with ratings ranging from 66.75kN (15,500lb) to 77.9kN (17,500lb), and the intercontinental Srs 30 and Srs 40 featured extended wing tips and the so-called 'four per cent' wing, the leading edge being modified to increase chord by this amount. The advent of turbofan adaptation of the JT-3C in the form of the JT-3D led to the appearance of the DC-8 Srs 50, first flown on 20 December 1960, and this was also the basis for the Jet Trader (DC-8 Srs 55) with a side-loading freight door, reinforced floor and cargo-handling provisions, first flown on 29 October 1962. Up to this point, all DC-8 variants had the same fuselage length, but in April 1965 three new variants were launched, introducing two new fuselage lengths. Known generically as the Sixty Series, these comprised the DC-8 Srs 61 first flown on 14 March 1966, the DC-8 Srs 63 first flown on 10 April 1967 with the same

1.18m (3ft 8in) fuselage stretch but a number of aerodynamic improvements, nd the DC-8 Srs 62 with only a 2.03m (6ft 8in) stretch but the same erodynamic changes, including an increase of 1.83m (6ft) in wingspan. onvertible (CF) and all-freight (AF) versions of all three were later offered. In 979, the Cammacorp company launched a conversion programme to fit FM56 turbofans to the Sixty Series aircraft, with substantial benefit to conomics. The first conversion flew on 15 August 1981 and the designations C-8 Srs 71, 72 and 73 were adopted for the converted aircraft.

ERVICE USE

he DC-8 Srs 10 was certificated on 31 August 1959, and United Air Lines and elta Air Lines flew the first revenue services on 18 September. The DC-8 Srs 0 was certificated on 1 February 1960 and was in service with KLM and Pan merican on transatlantic services in April. Certification of the DC-8 Srs 40 on 4 March 1960 allowed TCA (now Air Canada) to put this version into operation April. The DC-8 Srs 50 was certificated on 10 October 1961, and the DC-8 Srs 5 Jet Trader on 29 January 1963. Certification dates for the Sixty Series were September 1966, 27 April 1967 and 30 June 1967, and entry into service ates were 25 February, 22 May and 27 July respectively. The DC-8 Super 71, 2 and 73 were certificated in April, June and September 1982. Production of e DC-8 totalled 556 and ended in May 1972, including 263 of the Super Sixty eries, of which 110 had been converted to Super Seventy series when the ammacorp programme came to an end in March 1986. Some 230 DC-8s main in service, almost exclusively as cargo aircraft.

elow: Ivory Coast based multi-national carrier Air Afrique was the only frican airline to purchase new DC-8s for its passenger services. This DC- -50 was its first to be delivered in October 1963.

McDonnell Douglas DC-9

SPECIFICATION

(McDonnell Douglas DC-9-51)

Dimensions: Wingspan 28.47m (93ft 5in); length overall 40.71m (133ft 7in); height overall 8.56m (28ft 1in), wing area 92.97m² (1,001.7ft²).

Power Plant: Two 71.17kN (16,000lb) Pratt & Whitney JT8D-17 turbofans.

Weights: Operating weight empty 29,484kg (65,000lb); max take-off 54,885k (121,000lb); max landing 49,895kg (110,000lb); max payload 15,343kg (33,825lb).

Performance: Max cruising speed 490kts (907km/h); max rate of climb 14.7m/s (2,900ft/min); take-off field length 2,500m (8,200ft); range with max payload 700nm (1,295km).

Accommodation: Flight crew of two. Seating for up to 139 passengers, five-abreast with single aisle.

Douglas project studies in the early 1950s for an aircraft to complement th then recently-launched DC-8 concentrated upon a scaled-down version that type to operate over medium ranges. Intensive market studies over period of several years led the company to extend the timescale for the launc of this new type, and to initiate a wholly original design rather than attempt use DC-8 components. As the DC-9, the new jetliner was firmed up in 1963 an was formally launched on 8 April of that year as a short/medium range aircra with about 75 seats in typical mixed-class arrangement. In configuration th DC-9 closely resembled the BAC One-Eleven, with rear-mounted engines an

T-tail. Delta Air Lines became the launch airline with an order for 15, and the first of five aircraft for the certification programme flew on 25 February 1965. From the outset, Douglas planned to offer a variety of fuselage lengths and fuel capacities, with appropriate engine powers and operating weights, and this policy has helped to keep the DC-9 in production for a long period, with the very latest variants designated as the MD-80 series and yet more derivatives in the MD-90 series, both described separately.

VARIANTS

With 53.4kN (12,000lb) Pratt & Whitney JT8D-5 engines, the DC-9 Srs 10 had an overall length of 31.82m (104ft 4¾in) and up to 90 seats. More powerful 63.3kN (14,000lb) JT8D-7 engines were also available. The DC-9 Srs 20 was similar with more powerful JT8D-9 or -11 engines and the increased wing span of the Srs 30 with full-span leading-edge slats, for hot-and-high performance. It first flew on 18 September 1968, preceded by the first DC-9 Srs 30 on 1 August 1966, with fuselage lengthened by 4.6m (14ft 11in) to seat up to 115 passengers. The DC-9-30 was available in several sub-variants with differing weights and engine combinations, and was also produced for the United States Air Force (USAF) as the C-9A Nightingale, and for the US Navy as the C-9B ▶

Below: US low-fare, no-frills airline ValuJet operated close on 50 DC-9s from a hub at Atlanta, before a much-publicised crash in Florida led to a temporary grounding of the airline.

Skytrain II. The C-9A was produced for aeromedical duties, while the C-9B wa
used as a logistic transport. To meet the needs of SAS, the Srs 30 was furthe
evolved in the mid-1960s to produce the DC-9 Srs 40 with another stretch c
1.87m (6ft 4in) and up to 125 seats. This version first flew on 28 Novembe
1967. Yet another fuselage stretch was announced in July 1973 when Swissa
ordered the DC-9 Srs 50, longer than the Srs 40 by 1.87m (6ft 4in) at an overa
length of 40.72m (133ft 7½in). The Srs 50 introduced the uprated -15 or -1
versions of the JT8D engine and several other engineering improvements
these engines later becoming options for the Srs 30 and 40. With a forwar
port-side freight loading door and appropriate cabin arrangements, convertib
(C) or all-freight (F) versions of the DC-9 Srs 10 and Srs 30 have also bee
delivered. These included the DC-9-15MC (multiple-change) and DC-9-15R
(rapid change) which had a roller floor for quick changes in configuration, an

e DC-9-30CF (convertible freighter) with no cargo door for small package use, d the all-freight DC-9-30AF, later DC-9-30F, with no windows. The final DC-9 riant emerged in 1979 as the Super 80 but was subsequently redesignated cDonnell Douglas MD-80 and is separately described as such.

ERVICE USE
ne DC-9 Srs 10 was approved by the FAA on 23 November 1965 and entered rvice with Delta Air Lines on 8 December. The DC-9 Srs 30 was certificated 19 December 1966 and entered service with Eastern Airlines in early 1967. ▶

elow: Scandinavian Airlines System (SAS) was the first and one of only vo airlines (with Toa Domestic of Japan) to order the 125-seat DC-9-41. traded range requirements for more seating and payload.

The DC-9 Srs 20 was bought only by SAS, entering service on 27 January 196
and SAS was also first to use the DC-9 Srs 40, starting on 12 March 196
after certification on 27 February. The DC-9 Srs 50 gained FAA approval
1975, to enter service with Swissair on 24 August of that year. Continent
Airlines was the first to receive the convertible DC-9C Srs 10 on 7 Marc
1966; Overseas National received the first convertible Srs 30 in Octobe
1967 and Alitalia accepted the first all-cargo DC-9 Srs 30F on 13 May 196

bove: Northwest Airlines continues to be a prolific user of the DC-9
cluding the smallest model, the DC-9-15.

roduction of all DC-9 variants totalled 976, including 137 Series 10, 10
eries 20, 662 Series 30 (including 24 C-9A and 17 C-9B), 71 Series 40 and
6 Series 50. Some 685 remained in service in 2001, several equipped with
ushkits.

McDonnell Douglas DC-10

SPECIFICATION

(McDonnell Douglas DC-10-30ER)

Dimensions: Wingspan 50.41m (165ft 4in); length overall 55.50m (182ft 1in); height overall 17.70m (58ft 1in), wing area 367.7m² (3,958ft²).

Power Plant: Three 240.2kN (54,000lb) General Electric CF6-50C2B turbofans.

Weights: Operating weight empty 121,198kg (267,197lb); max take-off 263,085kg (580,000lb); max landing 182,978kg (403,000lb); max payload 48,330kg (106,550lb).

Performance: Max cruising speed 530kts (982km/h); max rate of climb 14.7m/s (2,900ft/min); service ceiling 10,180m (33,400ft); take-off field length 3,170m (10,400ft); landing field length 1,630m (5,350ft); range with max payload 5,730nm (10,620km).

Accommodation: Flight crew of three. Seating for up to 380 passengers, nine-abreast with twin aisles. Total baggage/cargo bulk volume 155.4m³ (5,489ft³).

*N*ith the DC-8 in production and the DC-9 recently entering service, the Douglas Aircraft Company (not then merged with McDonnell), turned its tention in March 1966 to the so-called 'Jumbo Twin' specification prepared by merican Airlines. Subsequent discussions between the company and the rline, and an assessment of broader market needs, led to the final proposal ecoming a three-engined wide-body type of larger capacity than first planned, d in this form, the type became the DC-10 as ordered by American Airlines 19 February 1968. A full production launch was achieved in April, when nited Airlines also placed a large order. The configuration and size closely atched that of the TriStar which Lockheed launched in March 1968, the most ▶

elow: The ORBIS International DC-10-10 is fitted out as a flying eye ospital and teaching facility. Over a period of 15 years, the ORBIS team as made 250 flights to 71 countries around the world, enabling them to ave the eyesight of more than 20,000 people. The team has taught ght-saving skills to 32,000 doctors and nurses.

significant difference being that the rear engine of the DC-10 was located in a individual nacelle above the fuselage, on a short pylon, with the fin and rudder carried above this nacelle. The DC-10 had a 35 deg swept wing including full span leading-edge slats and large-chord double-slotted trailing-edge flaps for high lift and low approach speeds. Capacity was for up to 380 passengers in a economy seating. All early versions of the DC-10 were powered by General Electric CF6-50 turbofan engines, the Pratt & Whitney JT9D being offered as a option at a later time, and the flight test programme began on 29 August 1970 with the second and third aircraft, in American Airlines and United Airline colours respectively, following on 24 October and 23 December 1970. In th early 1980s, McDonnell Douglas introduced a common performanc improvement package (CPIP), aimed at reducing drag and consequent bettering cruise performance. The CPIP incorporated the elimination of spoile steps, improved slat rigging, the addition of stabiliser fillets and revise contouring of the horizontal stabiliser fairing. Additional drag improvemen changes were applied on an individual model basis.

VARIANTS
The launch version of the DC-10 was aimed at providing non-stop U transcontinental range and, after the subsequent introduction of longer-rang versions, this initial model became known as the DC-10 Series 10. This ha CF6-6D or 6D1 engines of 178kN or 182.45kN (40,000lb or 41,000l respectively and 185,976kg (410,000lb) or, later, 206,388kg (455,000lb) gros

eight. The DC-10 Srs 15 introduced CF6-50C2F engines at 206.9kN (46,500lb) r high-temperature, high-altitude operations by Mexican airlines, and first flew 8 January 1981. Both these variants had the original DC-10 wing with a span 47.35m (155ft 4in). For long-range operations, Douglas developed centre-ection and fuselage (underfloor) fuel tanks, and a 3.05m (10ft) increase in wing an to allow for higher weights; a third main landing gear leg was also troduced, on the fuselage centreline. With CF6-50 engines, this variant was e DC-10 Srs 30, first flown on 21 June 1972. With JT9D-20 engines, it was at st the DC-10 Srs 20, later changed to DC-10 Srs 40, first flown on 28 February 972; the first Srs 40 with JT9D-59 engines flew on 25 July 1975. Progressive creases in certificated weights and fuel capacities were made once the Srs) and 40 were in production, and in 1980 the designation DC-10 Srs 30ER was dopted for the extended-range variants. A convertible freighter version with a rward side cargo door was introduced as the DC-10 Srs 30CF, first flown on 3 February 1973, and a maximum take-off weight of 267,620kg (590,000lb) as certificated for this variant. Some DC-10 Srs 10CFs were also built. A indowless pure freighter, the DC-10 Srs 30F, appeared in 1985 to meet the quirements of Federal Express and could accommodate up to 36 standard ontainers. The KC-10A Extender tanker/cargo transport for the USAF was ased on the DC-10-30CF and first flew on 12 July 1980. Several improvements ►

elow: Gemini Air Cargo utilises the DC-10-30F on cargo flights, seen ere at Basel.

including a remote operator's station and advanced boom were introduced the KDC-10 for the Royal Netherlands Air Force. A number of fuselage stretched variants of the DC-10 was studied under the Srs 50 and 6 designations and as the MD-100, leading eventually to the McDonnell Dougl MD-11. In 1997, FedEx launched the MD-10 retrofit programme with a agreement for 70 airframes, and an option for 50 more. The MD-1 incorporates the Boeing two-crew advanced common flight deck (AFC) and wa granted an amended type certificate on 9 May 2000. Delivery of the first of 8 MD-10s to FedEx was made that same day.

SERVICE USE

The DC-10 Srs 10 was certificated on 29 July 1971, and entered service on August 1971 with American Airlines. The Srs 15 was certificated on 12 June 198 for service with Mexicana and Aeromexico. The Srs 30 was certificated 2

November 1972, with first deliveries to KLM and Swissair. The first Srs 30ER deliveries were made to Swissair, and the first Srs 30ER with maximum supplementary tankage was delivered to Finnair. The Srs 40 was certificated on 20 October 1972, with the first delivery following to Northwest Orient Airlines. The Srs 30CF was first delivered to TIA and ONA on 19 April and 21 April 1973 respectively. The first Srs 30F was delivered to Federal Express on 24 January 1986. DC-10 sales totalled 446 when production finished in December 1988, including 60 KC-10A tanker transports for the USAF. Some 315 were in commercial service in January 2001.

Below: The DC-10 has carved itself a buoyant second-hand market and many are chartered to provide additional capacity. This DC-10-30 belonging to Mexican airline TAESA was leased to Dominicana and photographed on a charter flight at Leipzig. (Lothar Müller)

NAMC YS-11

SPECIFICATION

(NAMC YS-11A-200)

Dimensions: Wingspan 32.00m (104ft 11¾in); length overall 26.30m (86ft 3½in); height overall 8.98m (29ft 5½in), wing area 94.8m² (1,020ft²).

Power Plant: Two 2,284kW (3,060shp) Rolls-Royce Dart Mk 542-10K (RDa.10/1) turboprops, with Rotol four-blade constant-speed feathering and reversing propellers.

Weights: Operating weight empty 15,419kg (33,993lb); max take-off 24,500kg (54,101lb); max landing 24,000kg (52,910lb); max payload 6,581kg (14,508lb).

Performance: Max cruising speed 253kts (469km/h); initial rate of climb 6.2m/s (1,220ft/min); service ceiling 6,980m (22,900ft); take-off field length 1,110m (3,650ft); landing field length 660m (2,170ft); range with max payload 590nm (1,090km).

Accommodation: Flight crew of two. Seating for up to 60 passengers, four-abreast with central aisle. Total baggage volume 10.67m³ (377.0ft³).

Six Japanese companies (Mitsubishi, Kawasaki, Fuji, Shin Meiwa, Showa and Japan Aircraft Manufacturing) began during 1956 to study the design of short/medium-range civil airliner as a wholly indigenous project, primarily with view to meeting the requirements of Japanese domestic airlines. The design emerged as a relatively large twin turboprop, for whose construction the six companies set up Nihon Aircraft Manufacturing Co Ltd (NAMC) in May 1957. The development programme embraced four airframes: two flying prototypes and two structural test specimens. The first flights were made on 30 August

d 28 December 1962, by which time plans had been completed to launch oduction of the aircraft known as the YS-11. After production of 48 YS-11s, e first of which flew on 23 October 1964, NAMC developed the YS-11A with gher operating weights and increased payload. First flown on 27 November 967, the YS-11A was offered in three versions which became known as the s 200, 300 and 400, the original YS-11s then becoming Srs 100 aircraft. The S-11A-200 was the basic 60-passenger aircraft with a 1,350kg (2,700lb) crease in payload over that of the Srs 100, and 92 were built. With the same verall weights as the Srs 200, the YS-11A-300 was a mixed-traffic version aturing a side-loading cargo door in the forward side of the fuselage and able carry 46 passengers plus 15.3m³ (540 cu ft) of cargo. The YS-11A-300, which st flew on 17 September 1969, was an all-cargo variant, with the cargo door the forward fuselage side. The nine YS-11A-400s built were all for military se, as were a few of the earlier models. With an increase in maximum take-f weight of 500kg (1,105lb) to 25,000kg (55,115lb), the YS-11A-500, 600 and 00 were otherwise similar, respectively, to the Srs 200, 300 and 400. oduction of four Srs 500 and five Srs 600 aircraft brought the YS-11A ogramme to an end, totalling 182 aircraft. Japanese certification was obtained 25 August 1964, followed by FAA Type Approval on 7 September 1965. eliveries of the YS-11 began in March 1965. Around 50 remain in commercial rvice, mainly in Asia/Pacific.

elow: The indigenous YS-11 turboprop transport served many apanese domestic routes, here in Japan Domestic Airlines colours.

Piaggio P.180 Avanti

SPECIFICATION
(Piaggio P.180 Avanti)
Dimensions: Wingspan 14.41m (46ft 0½in); length 14.03m (47ft 3¼in); heig|
overall 3.98m (13ft 1in); wing area 16.00m² (172.2ft²).
Power Plant: Two 1,107kW (1,485) Pratt & Whitney PT6A066 turboprops.
Weights: Operating weight empty 3,402kg (7,500lb); max take-off 5,262kg
(11,600lb); max landing 4,965kg (10,945lb); max payload 907kg (2,000lb).
Performance: Max cruising speed 260kts (482km/h); service ceiling 12,500n
(41,000ft); take-off field length 869m (2,850ft); landing field length 872m
(2,860ft); range with typical payload 1,400nm (2,594km).
Accommodation: Flight crew of one or two. Max seating for nine
passengers. Baggage volume 1.25m³ (44ft³).

The history of this unusual twin-turboprop high-speed transport goes back
1982, when it was formally launched by Piaggio as the P-180 Avanti. Havir
already co-operated with a US company on an earlier design, the Italia
company joined forces with Gates Learjet in October 1983, which it considere
helpful in marketing the aircraft in the tough American market. Gates Learje
however, pulled out of the partnership on 13 January 1986, forcing Piaggio
go it alone. All tooling and the first three forward fuselages were transferred
Genoa in Italy, and the first two prototypes flew on 23 September 1986 and
May 1987. Initial Italian certification came on 7 March 1990, with full Italian ar
FAA approval given on 2 October that same year. The first Avanti had bee
delivered three days before. The P.180 has a high-aspect-ratio wing set high ar
well to the rear to allow an unobstructed cabin with maximum headroom f
seven passengers. Control is provided by the wing, a canard foreplane at th
extreme nose, and a T-tail. Lift from the canard allows the T-tail to act as a liftir
surface, thus reducing the required wing area. Both the canard and the T-ta
have a 5° anhedral, while the wing is slightly dihedral. Pratt & Whitney Canac
PT6A-66 turboprops are mounted in pusher configuration aft of the cabin ar

*Below: The unusual high-speed Piaggio Avanti has had a difficult
gestation, with very few entering service.*

Above: Piaggio has won new sales for its pusher turboprop-powered P.180 Avanti.

...e wing, to reduce cabin noise and propeller vortices on the wing. Increased ...eights and higher payload/range performance was introduced from 1991, and ...eights were again increased a year later. In spite of its attractive shape, sales ...er the early years were slow, and a modified version was launched in 1997. ...e main change was the construction of the fin, rudder and canard foreplane ...aluminium alloy, but fuel capacity was also increased to provide more range. ...onomy and deluxe interiors are now also being offerd. The changes added a ...w impetus to the programme, and appears to have given the aircraft a new ...ase of life. At 1 January 2001, around 25 Avantis were in service with a mix ...commercial and military customers. The Italian army and air forces operate ...for communications and civil protection service, and two have been ...livered to the Greek Ministry of Health in EMS configuration.

Pilatus PC-6 Turbo Porter

SPECIFICATION
(Pilatus PC-6/B2-H4 Turbo Porter)
Dimensions: Wingspan 15.87m (51ft 1in); length overall 10.90m (35ft 9in); height overall 3.20m (10ft 6in), wing area 30.15m² (324.5ft²).
Power Plant: One 507kW (680shp) Pratt & Whitney Canada PT6A-27 turboprop, with Hartzell three-blade constant-speed reversing propeller.
Weights: Operating weight empty 1,270kg (2,800lb); max take-off 2,800kg (6,173lb); max landing 2,660kg (5,864lb); max payload 945kg (2,083lb).
Performance: Max cruising speed 125kts (232km/h); max rate of climb 5.2m/s (1,010ft/min); service ceiling 8,840m (29,000ft); take-off field length 197m (646ft) landing field length 127m (417ft); range with typical payload 500nm (926km).
Accommodation: Flight crew of one. Seating for up to 10 passengers.

Design work on a single-engined utility aircraft with STOL capability began 1957, and developed into a braced high-wing monoplane of all-me construction with variable incidence tailplane. Its impressive STO characteristics permit operation from unprepared strips under harsh weath conditions and in inhospitable terrain. The PC-6 can operate from soft groun snow, glacier and water, and has been used for a multitude of aerial missio across the world, including passenger and cargo transport, and aeromedic roles, for which its box-like fuselage and large loading door are particula suitable. The first piston-engined PC-6 Porter flew on 4 May 1959 and Swi certification of the basic version was obtained in August 1959. Several engi and gross weight combinations were produced before the first PC-6/A-H1 Turt Porter with a 390kW (523shp) Turboméca Astazou IIE made its first flight on May 1961. A number of variants were built, with different Astazou and Pratt Whitney Canada turboprop engines, before the current production version, th PC-6/B2-H4, entered service in 1985. Compared with previous models, th introduced a 600kg (1,323lb) increase in maximum take-off weight, resulting a payload increase of 570kg (1,257lb), particularly for commercial passeng operations, achieved by strengthening of the airframe, improved aerodynam efficiency of the wings with new wingtip fairings, enlarged dorsal fin, an uprated mainwheel shock absorbers. Total production of Porters and Turt Porters exceeds 550 and the latter remains in limited production.

above: Able to operate from snow, glacier and water, the Turbo Porter has been used to good effect in the Alps.

below: New Zealand's Mount Cook Line operates the Turbo Porter in the country's South Island. Because it uses mountainous airstrips it has to be equipped with wheels in the summer and with skis in winter.

Pilatus PC-12

SPECIFICATION
(Pilatus PC-12)
Dimensions: Wingspan 16.23m (53ft 3in); length 14.40m (47ft 3in); height overall 4.26m (13ft 11¾in); wing area 25.81m² (227.8ft²).
Power Plant: One 1,197kW (1,605shp) Pratt & Whitney Canada PT6A-67B turboprops.
Weights: Operating weight empty 2,600kg (5,732lb); max take-off 4,500kg (9,920lb); max landing 4,500kg (9,920lb); max payload 1,410kg (3,108lb).
Performance: Max cruising speed 240kts (444km/h); service ceiling 9,150m (30,000ft); take-off field length 452m (1,480ft); landing field length 288m (945ft); range with typical payload 2,260nm (4,185km).
Accommodation: Flight crew of one or two. Max seating for nine passengers. Executive for six with toilet facilities. Baggage volume 1.13m³ (40ft³).

The single-engined PC-12 (or PC XII) was launched in October 1989 for executive use and to muscle in on the multi-purpose utility market successfully developed by the Cessna Caravan I. Combining a conventional airframe with a low-wing and T-tail configuration with advanced systems, has produced a fast, comfortable and rugged pressurised aircraft, able to operate from soft unprepared airstrip. Although largely of metal construction, the PC-

troduces composite winglets, engine cowling and dorsal and ventral fin
irings. Advanced flight avionics and instrumentation as standard, including
FIS primary displays, 3-axis autopilot, weather radar and global positioning
stem, allow routine single-pilot operation by day and night. A large cargo door
 the rear and flat strengthened cabin floor permit straight-in palletised loading.
ie PC-12 made its first flight on 31 May 1991 and received certification to FAR
 23 Amendment 42 on 30 March 1994. First deliveries took place in April, at
hich time 33 orders had been received. The critical certification for full
ommercial single-enged operations came in 1997, allowing the PC-12 to
perate to its full potential. The Pilatus PC-12 Corporate Commuter seats up to
ne passengers, while the PC-12 Executive normally offers customised
teriors for six people. A PC-12 Combi, typically carrying four passengers and
 95 m³ (210 cu ft) of cargo, and a PC-12F freighter version with a payload of
 000kg (3,086lb), are also available. Pilatus has also developed a special
issions version, known as the PC-12 Eagle, first announced at the Dubai Air
ow in November 1995. The Eagle is targeted at reconnaissance and
irveillance roles, for which it is fitted with a FLIR turret. The PC-12 winglets
ive been replaced by 'tiplets' (wingtips with small verticla winglets).

*elow: The fitting of advanced flight avionics allow single-pilot operation
 the Pilatus PC-12 by both day and night.*

Piper PA-31 Navajo/PA-31T Cheyenne

SPECIFICATION
(Piper T-1040)
Dimensions: Wingspan 12.52m (41ft 1in); length overall 11.18m (36ft 8in); height overall 3.96m (13ft 0in), wing area 21.27m² (229ft²).
Power Plant: Two 373kW (500shp) Pratt & Whitney Canada PT6A-11 turboprops with Hartzell three-blade constant-speed fully-feathering propeller
Weights: Operating weight empty 2,097kg (4,624lb); max take-off 4,082kg (9,000lb); max landing 4,082kg (9,000lb); max payload 1,350kg (2,976lb).
Performance: Max cruising speed 236kts (437km/h); initial rate of climb 8.2m/s (1,610ft/min); service ceiling 7,315m (24,000ft); take-off field length 810m (2,650ft); landing field length 640m (2,100ft); range with max payload 590nm (1,093km).
Accommodation: Flight crew of one or two and seating for up to 9 passengers on individual side-by-side seats with no aisle. Baggage compartments front and rear volume 0.96m³ (34ft³).

A number of related light twins produced by Piper in the PA-31 family can traced back to the original Navajo, which first flew on 30 September 19 as a six/eight seater with a pair of 224kW (300hp) Lycoming IO-540-MI engines. Progressive variants over the next decade included a turbocharge

Below: The Piper Navajo proved very adaptable to a number of roles, including air taxi, light freight and executive transport.

*bove: Key Airlines used the Piper Navajo on scheduled commuter
rvices out of Salt Lake City.

*ersion, the Turbo Navajo, with 231kW (310hp) TIO-540-A engines; the PA-31P
*ressurized Navajo with 317kW (425hp) TGO-540-E1A engines, and the PA-31-
*5 Turbo Navajo CR with 243kW (325hp) TIO-540-F2BD engines and handed
*ropellers. All these variants had applications in the air taxi and small third-level ▶

airline markets, but of more specific interest was the PA-31-350 Nava[jo] Chieftain, which was announced in September 1972 as a lengthened version [of] the Navajo C/R powered by 261kW (350hp) handed TIO-540-J2BD engines. [A] 610mm (2ft) lengthening of the fuselage allowed the Chieftain (as it is no[w] usually known) to seat up to 10 occupants including the pilot, and all-carg[o] versions were also developed. The success of this type in the commercial a[ir] transport market led Piper to set up an Airline Division in 1981 to suppo[rt] Chieftain operations and to evolve PA-31 derivatives more specifically intend[ed] for airline use, as described below.

VARIANTS

The PA-31-350, first flown on 25 September 1981, is known as the T-1020 an[d] is a Chieftain with special interior and structural modifications to suit short-ha[ul] commuter airline operation, with a high rate of landings to flight hours. Up to 1[0] passengers can be accommodated in addition to the pilot, and the T-1020 ha[s] a maximum take-off weight of 3,175kg (7,000lb). In parallel with the T-102[0] Piper evolved the T-1040 as an aircraft of similar capacity but offering th[e] advantages of turboprop power. For speed of development and minimum cos[t] the T-1040 made use, so far as possible, of existing Piper components, b[y] combining the fuselage of the T-1020 and Chieftain with the PT6A-11 engine[s] of the Cheyenne I (itself a Navajo derivative, as indicated by the PA-31T[-1] designation), the wings and landing gear of the Cheyenne IIXL (PA-31T-2) an[d] the engine nacelles with baggage lockers of the larger Cheyenne IIIA (PA-42[).

mall improvements were made, especially to the design of the air inlets, and
he first of three pre-production T-1040 airframes flew on 17 July 1981. The
esignation for this member of the Navajo/Cheyenne family is PA-31T-3. After
eliveries had begun, Piper obtained certification of a wingtip tank installation,
iving the T-1040 an extension of some 300nm (555km) in range, and another
otion was a cargo pod which, fitted under the fuselage, has a volume of
.85m³ (30cu ft). In all-cargo configuration, the T-1040's cabin offers a volume
f 7m³ (246cu ft) and the cargo payload is nearly 1,315kg (2,900lb). Access to
he cabin is facilitated by the 'Dutch' door, the top half of which hinges up and
he bottom half (incorporating steps) down. Adjacent and to the rear of this door
  a second, upward-hinged hatch giving access to the rear baggage
ompartment.

ERVICE USE

ome 500 Chieftains have been delivered specifically for commuter airline use
nce production of this PA-31 variant began. The T-1020 was certificated to
AR Pt 23 during 1982 and 22 were built. The T-1040 obtained FAA Type
pproval, to CAR Pt 3, FAR Pt 23, FAR Pt 36 and SFAR Pt 27 as appropriate, on
5 February 1982 and first deliveries were made in May 1982. Piper built 23 T-
040s before ending production of both it and the T-1020.

elow: Adelaide, South Australia-based Williams Airlines was one of many
mall operators using the PA-31-350 Navajo Chieftain on commuter services.

PZL-M-28 (Antonov An-28)

SPECIFICATION
(M-28 Skytruck PT)

Dimensions: Wingspan 22.07m (72ft 5in); length overall 13.10m (43ft 0in); height overall 4.90m (16ft 1 in), wing area 39.7m² (427.5ft²).

Power Plant: Two 820kW (1,100shp) Pratt & Whitney Canada PT6A-65B turboprops

Weights: Operating weight empty 3,917kg (8,635lb); max take-off 7,000kg (15,432lb); max landing 6,650kg (14,661lb); max payload 2,000kg (4,409lb).

Performance: Max cruising speed 181kts (335km/h); service ceiling 6,200m (20,340ft); take-off field length 265m (870ft); landing field length 185m (607ft) range with typical payload 765nm (1,417km).

Accommodation: Flight crew of two. Seating for up to 18 passengers.

A braced high-wing monoplane, the An-28 made its first flight appearance i September 1969, then known as the An-14M, indicating its relationshi with the earlier An-14 piston-engined light transport. Intended to replace th ubiquitous An-2 biplane, offering higher standards of comfort and performanc but comparable short take-off and landing capabilities, the An-28 underwent lengthy period of flight development and proving trials before entering production. Following the first flight of the Antonov-built An-28 prototype on 2 April 1975, production was assigned to PZL in Poland in February 1978, wher the first of a pilot-batch of 15 (including one for static testing) flew on 22 Jul

Below: After having built some 100 18-seat M-28s, PZL-Mielec is now working on a stretched Skytruck to carry up to 30 passengers in a larger, stand-up cabin, or three LD-3 cargo containers.

Top: The prototype Skytruck conversion first flew in July 1993.

Above: The M-28, still designated An-28, in the markings of Sprint Airlines.

1984. Certification was obtained on 7 February 1986. PZL production plan envisaged a total of 1,200 in the first five years, but less than 100 were delivered to Aeroflot before the collapse of the Soviet Union. Since then, small quantities have been built for the Polish armed forces in a range of different variants. Commercial variants (now all prefixed M) include the basic M-28 transport model with 705kW (945shp) TVD-10B turboprops; M-28A for polar use with increased fuel capacity; and the M-28 Skytruck PT. PZL is now planning to produce two stretched versions of the Skytruck for 30 passengers. The new models are the M28-03 and M28-04, both of which will be stretched by 1.84m (6ft) and have a 0.25m (10in) higher ceiling to allow passengers to stand upright. The M28-03 has rear clamshell doors, while the M28-04 has a side cargo door. Both models have uprated 880kW (1,200shp) PT6A-65B engines. Three prototypes were planned for first flight in mid-1998 and deliveries in 1999 but had not flown by end of 2000. NATO reporting name for the M-28/An-28 is 'Cash'.

Raytheon (BAe) Hawker 800

SPECIFICATION
(Raytheon Hawker 800XP)
Dimensions: Wingspan 15.66m (51ft 4½in); length 15.60m (51ft 2in); height overall 5.36m (17ft 7in); wing area 34.75m² (374.0ft²).
Power Plant: Two 20.73kN 4,660lb) thrust GE/Honeywell TFE731-5BR-1H turbofans.
Weights: Operating weight empty 7,303kg (16,100lb); max take-off 12,701kg (28,000lb); max landing 10,591kg (23,350lb); max payload 989kg (2,180lb).
Performance: Max cruising speed 456kts (845km/h); service ceiling 13,100m 43,000ft); take-off field length 1,640m (5,380ft); landing field length 1,372m (4,500ft); range with typical payload 2,280nm (4,222km).
Accommodation: Flight crew of two. Typical seating for eight passengers. Max high-density seating for 14 passengers. Baggage volume 1.67m³ (59ft³).

The Hawker 800 twin-turbofan business jet is the latest production aircraft in a long line that began with the de Havilland DH.125 Jet Dragon, designed as a pressurised six to eight-seat executive transport. The aircraft, powered by two Rolls-Royce Viper 520 turbojets, flew on 13 August 1962, and by the time deliveries started in autumn 1964, de Havilland had become part of Hawker Siddeley and the aircraft was re-designated HS.125. Only eight of the initial Series 1 were built, being quickly superseded from 1965 by the Series 1A with

increase in power and modifications to meet FAA requirements for the
merican market. For sale elsewhere, without FAA requirements, it was
esignated Series 1B. The Series 2 was built as the Dominie T.Mk 1 navigation
ainer for the UK Royal Air Force, which took delivery of 20 units. Production
ontinued with 39 Series 3, 3A and 3B, powered by Viper 522s and
corporating progressive refinements, with longer range introduced in the 3A-
A and 3B-RA models. Next came the HS125-400 with uprated engines,
furbished cabin and flight deck enhancements, of which 116 were built. The
eries 600, first flown on 21 January 1971, introduced a 0.95m (3ft 1in)
selage stretch to seat eight in an executive layout and 14 in high-density
eating, and Viper 601-22 engines. Production amounted to 72, before it was
placed by the Garrett AiResearch TFE731 turbofan-powered Series 700,
hich provided dramatically improved performance. A total of 215 was built.
any more improvements, including a 'glass' cockpit, produced the Series 800,
st flown on 26 May 1983 and then known as the British Aerospace BAe 125-
00. To meet competition from larger and longer-range business jets, British
erospace developed the BAe 1000, by stretching the 800 fuselage by 0.84m
ft 9in), and adding Pratt & Whitney Canada PW305 turbofans and extra fuel ▶

*elow: The Hawker 800XP is the latest in a long line of business jets
oing back to the early 1960s.*

for intercontinental range. First flown on 16 June 1990, the BAe 1000 wa
axed following the acquisition of the BAe Corporate Jets division b
Raytheon in 1993. The Wichita-based company continued with the Serie
800, renamed Hawker 800. The original version was superseded by th
Hawker 800XP (extended performance), first delivered in October 199
The XP model is powered by TFE731-5BR-1H turbofans, which provide
considerable boost in speed, take-off and climb performance, and also ha
a greater payload capacity and many other refinements. The Hawker 800

Above: The Hawker 800XP is powered by TFE731-5BR-1H turbofans, which provide a considerable boost in speed, take-off and climb performance.

USAF designation C-29A), 800SM (JASDSF designation U-125A), 800RA, nd 800SIG, are special missions variants for military customers. At 1 anuary 2001, a total of 460 BAe 125-800/Hawker 800 series were in ervice.

Raytheon Hawker Horizon

SPECIFICATION

(Raytheon Hawker Horizon)

Dimensions: Wingspan 18.82m (61ft 9in); length 21.08m (69ft 2in); height overall 5.97m (19ft 7in); wing area 49.3m^2 (531.0ft^2).

Power Plant: Two 28.9kN (6,500lb) thrust Pratt & Whitney Canada PW308A turbofans with FADEC.

Weights: Operating weight empty 9,494kg (20,930lb); max take-off 16,329kg (36,000lb); payload with max fuel 544kg (1,200lb).

Performance: Max cruising speed Mach 0.84; service ceiling 13,715m (45,000ft); take-off field length 1,600m (5,250ft); landing field length 713m (2,340ft); range with typical payload 3,100nm (5,741km).

Accommodation: Flight crew of two. Typical seating for eight-12 passengers Baggage volume 2.83m^3 (100ft^3).

All-new design on this 10-12 passenger business jet started in 1993, the under the preliminary designation of PD376 and briefly identified as th Hawker 1000. Its go-ahead was officially announced at the NBAA convention Orlando, Florida on 19 November 1996, and at the following year's conference Raytheon exhibited a full-size cabin mock-up. Standard accommodation provided for eight passengers in a double 'club four' arrangement in a stand-u cabin, with toilets and baggage compartment at the rear. Developmental ris sharing partners on the Horizon include Fuji Heavy Industries, which is buildin

Below: Raytheon Hawker Horizon super mid-size jet.

Above: Hawker Horizon stand-up cabin can seat up to 12 passengers.

ne wing, Pratt & Whitney Canada for the PW308A FADEC-equipped power
lant, and GE/Honeywell for the avionics suite. Landing gear will be supplied by
Messier-Dowty, while Honeywell will provide environmental and auxiliary
ower unit systems for the aircraft. The Hawker Horizon has a conventional
wept wing with a supercritical aerofoil section, and a T-tail with a small overfin
ntenna housing for an optional satellite communication system. Both the wing
nd area ruled rear fuselage to minimise engine nacelle drag have been
esigned using computational fluid dynamics (CFD). This technique was also
sed to re-profile the Hawker 1000-based nose section. Unique to the Horizon
 the use of the Fuselage Automated Splice Tool, created with Nova-Tech
ngineering of Seattle. This machine aligns the three fuselage sections using a
omputer-aided laser alignment system, drills the required attachment holes
nd fits the aluminium splice plates, which act as structural frames to carry the
ving loads. According to Raytheon, the new splice tool will save the company
S$20 million over the life of the programme. The Horizon was scheduled to
nake its first flight early in 2001, with FAA certification following in the second
uarter that year. The order book in January 2001 stood at more than 150
ircraft, including options.

Raytheon Premier

SPECIFICATION
(Raytheon Premier I)
Dimensions: Wingspan 13.56m (44ft 6in); length 14.02m (46ft 0in); height overall 4.67m (15ft 4in); wing area 22.95m² (247.0ft²).
Power Plant: Two 10.23kN (2,300lb) thrust Williams FJ44-2A turbofans.
Weights: Operating weight empty 3,629kg (8,000lb); max take-off 5,670kg (12,500lb); max landing 5,386kg (11,875lb).
Performance: Max cruising speed 461kts (854km/h); service ceiling 12,500m (41,000ft); take-off field length 915m (3,000ft); landing field length 747m (2,450ft); range with typical payload 1,500nm (2,778km).
Accommodation: Flight crew of one or two. Typical seating for six passengers. Baggage volume 1.68m³ (60ft³).

Raytheon entered the light business jet market in 1994, when it started design on a new model, designated PD374 (later PD390). Brief detail were revealed in June 1995, before its official launch at the NBAA convention in Las Vegas on 26 September that year with a full-scale fuselage/cabin mock-up. Given the name Premier I, it was the first aircraft to carry only the Raytheon name, its other models originating either with Beech or in the UK. The Premier I was rolled at at Wichita on 19 August 1998 and made its maiden flight on 22 December 1998. The third aircraft with complete interior made its public debut at the NBAA convention at Atlanta Georgia, in October 1999. After a four-aircraft, 1,400 hour test programme the Premier I received its FAA certification in March 2001, with deliverie following soon afterwards. The Premier I is a conventional small busines jet, with rear pod-mounted Williams FJ44-2A turbofans, each developing static thrust of 10.23kN (2,300lb), T-tail configuration, and a 20° swept-back wing mounted below the fuselage for additional cabin space Accommodation is provided for one or two crew and up to six passengers with externally accessible main baggage compartment to the rear of th cabin. The aircraft is made almost entirely of composites materials, with th

fuselage built of graphite/epoxy laminate and honeycomb composites, formed by a Cincinnati Milacron Viper automatic fibre-placement machine, enabling the entire fuselage to be completed in just one week. The Premier I is the baseline aircraft, but Raytheon is already projecting a stretched version with increased cabin space and longer-range as the Premier II, as well as a Premier III. The Premier has become in instant hit with the corporate community, and at January 2001, the order book stood at more than 300 aircraft, with a backlog extending through 2005.

Above: The Premier I features advanced Williams-Rolls FJ44-2A turbofans.

Left: Raytheon Aircraft's Premier I entry-level jet.

Rockwell Sabreliner

SPECIFICATION
(Rockwell Sabreliner 75A)
Dimensions: Wingspan 13.61m (44ft 8in); length 14.38m (47ft 2in); height overall 5.26m (17ft 3in); wing area 31.8m² (342.1ft²).
Power Plant: Two 20.2kN (4,500lb) thrust General Electric CF700-2D-2 turbofans.
Weights: Operating weight empty 5,987kg (13,200lb); max take-off 10,432kg (23,000lb); max landing 9,979kg (22,000lb).
Performance: Max cruising speed Mach 0.80; service ceiling 13,715m (45,000ft); take-off field length 1,326m (4,350ft); landing field length 753m (2,470ft); range with typical payload 1.712nm (3,173km).
Accommodation: Flight crew of two. Typical seating for eight to 10 passengers.

Buoyed by the success of its F-86 Sabre fighter, North American Aviation (NAA) (merged with Rockwell in September 1967) began work in 1952 on twin turbojet transport, which it later developed to meet the USAF 'UTX' requirement for a combat readiness trainer and utility aircraft. NAA entered it earlier design as the NA.286 Sabreliner, which, powered by two General Electric J85 turbojets, made its first flight on 16 September 1958. The aircraft then powered by Pratt & Whitney JT12A-6A engines, later won substantial orders from the US forces as the T-39 Sabre. Models included the T-39 support aircraft, T-39B and T-39D radar and radar interception trainers, CT-39 rapid response airlifter, CT-39G fleet tactical support aircraft, and T-39 navigation trainer. In 1962, NAA turned its attention to the commercial market and launched the Sabreliner 40, largely based on the T.39, but with more powerful 14.7kN (3,000lb) JT12A-8 turbjets, new brakes, a third window on each side of the passenger cabin, and accommodation for up to nine

Below: The Sabreliner was designated the T-39 Sabre in United States Air Force service.

*bove: The Sabreliner 75 introduced a stand-up cabin and square
indows.*

assengers. The Sabreliner 60, introduced in 1967, was generally similar, but
ad its fuselage lengthened by 0.97m (3ft 2in) to provide accommodation for 10
assengers. It can also be distinguished from earlier models by its five cabin
indows on each side. Aerodynamic improvements resulted in the designation
abreliner 60A, which remained in production until May 1979, when it was
placed by the Garrett TFE731-3 geared turbofan-powered Sabreliner 65,
hich first flew on 29 June 1977 and was the last model to be built, with
oduction finally ending on 1 January 1982. Before the introduction of the

Sabreliner 65, Rockwell produced the
Sabreliner 70 (quickly redesignated
Sabreliner 75), which was
certificated on 17 June 1970 with a
stand-up cabin and square
windows in place of the rounded
triangular windows of earlier
models. The replacement of the
JT12A-8 turbojets by new General
Electric CF700-2D-2 turbofans
produced the Sabreliner 75A
(initially the Sabreliner 80) in 1972.
A total of 631 aircraft was built,
including 191 for the military, and
440 for commercial customers,
including 137 Sabreliner 40, one
Sabreliner 50 (used for test only),
145 Sabreliner 60, 76 Sabreliner
65/65A, nine Sabreliner 75, and 72
Sabreliner 75A. In January 2001,
some 330 were still in use. These
are being supported by the St
Louis-based Sabreliner Corporation.

Saab 340

SPECIFICATION
(Saab 340B)

Dimensions: Wingspan 22.75m (74ft 7¾in) with optional extensions; length overall 19.73m (64ft 8¾in); height overall 6.97m (22ft 10½in), wing area 41.81m (450ft²).

Power Plant: Two 1,305kW (1,750shp) General Electric CT7-9B turboprops with Dow four-blade slow-turning constant-speed reversible-pitch auto-feathering propellers.

Weights: Operating weight empty 8,225kg (18,133lb); max take-off 13,155kg (29,000lb); max landing 12,930kg (28,505lb); max payload 3,795kg (8,366lb).

Performance: Max cruising speed 282kts (522km/h); max rate of climb 10.2m/s (2,000ft/min); service ceiling 9,450m (31,000ft); take-off field length 1,135m (3,710ft); landing field length 995m (3,265ft); range with typical payload 870nm (1,611km).

Accommodation: Flight crew of two and seating for up to 37 passengers in three rows with aisle. Baggage compartment volume 8.30m³ (293.1ft³).

After studying project designs for a number of possible civil aircraft, including all-cargo types, Saab-Scania of Sweden concluded an agreement with Fairchild Industries of the USA to proceed with project definition of a regional airliner. Known as the SF-340, it was to be a fully collaborative venture – the first of its kind between a European and an American company – in which each company would be responsible for the design and production of a portion of the airframe, and marketing and sales activities would be shared. All aircraft were

Right: The Saab 340 was the first civil aircraft to be built by Saab since the Scandia in the immediate post-war years.

Below: More than half of the Saab 340s produced are operated in the Americas, including this 340A operated by Argentine airline TAN on regional services from its hub at Neuquen.

to be assembled in Sweden, but those for the North American customers we
to be finished and furnished by Fairchild in the USA. Project definition w
completed during 1980 and in September of that year the two compani
agreed to a full go-ahead for the SF-340, which had evolved as a twin-engine
low-wing monoplane with 34 passenger seats – hence the designatic
Features of the design included a circular-section pressurised fuselage, a hig
aspect ratio wing with long-span single-slotted flaps, extensive use
composite materials and adhesive bonding in the structure, and a desig
fatigue life of 45,000 flight hours and 90,000 landings. Three aircraft were use
for flight development and certification, these being first flown on 25 Januar
11 May and 25 August 1983 respectively. The first full production standar
aircraft flew on 5 March 1984. Saab-Scania assumed control of the SF-34
programme on 1 November 1985, after Fairchild indicated that it wished
relinquish its participation, and the aircraft was re-designated the Saab 340.

VARIANTS

Early deliveries of the initial production 340A had 1,215kW (1,630shp) Gener
Electric CT7-5A turboprops and a gross weight of 11,794kg (26,000lb), but fro
mid-1985, engine power was increased to 1,294kW (1,735shp) and propelle
enlarged. Aircraft built before then were subsequently retrofitted. The 340
was replaced from the 160th aircraft by the 340B, first flown in April 1989. Th
340B introduced CT7-9B engines with automatic power reserve, high
weights and increased tailspan, providing better payload/range performanc
and hot-and-high capability. The 340BPlus was launched in February 199
adding considerably to passenger comfort and performance. Main change
included a 'Generation III' interior with 15 per cent increase in overhead b
volume, improved lighting, re-designed seats and toilet, and an optional activ
noise control system. Further improvements to hot-and-high performance we
achieved with 610mm (2ft) wingtip extensions, permitting up to 680kg (1,500l
increase in take-off weight and reduction in field length of 122m (400f
Optional low pressure tyres and gravel runway protection kit were availabl
Corporate, QC (Quick-change) and Combi versions have also been produced, a
have two militarised versions, the 340AEW&C reconnaissance aircraft for th

wedish Air Force, and the 340BPlus SAR-200 rescue version for the Japan
Maritime Safety Agency.

SERVICE USE

Type certification was obtained in Sweden on 30 May 1984 and ratified by the
FAA in US and by nine other European authorities (members of the JAR – Joint
Airworthiness Requirements group) on 29 June 1984. Australian approval was
gained on October 1984. Revenue passenger service began with the 340A on
15 June 1984 in the hands of Crossair of Switzerland. Other early operators
were Comair of Cincinnati in the US, in October 1984, and Kendell Airlines of
Australia in March 1985. Finnaviation began operating the 340QC in September
1986. The 340B was certificated on 3 July 1989 and joined launch customer
Crossair on 15 September 1989. The clamour for regional jets forced Saab to
announce the closure of its turboprop line. The last 340B was delivered to
Hokkaido Air System in Japan on 4 June 1999, taking the production total to
459 aircraft. In January 2001, 420 remained in active service.

Above: American Eagle is the largest operator of the Saab 340, totalling 105 aircraft, including 24 of the 340Bplus, shown here.

Left: The Saab 340 also proved popular with regional airlines in Europe, including the Belgian carrier Air Exel.

Saab 2000

SPECIFICATION
(Saab 2000)

Dimensions: Wingspan 24.76m (81ft 2¾in); length overall 27.28m (89ft 6in); height overall 7.73m (25ft 4in), wing area 55.74m² (600ft²).

Power Plant: Two 3,096kW (4,152shp) Allison AE 2100A turboprops with FADEC. Dowty slow-turning constant-speed propellers with six swept blades, full auto-feathering and revese pitch.

Weights: Operating weight empty 13,800kg (30,423lb); max take-off 22,800k (50,265lb); max landing 22,000kg (48,501lb); max payload 5,900kg (13,007lb).

Performance: Max cruising speed 368kts (682km/h); max rate of climb 11.4m/s (2,250ft/min); service ceiling 9,450m (31,000ft); take-off field length 1,285m (4,220ft); landing field length 1,245m (4,085ft); range with max payload 1,200nm (2,222km).

Accommodation: Flight crew of two and seating for up to 58 passengers, three-abreast with aisle. Baggage/cargo compartment volume 10.2m³ (360ft³)

The general trend for greater capacity aircraft in the regional marke coupled with the growing success of its 34-seat 340 model, convince Saab of the viability of producing a 50-seat aircraft as a complement to th 340. In sharp contrast to other manufacturers which were developin regional jets, the Swedish company opted for a turboprop-powered aircraf although its principal design objective was to combine jet speeds wit turboprop economy, aiming at a 370 knots (685km/h) cruising speed, fas climb and high-altitude operation up to 9,450m (31,000ft). On hindsight, i decision appears to have been the wrong one, as sales petered out to trickle, when the Canadair and Embraer regional jets, both 50-seater entered service. Design definition started in the autumn of 1988, and th programme was formally launched on 15 December 1988, on the back of

Below: The only airline customer outside Europe for the Saab 2000 was AirMarshall Islands, which used the aircraft on inter-island services in the Pacific.

bove: Second prototype of the Saab 2000 on test flight.

rm commitment from Crossair (which had also been the launch customer
or the 340) for 25 aircraft, plus 25 options. Formal go-ahead was made in
May 1989, and the Allison GMA (now AE) 2100 engine, driving six-bladed
ropellers, was selected in July. Contracts were also signed with other
najor subcontractors to spread the development risk. These include CASA
f Spain which builds the wing, Finland's Valmet, producing the tail unit and
elevators, and Westland Engineering in the UK for the rear fuselage. The
ame fuselage cross-section of the 340 was chosen for the Model 2000, ▶

but another 7.55m (24ft 9¼in) was added to the length to provic accommodation for 50 passengers, although an extra eight passengers ca be accommodated by moving the rear bulkhead into the baggage space The span was also stretched by 3.32m (10ft 10¾in) to increase wing are by 33 per cent. External and cabin noise reduction was a major design go and, apart from choosing the Allison engine and slow-turning Dow propellers with six swept blades, the engines were moved further outboar and an Ultra Electronics active noise control (ANC) system was fitted in th cabin. The ANC employs 72 microphones and 36 loudspeakers whic continually monitor noise levels and generate, via an electronics syster controller, an anti-phase sound field to lower interior noise levels. The firs Saab 2000 was rolled out on 14 December 1991 and made its first flight c 26 March 1992. Two further aircraft in the certification programme flew c 3 July and 28 August 1992. The certification programme was delayed t problems with the aircraft's high-speed longitudinal stability, but this wa overcome by a new Powered Elevator Control System (PECS), first flow on 19 May 1994. European certification to JAR 25 (Amendment 13) wa obtained on 31 March 1994, followed by US certification to FAR 2

mendment 70) on 29 April. Full PECS certification was granted in ecember 1994.

ARIANTS

nly one basic Saab 2000 passenger model was available, delivered to both rlines and corporate customers. First five aircraft delivered with manual evator controls, but subsequently retrofitted with PECS.

ERVICE USE

rst aircraft was delivered to launch customer Crossair, which put the type into ervice in September 1994. The second airline, Deutsche BA, took delivery on 17 arch 1995, and the first corporate customer, General Motors, accepted the 20th rcraft off the production line on 30 October 1995. The Saab 2000 also found it possible to compete with the new regional jets and production ceased in 1998 ter completion of the 63rd aircraft. The final delivery was made to Crossair on 29 pril 1999. In January 2001, 54 remained in airline service.

elow: Swiss regional Crossair is the largest operator of the Saab 2000.

Shorts 330

SPECIFICATION
(Shorts 330–200)
Dimensions: Wingspan 22.76m (74ft 8in); length overall 17.69m (58ft 0in);
height overall 4.95m (16ft 3in), wing area 42.1m² (453.0ft²).
Power Plant: Two 893kW (1,198shp) Pratt & Whitney Canada PT6A-45R
turboprops, with Hartzell five-blade constant-speed fully-feathering and
reversing propellers.
Weights: Operating weight empty 6,680kg (14,727lb); max take-off 10,387kg
(22,900lb); max payload 2,653kg (5,850lb).
Performance: Max cruising speed 190kts (352km/h); initial rate of climb
6.0m/s (1,180ft/min); take-off field length 1,040m (3,420ft); landing field length
1,030m (3,380ft); range with max payload 473nm (876km).
Accommodation: Flight crew of two. Seating for up to 30 passengers in two
plus one arrangement with offset aisle. Total baggage compartment volume
4.10m³ (145.0ft³).

Based on its experience in the design and operation of the Skyvan, Shorts began
to study, in the early 1970s, the possibility of developing a larger commuter
airliner, in the 30-seat category, for which there then appeared to be an emerging
market. To make such an aircraft attractive to a market that was traditionally unlikely
to be able to finance expensive new equipment, the company set itself the target
of producing an aircraft having a first cost no greater than $1 million (about
£400,000) in 1973 values. Such a restraint ruled out any possibility of starting the
design of a new type from scratch. Instead, what became known initially as the
SD3-30 evolved as an aircraft sharing several features with the Skyvan: it used the
same outer wing panels, on a longer centre wing; had the same, basically square
cross-section for the fuselage, which was 3.78m (12ft 5in) longer; and used

*Below: Its simplicity and low cost have made the Shorts 330 attractive
for commuter services between smaller towns and cities. Flying
Enterprise operated them in southern Sweden.*

imilar, though enlarged, tail unit. Improving the appearance of the SD3-30 (compared with that of its progenitor) was a longer nose and a longer top fuselage airing, extending from the flight deck to the tail. Other significant changes were the introduction of retractable landing gear and a switch from the Skyvan's Garrett engines to Pratt & Whitney Canada PT6As, judged to be more acceptable to the regional airline industry and more readily able to meet the power requirements of the enlarged aircraft, since suitably uprated PT6A-45s were already under development for the de Havilland Canada Dash 7. Helped by a UK government grant towards launching costs (to be repaid through a levy on subsequent sales) Shorts was able to announce a formal go-ahead for the SD3-30 on 23 May 1973, and construction of prototypes and pre-production aircraft was put in hand at the Queen's Island, Belfast, factory in Northern Ireland. The first and second aircraft made their initial flights there on 22 August 1974 and 8 July 1975 respectively. The first production aircraft, flown on 15 December 1975, was also used to complete the final stages of certification.

VARIANTS

The SD3-30, which was re-styled as Shorts 330 soon after entering service, was initially powered by 862kW (1,156shp) PT6A-45A engines. After delivering 6 aircraft with these engines, Shorts introduced the slightly modified PT6A-45B, and these were used in the next 40 aircraft. A switch was then made to the PT6A-45R, with slightly higher flat-rated power and a power reserve system and some previously optional items of equipment became standard. The power increase allowed the gross weight to go up by 95.3kg (210lb) from the original certification weight of 10,292kg (22,690lb). Fuel capacity in the Shorts 330 was increased in January 1985 and in this form, the aircraft was known as the Shorts 330-200. Although the Shorts 330 was primarily a regional airliner, it was readily adaptable for all-cargo and military transport roles. Specifically for military use, the Shorts 330-UTT (Utility Tactical Transport) has a strengthened floor, inward-opening rear cabin doors for paradropping, and structural reinforcement for a max take-off weight of 11,158kg (24,600lb). The C-23A ▶

Sherpa flew on 23 December 1982 and was sold to the USAF as a military freighter with a full width rear cargo ramp/door.

SERVICE USE
The SD3-30 gained full UK certification in the transport category on 18 February 1976, and won FAA type approval to FAR Pt 25 and FAR Pt 36 on 18 June 1976

Above: This head-on shot shows the box-like cross-section of the Shorts 330 (Photo Link).

Deliveries began in the same month, and revenue service was inaugurated by Time Air in Canada on 24 August 1976. A total of 139 Shorts 330 were built, and some 35 remained in airline use in 1998.

Shorts 360

SPECIFICATION
(Shorts 360-300)
Dimensions: Wingspan 22.80m (74ft 9½in); length overall 21.58m (70ft 9½in); height overall 7.27m (23ft 10¼in), wing area 42.18m² (454.0ft²).
Power Plant: Two 1,062kW (1,424shp) Pratt & Whitney Canada PT6A-67R turboprops, with Hartzell six-blade constant-speed fully-feathering propellers.
Weights: Operating weight empty 7,870kg (17,350lb); max take-off 12,292kg (27,100lb); max payload 12,020kg (26,500lb).
Performance: Max cruising speed 216kts (400km/h); max rate of climb 4.8m/s (952ft/min); take-off field length 1,305m (4,280ft); landing field length 1,220m (4,000ft); range with max payload 402nm (745km).
Accommodation: Flight crew of two. Seating for up to 36 passengers in two plus one arrangement with offset aisle. Total baggage compartment volume 6.10m³ (215.0ft³).

For many years, operators of commuter-style services in the USA (where a large proportion of the market for this type of aircraft exists) had been limited by the terms of the CAB Economic Regulation 298 to flying aircraft with no more than 30 passenger seats. To fly larger types required the airline to seek authority under a substantially different set of operating regulations, compliance with which frequently imposed extra costs which were necessarily passed on to the traveller and thus served to diminish the

number of passengers carried. The deregulation of the US airline industry in 1978 brought a relaxation of these rules and made it possible for many third-level airlines to contemplate growth of a kind previously thought impossible. One obvious impact of this sea-change in the fortunes of at least some of the commuter specialists was that the aircraft manufacturers found a new opportunity to market aircraft of more than 30-seat capacity. In the late 1970s Shorts had already been studying several ways of improving the basic Shorts 330 without increasing capacity, one such option being to use more powerful PT6A-65 engines in order to achieve higher operating weights. When the limit on capacity became less important, it became possible to combine this new engine installation (with a modified cowling and improved air intake) with a new or modified fuselage. As a first step, it was decided to restrict the 'stretch' to a modest six seats, emphasis being placed upon improvement to the rear fuselage profile to reduce drag and thus improve operating economics. Wind tunnel testing embraced several options, including a T-tail layout, but an entirely conventional low-mounted tailplane and single fin-and-rudder finally met the design objectives, allied to a somewhat lengthened rear fuselage of improved aerodynamic form. This redesign allowed one extra seat row (three passengers) at the rear of the cabin; a 915mm (36in) plug ahead of the wing provided for another seat row. For the most part, the remainder of the airframe was little changed from that of the Shorts 330, although Dowty landing gear was chosen to replace the earlier Menasco gear, and improved Hartzell propellers were ▶

Left: Many major US airlines used the Shorts 360 in the fleets of their commuter associates.

matched to the new power plant, which incorporated an emergency reserve feature to provide a power boost in the event of one engine failing during the critical stages of take-off. Since the Shorts 330 designation was indicative of a 30-seat version of the basic SD-3 design, the new 36-seat project became known as the Shorts 336 in the drawing office, but this was changed to Shorts 360 for marketing purposes. The go-ahead for the Shorts 360 was given in January 1981, and a first flight was achieved on 1 June of the same year, indicating the extent to which standard components of the Shorts 330 were applicable to the new aircraft. In the prototype, this commonality extended to the PT6A-45R engines fitted for the first six months of flight testing, the definitive PT6A-65Rs first being flown in January 1982.

VARIANTS

Between prototype first flight and production definition, some small changes were made in the control system of the Shorts 360, including deletion of one of the two trim tabs from each elevator. The first production batch of aircraft had PT6A-65R engines each rated at 875kW (1,173shp) for maximum continuous operation and at 990kW (1,327shp) with emergency

serve for take-off. During 1986, the more powerful PT6A-65AR engines were introduced in aircraft designated Shorts 360 Advanced. The final variant was the 360-300 in 1987, which featured new PT6A-67ARs, autopilot and substantially enhanced passenger comfort. Earlier models were then re-dubbed 360-100 and 360-200.

SERVICE USE

The first production Shorts 360 flew on 19 August 1982 and UK certification was obtained on 3 September of that year, followed in November by FAA approval to FAR Pts 25 and 36. The first delivery was made to Suburban Airlines at Reading, Pennsylvania on 11 November 1982, and service use began on 1 December. The first Shorts 360 Advanced went to Thai Airways in early 1986. Shorts had built 164 aircraft when production ceased in 1992. Around 115 are still in service.

Below: Although the Shorts 360 has now been supplanted in front line service by newer and faster types, it can still be seen on many third-level routes. BAC Express Airlines uses its 360s on passenger flights by day and freight flights at night

Shorts SC.5 Belfast

SPECIFICATION
(Shorts SC.5 Belfast)

Dimensions: Wingspan 48.41m158ft 10in); length overall 41.58m (136ft 5in); height overall 14.33m (47ft 0in), wing area 229.1m² (2,465ft²).

Power Plant: Four 4,276kW (5,730shp) Rolls-Royce Tyne RTy.12 turboprops, with four-blade Hawker Siddeley (DH) constant-speed feathering and reversing propellers.

Weights: Operating weight empty 58.967kg (130,000lb); max take-off 104,325kg (230,000lb); max landing 97,520kg (215,000lb); max payload 34,020kg (75,000lb).

Performance: Normal cruising speed 275kts (510km/h); take-off field length 2,500m (8,200ft); landing field length 2,075m (6,800ft); range with max payload 850nm (1,575km).

Accommodation: Flight crew of three or four. Total usable cabin cargo volume 321.4m³ (11,350ft³), with provision for up to 19 passengers on upper deck.

The Belfast was developed to meet an RAF requirement for a heav strategic freighter, and the first of 10 ordered for military use flew on January 1964. Deliveries to the RAF began on 20 January 1966 and all 1 aircraft were operated by No. 53 Squadron until retirement in Septembe 1976. Design features included four Rolls-Royce Tyne turboprops mounte on a high wing, and 18-wheel undercarriage, and beaver tail rear loadin doors and ramp. Five of the ex-RAF aircraft were then acquired fo conversion for operation in civil guise as all-cargo transports carrying outsiz loads. Conversion design, engineering and certification was handled b Marshall of Cambridge (Engineering) and involved changes to the autopilo

Below: A total of five Belfasts were converted for civil use by HeavyLift.

Above: The Belfast, once the largest aircraft in service with the RAF, has a payload exceeding 34 tonnes.

vionics, power plant and flight control systems to meet civil certification standard, CAA approval being obtained on 6 March 1980. Commercial operation of the Belfast began later in March 1980, the company at first being known as TAC HeavyLift, subsequently simply as Heavylift after the parent TAC had gone out of business. Two Belfasts remain in full-time service with Heavylift, carrying awkward and outsize loads to many different parts of the world.

Shorts SC.7 Skyvan

SPECIFICATION

(Shorts SC.7 Skyvan 3)

Dimensions: Wingspan 19.79m (64ft 11in); length overall 12.21m (40ft 1in); height overall 4.60m (15ft 1in), wing area 35.1m² (378.0ft²).

Power Plant: Two 533kW (715shp) Garrett TPE331-2-201A turboprops, with Hartzell three-blade variable-pitch propellers.

Weights: Operating weight empty 3,674kg (8,100lb); max take-off 5,670kg 12,500(lb); max landing 5,670kg (12,500lb); max payload 2,086kg (4,600lb).

Performance: Max cruising speed 175kts (324km/h); initial rate of climb 8.3m/s (1,640ft/min); service ceiling 6,860m (22,500ft); take-off field length 490m (1,600ft); landing field length 450m (1,480ft); range with typical payload 162nm (300km).

Accommodation: Flight crew of one or two. Seating for up to 19 passengers in a two plus one arrangement with offset aisle.

Plans by Belfast-based Short Brothers for a small multi-role STOL freighter took shape as the PD.36 project design and acquired the engineering number SC.7, when construction of a prototype was launched in 1959. The Skyvan, as it was later dubbed, had a conventional fuselage based on a payload 'box' with a 1.98m (6ft 5in) square cross-section, and also featured a high aspect ratio, untapered, strut-braced high wing, incorporating the results of research by F G Miles, and a fixed landing gear. The prototype first flew on 1 January 1963 with a pair of 291kW (390hp) Continental GTSIO-520 piston engines, but these were replaced with Turbomeca Astazou II turboprops, with which the aircraft flew again on 2 October 1963. An initial production batch of 19 Skyvan Srs IIs was built with 545kW (730shp) Astazou XII engines, the first

Below: Del-Air (Delaware Air Freight Company) acquired nine Shorts Skyvans in 1970 and operated them on local scheduled cargo services, before acquiring Convair 580s.

Above: The Skyvan's square fuselage, rear loading ramp and excellent STOL performance made it popular with operators in difficult terrain.

ght being made on 29 October 1965. The type could carry 19 passengers or ,815kg (4,000lb) of freight and was used by several commercial operators. To roduce a definitive version of the Skyvan, Shorts then switched to the Garrett PE331-201 engine to produce the Skyvan Srs 3 which first flew on 15 ecember 1967. Some Srs 2s were converted to have the Garrett engines, and ome aircraft were produced as Skyvan IIIAs with a 6,215kg (13,700lb) gross eight. Furnished to higher standard for airline use, the Skyliner version of the kyvan Srs 3 could carry up to 22 passengers. Several military variants were lso developed, as the Skyvan Srs 3M and Skyvan 3M-200, the latter with learance to operate at weights up to 6,804kg (15,000lb). Certification of the stazou-engined Skyvan Srs 2 was obtained early in 1966, and deliveries began t that time. The Skyvan Srs 3 entered service in 1968, and in 1970 it was ertificated in accordance with new UK civil airworthiness requirements for hort take-off and landing (STOL) operations. The Skyvan's total production was eventually in excess of 150 aircraft.

Sino Swearingen SJ30

SPECIFICATION

(Sino Swearingen SJ30-2)

Dimensions: Wingspan 12.90m (42ft 4in); length 14.31m (46ft 11½in); heigh
overall 4.34m (14ft 3in); wing area 17.72m² (190.7ft²).

Power Plant: Two 10.23kN (2,300lb) thrust Williams FJ44-2A turbofans.

Weights: Operating weight empty 3,583kg (7,900lb); max take-off 5,987kg
(13,200lb); max landing 5,688kg (12,540lb); max payload 635kg (1,400lb).

Performance: Max cruising speed Mach 0.80; service ceiling 14,935m
(49,000ft); take-off field length 1,167m (3,830ft); landing field length 1,042m
(3,420ft); range with typical payload 2,500nm (4,630m).

Accommodation: Flight crew one or two. Typical seating for six passengers
in cabin. Baggage volume 1.7m³ (60ft³).

The SJ30 twin turbofan-powered and pressurised business jet has had
long and difficult gestation, largely due to shortage of funds and frequen
changes of ownership and participants. It was first announced by Swearinge
on 30 October 1986 as the SA-30 Fanjet, and after Gulfstream Aerospac
Williams International and Rolls-Royce made public in October 1988 the
intention to join the programme, it became known as the Gulfstream SA-3
Gulfjet. Yet another change occurred on 1 September 1989, when Gulfstrear
pulled out and the Jaffe Group stepped in, renaming the aircraft th
Swearingen/Jaffe SJ30. The SJ30 finally flew on 13 February 1991 wit
Williams-Rolls FJ44-1 turbofan engines, but certification was delayed pendin
development of an improved model, the SJ30-2, which made its first flight o
8 November 1996. In the meantime, Swearingen Aircraft had been reforme
as a joint venture company with Sino Aerospace of Taiwan. The high-spee
SJ30-2 differs from the original model by having a longer fuselage (stretche
by 1.83m/6ft 0in), increased wing dihedral, more fuel, and more powerf
FJ44-2A engines. After several years of test flying the prototype wa
withdrawn from use in mid-1999. The first of three new prototypes flew fron

*Below: The SJ30-2 business jet became the first aircraft to fly with the
Williams Rolls FJ44-2A turbofan engine on 4 September 1997.*

Above: The SJ-30-2 is claimed to fly further, faster and higher than other business jets.

an Antonio, Texas, on 30 November 2000, marking the beginning of the J30-2s FAA certification flight test programme, which is expected to last a ear and include 1,400 flight hours. The SJ30-2 will be the first business jet to e certified under FAR 23 Commuter Category regulations, and is also the first o be certified by a new manufacturer in almost 40 years. Sino Swearingen laims orders for 175 of the seven-seat jet. First deliveries could be made by he end of 2001.

Sukhoi S-80

SPECIFICATION

(Sukhoi S-80GP)

Dimensions: Wingspan 23.18m (76ft 0½in); length 16.68m (54ft 8¾in); height overall 5.48m (17ft 11¾in); wing area 44.00m² (473.6ft²).

Power Plant: Two 1,394kW (1,870shp) General Electric CT7-9B turboprops.

Weights: Operating weight empty 8,350kg (18,408lb); max take-off 12,500kg (27,557lb); max payload 3,500kg (7,716lb).

Performance: Max cruising speed 289kts (535km/h); service ceiling 6,000m (19,680ft); take-off field length 555m (1,820ft); landing field length 280m (920ft); range with typical payload 1,393nm (2,580km).

Accommodation: Flight crew of one or two. Typically 26 passengers in a single-aisle cabin.

The Sukhoi S-80 is a twin-turboprop multipurpose STOL aircraft developed by the Sukhoi Design Bureau and the Komsomolsk-on-Amur Aircraft Production Association (KnAAPO), primarily as a replacement for the Let L-410 Turbolet, more than 800 of which were delivered to the then Soviet Union. Work initially began in 1989 under contract to the Ministry of Health for an EMS aircraft, and first introduced to Western audiences in model form at the Paris Air Show that same year. However, with the collapse of the Soviet Union funding dried up, and nothing further was heard until the project was revived

092. The intention then was to produce an aircraft capable of fulfilling a variety
roles, including passenger and cargo transport, commuter aircraft for
omestic use, and aerial work applications. Manufacture of the prototype was
egun in 1993, but continuing refinements of the design, including the fitting of
eneral Electric CT7-9 turboprops, made for slow progress. The first flight was
cheduled for late 1996, but was further postponed until the end of 2000. The
80 is a conventional high-wing, twin-boom aircraft with short tandem-wing
rfaces between each tailboom and the rear fuselage, and septback vertical
il with horizontal bridging. It has unobstructed rear loading for freight.
ccommodation is provided for one or two crew, and up to 26 passengers, or
0 stretcher patients in main cabin. In the utility role, it can uplift 3,100kg
,834lb) of freight or equipment. A number of variants are proposed, starting with
e baseline S-80GP cargo/passenger version. The S-80A is generally similar, but
ptimised for Arctic operations. Others are the S-80GR for geological surveys, S-
0M for medical evacuation, S-80P pure passenger version, the slightly longer S-
0PT for patrol missions, equipped with FLIR, and the S-80TD 21-seat troop
ansport with mechanised handling equipment. A 32-passenger stretched version
also projected. No details of orders are available, but the market has been
stimated at 400 for Russia/CIS, and another 250+ for export.

elow: The 26-seat S-80 marks Sukhoi's entry into the civil market.

Tupolev Tu-134

SPECIFICATION
(Tupolev Tu-134A)
Dimensions: Wingspan 29.00m (95ft 1¾in); length overall 37.05m (121ft 6½in); height overall 9.14m (30ft 0in), wing area 127.3m² (1,370.3ft²).
Power Plant: Two 64.5kN (14,990lb) Soloviev D-30 Series II turbofans.
Weights: Operating weight empty 29,050kg (64,045lb); max take-off 47,000k (103,600lb); max landing 43,000kg (94,800lb); max payload 8,200kg (18,075lb
Performance: Max cruising speed 486kts (898km/h); service ceiling 11,900m (39,040ft); take-off field length 2,400m (7,875ft); landing field length 2,200m (7,220ft); range with max payload 1,020nm (1,890km).
Accommodation: Flight crew of three. Seating for up to 84 passengers, four-abreast with central aisle. Total baggage/cargo volume 14.16m³ (500ft³).

The Tupolev design bureau began development of this twin-engine short/medium-range jetliner in the early 1960s, in an effort to provide Aeroflot with an aircraft of better performance than the Tu-124, which had on then recently entered service. The Tu-124 was essentially a scaled-down derivative of the first Soviet jet transport, the Tu-104, which itself was adapted from the Tu-16 jet bomber and therefore lacked some of the refinements th were coming to be taken for granted by airline passengers in the west. The T 134, initially designated Tu-124A, emerged in September 1964, by which tim a prototype was reputed to have completed more than 100 test flights, 1 show that its configuration matched quite closely that chosen by BAC ar Douglas for, respectively, the One-Eleven and the DC-9, aircraft both in similar category to the Tu-134. The Soviet aircraft had more wir sweepback, however, combining this with a rugged tricycle landing gea design to allow short-field and rough-field operation, in line with Aerofl requirements. It also had the characteristic Tupolev fairings at the wir

Below: Aeroflot inaugurated commercial Tu-134 service in September 1967.

*bove: Lithuanian Airlines operated this Tu-134A-3 on its scheduled
ervices, acquiring a number from the local division of Aeroflot.*

ailing edge to house main units of the landing gear when retracted. Six
ototypes or pre-production aircraft are reported to have been used in
evelopment of the Tu-134, which is believed to have made its first flight in
ecember 1963. Production was launched in 1964 at Kharkhov.

ARIANTS

1e first production batch was followed by the appearance, in the second half
* 1970, of the Tu-134A, featuring a 2.10m (6ft 10½in) fuselage 'stretch', ▶

providing for eight extra passengers (two seat rows) in the maximum-dens[
one-class layout. All early Tu-134s and some Tu-134As had the Tupolev glaz[
nose, similar to that of the original Tu-16 bomber, but later aircraft had a 'sol[
nose radome containing weather radar. Soloviev D-30 Srs II engines we[
introduced on the Tu-134A, as was a locally-strengthened wing and improv[
avionics. Further versions of the aircraft began to appear from the autumn [
1981 onwards, but these were the result of modification programmes rath[
than new production, which is believed to have ended in 1978. These varian[
included the Tu-134B with spoilers for direct lift control, and a forward-facin[
crew compartment including engine controls and navigation instruments on th[
centre panel, with a jump seat (between the two pilots' seats) for th[
navigator/flight engineer. The Tu-134B-1 had interior revisions, including a sm[
reduction in toilet size, to allow an increase in basic capacity to 84 passenger[
or a maximum of 90 if galley facilities were removed. The Tu-134A-3 introduce[
new lightweight seats permitting five-abreast seating for 96 passengers, wi[
full toilet and galley provisions retained; improved D-30-III engines were als[
introduced.

SERVICE USE

Proving flights with the Tu-134 on Aeroflot routes were made before the fir[
commercial service began in September 1967, between Moscow an[
Stockholm. The Tu-134A went into service in the second half of 197[
Production of all versions of the Tu-134 is estimated at more than 700, of whi[
up to 100 were exported, for use by most of the East European airlines, an[
other Soviet satellite countries. More than 320 are still in service, mostly [
Russia and the CIS.

bove: Early Tu-134s and some Tu-134As had the signature Tupolev
lazed nose.

elow: The Tu-134, once standard on the scheduled services networks of
eroflot, has found its way into the fleets of charter airlines which
merged out of its shadows. This Tu-134B of Latcharter was fitted out by
ritish Aerospace with a VIP interior.

Tupolev Tu-154/155/156

SPECIFICATION
(Tupolev Tu-154M)
Dimensions: Wingspan 37.55m (123ft 2½in); length overall 47.90m (157ft 1¾in); height overall 11.40m (37ft 4¾in), wing area 201.45m² (2,168ft²).
Power Plant: Three 104kN (23,380lb) Aviadvigatel D-30KU-154-II turbofans.
Weights: Operating weight empty 55,300kg (121,915lb); max take-off 100,000kg (220,460lb); max landing 80,000kg (176,365lb); max payload 18,000kg (39,680lb).
Performance: Max cruising speed 504kts (935km/h); service ceiling 12,100m (39,700ft); take-off field length 2,500m (8,200ft); landing field length 2,500m (8,200ft); range with max payload 1,997nm (3,700km).
Accommodation: Flight crew of three. Seating for up to 166 passengers, six-abreast with central aisle. Total baggage/cargo volume 43.0m³ (1,517ft³).

Intended to take the modernisation of Aeroflot a step further following the introduction of the first generation of turbojet and turboprop transports, the Tu-154 had the same overall configuration as its two Western contemporaries, the Boeing 727 and Hawker Siddeley Trident, but also some significant differences to meet the operational requirements of Soviet air transport. In particular, the power-to-weight ratio is considerably higher than that of the Model 727, giving the aircraft a lively airfield performance and allowing it to operate from the relatively short and poorly surfaced Class 2 airfields at many Russian cities. The wing pods for landing gear stowage are also a distinctive feature of the Tupolev design. Flight development involved six prototypes and pre-production aircraft, and the first prototype took to the air on 4 October 1968, powered by three 93.2kN (20,950lb) Kuznetsov NK-8-2 turbofans, similar to those being developed for the Ilyushin IL-62.

Below: Flagship of the Tajikstan Airlines fleet is the three-engined Tupolev Tu-154M.

VARIANTS

The initial production version, identified simply as Tu-154, had 93.2kN (20,950lb) Kuznetsov NK-8-2 engines, and a number of possible interior layouts, ranging from 128 to 167 seats. The standard all-economy layout had 160 seats, and a typical mixed-class arrangement provided 24 first-class seats in the forward cabin in place of 54 economy-class. Soviet sources indicated the availability of an all-cargo version, but this may not have appeared in definitive form until the Tu-154C was developed as a Tu-154B derivative, as noted below. The Tu-154A was the first improved version to appear, in 1973, with its uprated NK-8-2U engines, and maximum take-off weight increased from 90,000kg (198,416lb) to 94,000kg (207,235lb). This allowed an increase in fuel capacity, from the original 33,150kg (73,082lb), with provision for 6,600kg (14,550lb) in a centre-section tank that was not connected to the aircraft's main fuel system but the contents of which could be transferred to the main tanks at destination airports where refuelling facilities were restricted or expensive. Numerous changes and improvements were made in the avionics and other systems and the cabin interior. The Tu-154B superseded the Tu-154A in 1977, and was followed by the slightly refined Tu-154B-2. This introduced a Thomson-CSF/SFIM automatic flight control and navigation system for Cat II landings and had higher operating weights, matched to a rearranged cabin layout that increased maximum seating to 180. The supplementary tank of the Tu-154A was also fully integrated into the aircraft's fuel system. As a conversion of the Tu-154B, the Tu-154C is an all-cargo carrier with a side-loading door ahead of the wing and a 1,565nm (2,900km) range with 20,000kg (44,100lb) payload. The latest development is the Tu-154M (sometimes described as the Tu-164 in early references), which appeared in 1982 with Soloviev D-30KU-154-II engines derived from those of the Il-62M and each rated at 104kN (23,380lb). Overall dimensions were unchanged but the tailplane was redesigned, and wing slats and spoilers modified. The Tu-154M-100 with upgraded Zhasmin avionics was delivered to ▶

EY-85717

459

iran in 1998, while the Tu-154M-200 is a projected version with Samara NK-8
turbofans. Two aircraft have been built for VVIP use as the Tu-154M-LK-1.
modernised Tu-154M2 with more fuel efficient 156.9kN (35,274l
Aviadvigatel/Perm PS-90A turbofans and area navigation system was und
development but has now been abandoned. A special version for 'Open Skie
treaty observations flights, with side-looking synthetic aperture radar, is bein
developed under a co-operative agreement between Russia and German
Known as the Tu-154M/OS, the aircraft is being used to trial the new radar, fo
incorporation into the Tu-154M. The Tu-155 was a development aircraft wit
Kuznetsov NK-88 turbofans operating on liquid hydrogen and liquified natur
gas (LNG), flown on 15 April 1988. This is now being proposed to be replace
by the Tu-156, several versions of which were to be made available from 199
although no progress had been made by the end of 2000. These are the 13(
seat Tu-156S with NK-89 turbofans, a kerosene/LNG-powered conversion c
the Tu-154B; the Tu-156M, a similar conversion from the Tu-154M; and the T

56M2 with NK-94 turbofans operating on LNG only.

SERVICE USE

Aeroflot conducted Tu-154 proving flights early in 1971 and began services in mid-year on an *ad hoc* basis, with full commercial exploitation starting on 9 February 1972 on the Moscow-Mineralnye Vody route. First international services were on the Moscow-Prague route, starting on 1 August 1972. The Tu-154A entered service in April 1974, the Tu-154B in 1977 and the Tu-154M at the beginning of 1985. The Tu-154M remains in production and continues to find export customers, being in service with many airlines in Europe, Asia and with Cubana in Central America. Production is approaching 950 units of all models, with some 570 in active service.

Below: Among the large fleet of government-owned Air Ukraine are more than 20 Tupolev Tu-154Bs.

Tupolev Tu-204/214/224/234

SPECIFICATION
(Tupolev Tu-204-200)
Dimensions: Wingspan 42.00m (137ft 9½in); length overall 46.00m (150ft 11in); height overall 13.90m (45ft ¼in), wing area 182.4m² (1,963ft²).
Power Plant: Two 158.3kN (35,580lb) Aviadvigatel PS-90A turbofans.
Weights: Operating weight empty 59,000kg (130,070lb); max take-off 110,750kg (244,155lb); max landing 89,500kg (197,310lb); max payload 25,200kg (55,555lb).
Performance: Max cruising speed 448kts (830km/h); service ceiling 12,600m (41,340ft); required runway length 2,250m (7,380ft); range with max payload 3,415nm (6,330km).
Accommodation: Flight crew of two or three. Seating for up to 212 passengers, six-abreast with central aisle. Total baggage/cargo volume 30.8m² (1,088ft³).

Below: Vnukovo Airlines, one of Russia's major trunk airlines, became the first operator of the Tu-204 in 1993, when it received the type for operational trials, before inaugurating offical scheduled passenger services in February 1996. The most likely version to succeed in the market, especially for use on international routes, is the Tu-204-120 with Western engines and avionics being marketed by Sirocco Aerospace International which sold the first 10 to Russia's KrasAir in August 1997.

Above: The Tu-214C³ combi version based on the Tu-204-200 first flew on 21 March 1996. (Paul Jackson/Jane's.)

Russia's first truly modern airliner, the twin-engined Tu-204 was announced 1983 as a replacement for the Tu-154 and Il-62 in Aeroflot service Dimensionally and in appearance similar to the Boeing 757, noticeable extern differences are a slightly greater 28 deg sweepback and winglets. The Tu-20 has a wing of supercritical aerofoil section, with a relatively high aspect rati and makes extensive use of composites in wing control surfaces, wingroo fairings, nose radome and the tail unit, making up about 18 per cent of th structural weight. It features a triplex digital fly-by-wire control system wit triplex analog back-up, and EFIS cockpit with two-colour CRTs for fligh navigation, engine and systems displays. Sidestick controllers were evaluate on a Tu-154 testbed, but these were rejected in favour of conventional 'v control yokes. The first prototype, powered by Aviadvigatel PS-90AT turbofans made its maiden flight on 2 January 1989, flown by Tupolev's chief test pilot A Talakine. It was followed by three more prototypes, and the first aircraft wit Rolls-Royce RB.211-535E4-B engines flew on 14 August 1992, prior to bein introduced at the Farnborough air show three weeks later. Small-scal production of the basic version began at Ulyanovsk in 1990.

VARIANTS

The basic Tu-204 for 214 passengers with twin PS-90A engines and a take-o weight of 94,500kg (208,557lb) was supplemented in 1993 by the extende range Tu-204-100, which differs largely in having additional fuel and a highe weight of 103,000kg (227,070lb). The Tu-204-120 is similar to the -100 but ha Rolls-Royce engines and Russian avionics.. Further increase in payload an gross weight produced the Tu-204-200, first flown on 21 March 1996 as such but now marketed as the Tu-214. The same designation has also been given t

he Tu-204-200C with more payload, and the Tu-204C³ (cargo, converted, containerised) proposal. The Tu-204-220 is similar to the -200 but is powered by 191.7kN (43,100lb) Rolls-Royce RB.211-535E4 or 535F5 turbofans. Variants with Rolls-Royce engines and Rockwell Collins avionics are marketed as the Tu-204-122 and Tu-203-222. Several other specific models are proposed under the Tu-204 designation. These include the Tu-204P military patrol version of the Tu-204-200, the Tu-204-230 with 176.5kN (39,683lb) Samara NK-93 turbofans, the Tu-204 business jet, and the stretched Tu-204-400 for 250 passengers. Longer-term plans include several models powered by liquid natural gas (LNG), currently referred to as the Tu-206, Tu-216, Tu-306 and Tu-316.. Shorter fuselage versions for up to 166 passengers with RB.211-535E4 and 158.3kN (35,580lb) PS-90P engines respectively are the Tu-224 (formerly Tu-204-320) and Tu-234 (formerly Tu-204-300). Windowless all-cargo versions direct from the factory, suffixed C, are available for all main models, as is a conversion programme undertaken by Oriol-Avia. Production of all Tu-204 models is shared between plants at Kazan and Ulyanovsk.

SERVICE USE

Initially used on freight services following Russian certification for the basic type on 12 January 1995. First revenue passenger flight between Moscow and Mineralnye Vody operated by Vnukovo Airlines on 23 February 1996. First Tu-204-120 with Rolls-Royce engines entered KrasAir service at the end of 1997. Only around 15 Tu-204s are believed to be in service.

Below: The Rolls-Royce RB211-535-powered Tu-204 was the fourth prototype to fly on 14 August 1992.

Tupolev Tu-324

PRELIMINARY SPECIFICATION
(Tupolev Tu-324R)
Dimensions: Wingspan 23.20m (76ft 1½in); length 25.50m (83ft 8in); height overall 7.10m (23ft 3½in).
Power Plant: Two 41.0kN (9,220lb) thrust General Electric CF34-3B1 turbofans.
Weights: Max take-off 23,700kg (52,249lb); max payload 5,500kg (12,125lb).
Performance: Max cruising speed 448kts (830km/h); take-off field length 1,800m (5,910ft); range with typical payload 1,619nm (3,000km); range with maximum payload 1,349nm (2,500km).
Accommodation: Flight crew of two. Single-aisle cabin layout, seating typically 44 passengers in a two-class configuration. Max high-density seating for 52 passengers.

The Tu-324 is a proposed twin-turbofan regional transport, first announced at the Paris Air Show in June 1995. The specification was revised in 1996, and further refined in 1997, when the governments of Russia and Tatarstan signed an agreement on 20 August for the joint development of the new aircraft. The Tatarstan Government signed a symbolic contract for one presidential aircraft

on the same day. A mock-up was completed later that year, and the latest known plans are for the construction of five prototypes in 2001, with the first flight before the end of the year. Certification is expected in 2003, with deliveries to airlines starting in 2004. Manufacture will be by Kazan Aircraft Production Association (KAPO) at Kazan. The Tu-324 is of conventional configuration with scaled-down Tu-204 wings, T-tail, and two turbofan engines mounted on the sides of the rear fuselage. Wings have been shown with and without winglets, suggesting that the design is anything but complete. The engine choice lies between the preferred Ivchenko Progress AI-22 or Soyuz TRDD R-126-300 turbofans, but the 41.0kN (9,220lb) thrust General Electric CF34-3B1 could be fitted on export models. Landing gear is being supplied by Messier-Dowty, while Honeywell is the main avionics supplier. The initial versions will be the Tu-324A VIP transport fitted out for 10 passengers, and the TU-324R regional airliner with 10+34 passengers in a two-class cabin, or 52 in a high-density layout. Longer term plans focus on a stretch to 72-76 seats, possibly with Rolls-Royce Deutschland BR710-48 turbofans.

Below: Model of the Tupolev Tu-324A project with General Electric CF34 turbofan engines.

Tupolev Tu-330/338

PRELIMINARY SPECIFICATION
(Tu-330)
Dimensions: Wingspan 43.50m (142ft 8½in); length overall 42.00m (137ft 9½in); height overall 14.00m (45ft 11¼in); wing area 196.50m² (2,115.2ft²).
Power Plant: Two 158kN (35,500lb) Aviadvigatel PS-90A turbofans.
Weights: Max take-off 103,500kg (228,175lb); max payload 35,000kg (77,160lb).
Performance: Cruising speed 458kt (850km/h); Range with 30t payload 1,620nm (3,000km).

The Tu-330 was announced in early 1993 as a replacement for the large numbers of Antonov An-12s still flying in Russia and the CIS. The first flight had not been made by the end of 1997, one of the conditions imposed by the Russian Government in a resolution dated 23 April 1994 to finance the aircraft. No new timetable has been released, and the aircraft had not flown at the end of 2000. Design is based on the Tu-204 with a similar, but high-mounted wing and two turbofan engines on pylons, with a large over-fuselage fairing to

erodynamically blend the carry-through structure. A 4.0 x 4.0m (rear-loading amp facilitates loading and unloading of freight. For the local market, the rcraft will have two Aviadvigatel PS-90A turbofans, but Rolls-Royce RB.211-35 or Pratt & Whitney PW2000 engines are being considered to enhance the ew aircraft's appeal in the foreign market. The aircraft has been designed to nd on grass runways. No variants have yet been disclosed, although a ryogenic-fuelled version with Samara NK-94 engines and 20,000kg (44,092lb) f liquefied natural gas (LNG) is proposed as the Tu-338. Another possibility is derivative of the standard Tu-330 for the carriage of LNG, which would be ccommodated in three tanks in the cabin with a total capacity of 22,800kg 50,265lb). Production of the Tu-330 will be undertaken at Kazan, where 10 are elieved to be in various stages of construction. Tupolev forecasts a market for argo aircraft of the Tu-330 type of 1,000 aircraft, for both civil and military pplications.

Below: Model of the Tu 330 cargo aircraft, believed to be under onstruction in Kazan.

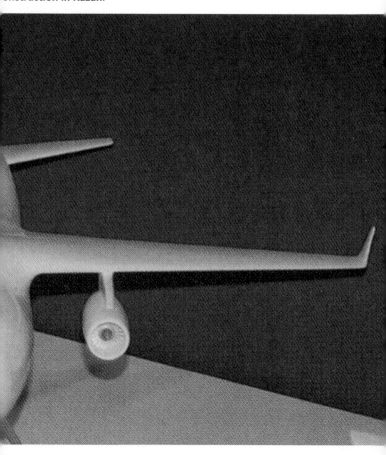

Tupolev Tu-334/336/354

PRELIMINARY SPECIFICATION
(Tu-334-100D)
Dimensions: Wingspan 32.61m (107ft 0in); length overall 31.80m (104ft 4in); height overall 9.38m (30ft 9¾in); wing area 100.0m² (1,076.4ft²).
Power Plant: Two 80.5kN (18,100lb) Ivchenko Progress D-436T2 turbofans.
Weights: Max take-off 54,420kg (119,975lb); max payload 11,000kg (24,250lb).
Performance: Cruising speed 442kt (820km/h); take-off and landing field length 2,200m (7,220ft); Range with typical payload 2,213nm (4,100km).
Accommodation: Flight crew of two. Seating for up to 102 passengers, six-abreast with central aisle.

This twin-fan replacement for the Tu-134 and Yak-42 on domestic routes in the Russian Federation and the CIS countries, has been under development since the late 1980s. Although the prototype was rolled out at Zhukovsky during the Moscow air show on 25 August 1995, funding shortages held up production, and the first aircraft did not make its maiden flight until 8 February 1999. The three-aircraft, 1,000-hour flight test programme is expected to last until the end of 2001, with deliveries to airlines starting in 2003. Based on the Tu-204, but with a considerably shortened fuselage for up to 102 passengers, the Tu-334 uses many of the Tu-204's systems and has an identical flight deck. Design features include a supercritical dihedral wing with 24-deg sweepback.

nd winglets, rear-mounted engines and a T-tail and fly-by-wire controls. Composites and other lightweight materials make up around 20 per cent of the tructural weight. Retractable tricycle landing gear is fitted with a slush and ice eflector grille behind the mainwheels. Several models are available to airlines, part from the basic 102-seat Tu-334-100 with two Ivchenko Progress D-436T1 urbofans, rated at 73.5kN (16,535lb) static thrust each. These include the Tu-34-100D extended-range version with uprated 80.5kN (18,100lb) D-436T2 urbofans, increased gross weight and fuel; the Tu-334C cargo variant; and the u-354, originally designated Tu-334-200. The latter is being offered with either he D-436T2 or 88.95kN (19,995lb) Rolls-Royce Deutschland BR 715-55 (as the U-334-220), and has an increased wingspan and a lengthened fuselage to ccommodate up to 126 passengers. Also projected are the Tu-334-100C Combi, the Tu-134-100M with a higher gross weight, and the Tu-334-120 with BR710-48 engines. The Tu-336 is a long-term plan for a cryogenic-fuelled ersion. Letters of intent have been received for some 160 aircraft from Rossiya Airlines, Bashkiri Airlines, Tatarstan Airlines, Tyumen Airlines and nother 10 airlines, but the home market in Russia and the CIS is estimated to e at least 600 aircraft.

Below: The short-range Tu-334 made its public debut at Zhukovsky n 1995.

Vickers V700/800 Viscount

SPECIFICATION
(Vickers V.800 Viscount)

Dimensions: Wingspan 28.55m (93ft 8in); length overall 26.11m (85ft 8in); height overall 8.15m (26ft 9in), wing area 89.4m² (963.0ft²).

Power Plant: Four 1,300kW (1,740shp) Rolls-Royce Dart Mk 510 (RDa.6) turboprops, with Rotol four-blade constant-speed fully-feathering propellers.

Weights: Operating weight empty 18,600kg (41,000lb); max take-off 29,260kg (64,500lb); max landing 26,535kg (58,500lb); max payload 6,000kg (13,224lb).

Performance: Max cruising speed 282kts (523km/h); service ceiling 7,620m (25,000ft); take-off field length 1,620m (5,310ft); landing field length 1,510m (4,950ft); range with max payload 565nm (1,050km).

Accommodation: Flight crew of three. Seating for up to 71 passengers, five-abreast with offset aisle. Total baggage volume 10.48m³ (370.0ft³).

The result of project design work that began before the end of World War II under the aegis of the Brabazon Committee, the Viscount emerged in 1948 as the world's first airliner with turboprop engines, and went on to become the UK's most successful commercial aircraft production programme. With government backing Vickers launched construction of two prototypes in March 1946 and the first of these (Vickers 630) flew on 16 July 1948, with Dart RDa.1 engines and accommodation for 32 passengers. The first enlarged production standard was defined as the Viscount 700, with Dart Mk 505 engines (replacing Dart Mk 504s in the prototype), a gross weight of 240,040kg (53,000lb) and 47 seats five-abreast. Individual 700-series type numbers applied to each customer variant, starting with 701 for the BEA aircraft. In the mid-1950s Vickers stretched the Viscount's fuselage by 1.17m (3ft 10in) and moved the rear cabin bulkhead aft to obtain enough space to seat up to 71 passengers. With RDa.6 engines and 29,256kg (64,500lb) gross weight this was the Viscount 800, first flown on 27 July 1956, and with more

Below: South African Airways was one of many major operators of the Viscount, the first turboprop airliner.

Above: An order for 75 Viscount 745s from Capital Airlines marked the type's breakthrough into the US market.

powerful RDa.7 Mk 520 engines it was the Type 806, a BEA 'special'. The Type 806A prototype first flew on 9 August 1957. Based on the Type 806, the Viscount 810 series combined RDa.7/1 engines with structural modifications to allow the maximum take-off weight to increase to 32,885kg (72,500lb). A prototype of the Viscount 810 flew on 23 December 1957, and most of the final production batches, for several overseas operators, were of this type. Viscount production ended in 1964 with 444 built. The Viscount 700 obtained its UK certificate of airworthiness on 17 April 1953 and BEA put the type into service between London and Cyprus on the following day, which was the world's first revenue airline service by turboprop airliner. In the US, FAA approval of the Type 745 for Capital Airlines was obtained on 7 November 1955. Deliveries of the Type 802 began (to BEA) on 11 January 1957, and of the Type 806 (also to BEA) on 1 January 1958. Continental Airlines received the first of the 810-series (Type 812) in May 1958 and revenue service began on 28 May. Less than a handful are still in service.

Yakovlev Yak-40

SPECIFICATION
(Yakovlev Yak-40)

Dimensions: Wingspan 25.00m (82ft 0¼in); length overall 20.36m (66ft 9½in); height overall 6.50m (21ft 4in), wing area 70.0m² (753.5ft²).

Power Plant: Three 14.7kN (3,300lb) Ivchenko AI-25 turbofans.

Weights: Operating weight empty 9,400kg (20,725lb); max take-off 16,000kg (35,275lb); max payload 2,720kg (6,000lb).

Performance: Max cruising speed 297kts (550km/h); initial rate of climb 8.0m/s (1,575ft/min); take-off field length 700m (2,295ft); landing field length 360m (1,180ft); range with max payload 950nm (1,758km).

Accommodation: Flight crew of two. Seating for up to 32 passengers, four-abreast with central aisle.

B est-known for its long series of piston-engined fighters and later for jet fighters including the first Soviet VTOL types, the Yakovlev design bureau turned its attention to the small airliner class of aircraft in the early 1960s. Its interest in this category of aircraft had been shown during the 1940s with the design of several light transports, but as a replacement for the many Lisunov Li-2 (licence-built DC-3) aircraft still then in service in the Soviet Union, the Yak-40 broke new ground both for the design bureau and for Aeroflot, its principal operator. A major requirement, in this context, was that the new aircraft should be able to operate from Class 5 airfields, having no paved runways – a requirement reflecting the special needs of the Soviet Union and one which was unmatched in any contemporary jet aircraft of Western origin. With the emphasis upon good field performance, the Yakovlev design team chose a three-engined configuration for the new transport. This meant that take-off weights and runway lengths could be calculated for the 'engine out' case with the loss of only one third, rather than one half (as in a twin-engined design) of available engine power. The rear engine location also has advantages over podded engines beneath the wings in terms of possible ingestion of debris when operating on grass and gravel strips. In common with most other Soviet jet transports, the Yak-40 was designed to have a relatively high thrust-to-weight ratio, again with benefit to airfield performance (including operation at

Below: The three-engined Yak-40 is now rarely seen outside Russia and the CIS, although small numbers continue to be operated. The Bulgarian airline Hemus Air is one of the largest operators, flying seven aircraft out of its base at Sofia.

Above: In 10 years, Yakovlev built around 1,000 Yak-40s, the first entering service with Aeroflot in September 1968.

igh altitude airfields), albeit with some sacrifice in operating economy. To ower the aircraft as planned by Yakovlev, turbofans of about 13.35kN-15.60kN 3,000-3,500lb) were required, and the Ivchenko bureau undertook the evelopment of a suitable engine specifically for this purpose, the AI-25 two-haft turbofan. To minimise the requirement for ground equipment to support peration of the Yak-40 at smaller airfields, an APU was fitted as standard, rimarily for engine starting, and access to the cabin was by way of a ventral irstair/door in the rear fuselage. Five prototypes were used to develop the Yak-0, whose first flight was made on 21 October 1966. The type was assigned he NATO reporting name 'Codling'.

VARIANTS

Modifications to the basic Yak-40 in the course of the production run included he introduction of a clam-shell thrust reverser on the centre engine, and eletion of an acorn fairing at the fin/tailplane leading-edge junction. Other than hese, all production Yak-40s were externally similar, although several lternative interior layouts were available. Freight-carrying and ambulance ersions also were produced. In 1970, a Yak-40M was projected, with a engthened fuselage, to carry 40 passengers. This may have reached prototype esting, but in any case did not proceed to production. The Yak-40V designation vas used to identify an export variant, powered by AI-25T engines rated at 7.2kN (3,858lb) each and with the maximum take-off weight increased to 6,500kg (36,376lb). The Yak-40 achieved reasonable export success, including he Yak-40EC with westernised avionics and in the early 1980s plans were nade for an 'Americanised' version to be developed and marketed by ICX Aviation in Washington. Known as the X-Avia, this was to have been re-engined vith Garrett TFE 731-2 turbofans and was projected in three variants: the 30-seat LC-3A, the 40-seat LC-3B and the all-cargo LC-3C. A conversion orogramme along similar lines, but replacing the Ivchenko power plants with 31.14kN (7,000lb) Textron Lycoming LF 507-1N turbofans, was projected in 991, but neither programme went ahead. The same fate befell the proposed win-engined Yak-40TL.

▶

SERVICE USE

The Yak-40 entered production at the Saratov factory in 1967 an
deliveries to Aeroflot began in 1968, with the first passenger-carryin
flight made on 30 September of that year. Production ended in 1978 wit
approximately 1,000 built; most entered service with Aeroflot but export
were made to Afghanistan, Bulgaria, Czechoslovakia, France, Wes
Germany, Italy, Poland and Yugoslavia for commercial use, and elsewher

or government or military operation in a VIP role. Use of this tri-jet is now diminishing, but around 700 remain in service. The vast majority operate in Russia and the CIS, with some 30 to be found in Africa, the Far East and Central America.

Below: Estonian Air took over a fleet of Yak-40s upon formation soon after independence.

Yakovlev Yak-42

SPECIFICATION
(Yakovlev Yak-42D)

Dimensions: Wingspan 34.88m (114ft 5¼in); length overall 36.38m (119ft 4¼in); height overall 9.83m (32ft 3in), wing area 150.0m² (1,614.6ft²).

Power Plant: Three 63.74kN (14,330lb) ZMKB Progress D-36 three-shaft turbofans.

Weights: Operating weight empty 34,515kg (76,092lb); max take-off 57,000kg (125,660lb); max landing 51,000kg (112,433lb); max payload 13,000kg (28,660lb).

Performance: Max cruising speed 437kts (810km/h); service ceiling 9,600m (31,500ft); take-off field length 2,200m (7,220ft); landing field length 1,100m (3,610ft); range with max payload 1,185nm (2,200km).

Accommodation: Flight crew of two or three. Seating for up to 120 passengers, six-abreast with central aisle. Total baggage volume front and rear 29.3m³ (1,035ft³).

The Yak-42 was developed as a short-haul, medium-capacity jetliner for Aeroflot, to replace the Tu-134, Il-18 and An-24 primarily on the shorter domestic routes within the Soviet Union. Design began in the early 1970s, with a mock-up displayed in Moscow in mid-1973, showing that the overall configuration closely resembled that of the Yak-40, including the three-engined layout and rear-fuselage ventral stairway for access to the cabin. A key design requirement for the Yak-42 was the ability to operate reliably in the more remote regions of the USSR, in a wide range of climates, with the minimum of ground support and maintenance facilities. At the project stage, the design bureau apparently had difficulty assessing the relative merits, particularly in terms of operating economy and performance, of alternative designs with different degrees of wing sweepback. The unusual step was taken of building ▶

Below: The Yak-42D is now operated on mainline services by many airlines in Russia and the CIS countries.

prototypes for comparative testing with 11 deg and 23 deg of sweepback, th first of these making its maiden flight on 7 March 1975. The 23-deg version wa found to be superior and the third prototype was completed to the sam standard while production plans were made and a first batch of 200 was put hand at the Smolensk factory. Initial production aircraft were similar to the thi prototype, but a switch was made from twin main wheels to four-wheel bog units on the main undercarriage.

VARIANTS

The first production Yak-42s had a wing span of 34.02m (111ft 7½in) an gross weight of 53,500kg (117,950lb). The bogie main landing gear wa standard, and alternative interiors were for 120 passengers in a one-clas layout or 104 two-class in a local-service configuration with carry-c baggage and coat stowage compartments at the front and rear of the cabi An enlarged loading door in the forward-fuselage port side could be fitted t allow the Yak-42 to operate in the convertible passenger/cargo role. modification programme was undertaken in 1983 to overcome handlin difficulties encountered during early service with Aeroflot, and led to a sma increase in wing area. The Yak-42 also had a higher maximum take-o weight than initially approved. The first major development was the Yak 42D, which offers increased fuel capacity extending range to 2,200km (1,185nm) with 120 passengers. Specialist versions are the Yak-42F wit large underwing sensor pods for Earth resources and environment. surveys and the Yak-42E-LL propfan testbed. A stretched Yak-42M development announced in 1987 has now been superseded by the planne Yak-42-200, while work continues on a Yak-42D-100 with Western avionics Production has started on the Yak-42A, an improved Yak-42D with a mor comfortable interior and better performance. Yakovlev is also developin the Yak-42T freighter with a side cargo door and payload of 12,000k (26,455lb).

SERVICE USE

First passenger proving flights were made by Yak-42s in late 1980, on the Moscow Krasnodar route, and about 20-30 aircraft were delivered to Aeroflot by the enc 1981. Following an accident in 1982, the Yak-42 was withdrawn until modifie aircraft were put back into operation in October 1984, starting with the Saratov Leningrad and Moscow-Pykovo routes. Yak-42 production continues at a slow rate a Saratov, and by January 2001, approximately 180 had been delivered.

Below: The improved Yak-42D touching down.